The Revolution of 1688 and the Birth of the English Political Nation

PROBLEMS IN EUROPEAN CIVILIZATION

Under the editorial direction of
John Ratté
Amherst College

The Revolution of 1688 and the Birth of the English Political Nation

Second Edition

Edited and with an introduction by
Gerald M. Straka
University of Delaware

D. C. HEATH AND COMPANY
Lexington, Massachusetts Toronto London

CONTENTS

III THE REVOLUTION AND THE EMERGENCE OF PARTY POLITICS

INTRODUCTION

It was called the "Glorious Revolution" from its onset. The glory therein consisted of a remarkable avoidance of the civil war expected by most contemporaries. Only ten years earlier the Exclusionists under Lord Shaftesbury had warned the country of a dreaded Catholic resurgence led by the court. He had tried in three desperate futile attempts to ram through Parliament an Exclusion Bill to remove the king's brother, the Catholic James, Duke of York, from the succession. But Charles II forestalled these "Whigs" (a Royalist insinuation that the Exclusionists were little better than Scottish brigands) and James II assumed the throne on Charles II's death in 1685. Plots against the court culminated in a major insurrection in the West Country led by Charles's illegitimate son, the Duke of Monmouth, in the first summer of James's short reign. Monmouth was destroyed and the "bloody assizes" condemned hundreds of his simple followers to death, prison, or exile. This the West Country folk were not to forget when William landed on their shores in 1688.

James began a series of actions through the courts and the church to wipe out the Whig strongholds in the towns and universities, the Army came under Catholic officers, and an attempt was made to grant religious toleration to Catholics through a Declaration of Indulgence that politicly included dissenters as well.

The lords, the gentry, and the general public were alarmed. While much of what James did was within lawful procedure, there was the growing feeling that his will should be exercised through a freely elected Parliament. The majority of the Anglican Church was in favor of some toleration for dissenters, but not if it meant the infiltration of the church by Catholics. Though James steered a far more neutral diplomatic course than had Charles II (with his reliance on

French subsidies), his standing army far exceeded his brother's, and its support did not come from parliamentary tax grants. By 1688 no Englishman would have followed a John Pym—much less an Oliver Cromwell—as in 1640 and 1650, but there was a general feeling that James had to be brought to some kind of reasonableness.

In 1688 three events turned the public's perturbation into alienation: the announcement of the birth of the king's son (thus entailing an interminable succession of Catholic monarchs), the promulgation of a second Declaration of Indulgence coupled with the order it be read from every pulpit in England, and the arrest and trial of "the Seven Bishops" for refusing to obey that order. A small group of both Whig and Tory lords, encouraged by an increasing animosity, pledged the country's support to the king's nephew and son-in-law, William of Orange, claiming if he would but cross over from the Netherlands with a protecting army, "there are nineteen parts of twenty of the people throughout the kingdom who . . . would willingly contribute to it, if they had such a protection to countenance their rising as would secure them from being destroyed before they could get to be in a posture to defend themselves."

And so William invaded in November, 1688. James II fled England for France just before Christmas. The Parliament that convened on William's order yielded him and his wife, Mary (James's daughter), a shared crown, the only joint reign in English history. It passed a Declaration of Rights (the Bill of Rights), a Mutiny Act abolishing standing armies, and a Toleration Act granting religious worship to dissenters, though not to Catholics.

Though it resolved a momentary crisis, the Revolution of 1688 is also thought of as the culmination of the seventeenth-century struggle between Parliament and the Stuarts over the issue of sovereignty. From the time James I came to the throne in 1603, legislature and crown debated and fought over which of them had ultimate control over the making of law. At times, as under Charles I and Strafford, the crown claimed and exercised the right; under Cromwell, Parliament triumphed. When the later Stuarts, Charles II and James II, attempted to match and then outdo their father in destroying parliamentary sovereignty, the Whigs and a majority of the Tories withdrew their support.

The Revolution, then as now, impresses students of history with its simplicity. It exhibits none of the complexities of the rebellion of 1643 or of the French Revolution a century later, for it consists mainly of one movement: the peaceful accession of the House of Orange. It is not a mass movement nor a class movement; individuals from many parties contributed to its success. It is not a "revolution" as that word is used today, for it resulted in a body of laws that strengthened rather than overthrew the old order. In a sense the "Glorious Revolution" prevented a real revolution. If any innovations can be found, they consist in the granting of toleration to dissenters, the regularization of parliamentary elections, and the establishment of a Protestant monarchy. The Revolution, then, means nothing more than that the English rejected a specific man as unfit to rule, repudiated his foreign and domestic policy, and got themselves a king who pleased them better.

Then why do historians give a significant place to a "palace revolution"? Precisely because Parliament was able to make such a choice. When the Convention Parliament met in February, 1689, it declared that James II had "abdicated" when he escaped to France, but regardless of the explanation, Parliament assumed that it had the power to replace one king with another. Here was an ultimate power over the throne—the power of deposition. Many have assumed, furthermore, then and now, that Parliament's grant of the throne to William implied that the use of kingly prerogatives in the future would be a trust given by Parliament; since Parliament represented the people of England, ultimate governmental power was believed to be the people's. Thus the Revolution of 1688 has come to mean, through implication, that modern political democracy and limited monarchy began with the Revolution Settlement.

Still, it must be remembered that these last-mentioned interpretations have meaning only through implication. This was not a democratic revolution, for it safeguarded rights only to those who had them before 1688—the nobles and landowners of England. There is little to distinguish this event from the medieval battle the barons waged with King John; in spirit the Bill of Rights resembles Magna Carta more than it does the Declaration of Independence or the Communist Manifesto. One thing only distinguishes the Glorious Revolution from earlier constitutional conflicts between the king and his leading subjects: this was to be the last struggle over the medieval problem of sovereignty in England. Politically speaking the Middle Ages in England do not end in 1485, but in 1688; only after this date do the English begin to occupy themselves with perfecting the cabinet system, parliamentary reform, and extending the franchise, having finally declared that the king is not the sole source of law.

The structure of this anthology reflects three major approaches that dominate studies of the Revolution. Part I, "The Revolution and the Nation," opens with a first-hand account by the botanist-diarist, John Evelyn. The sixty-eight-year-old conservative had lived through the civil wars and the Restoration, and his composure was only slightly ruffled by the events of 1688–1689. Many of the revolutionaries were friends and acquaintances, so that much of what he describes is an eyewitness account. His narrative tells not of a conspiracy, but rather of a nation injured by a precipitate king. If Evelyn expresses any opinion it is implied through his description of the sudden and massive nature of the nation's retaliation against James II.

Two hundred and fifty years after the Revolution, England's august historian, George Macaulay Trevelyan, elevated the entire episode to the stature of a national unification movement. The very title he chose—*The English Revolution, 1688–89*—signals his theme, that the Revolution was the great bonding agent unifying classes and interests behind one great institutional achievement, the Revolution Settlement. Trevelyan had written three books on the emergence of Italian nationalism in the nineteenth century, and he felt pride that England achieved status as a nation 200 years before Italy and Germany. He stands in the tradition of George Babington Macaulay and the great Whig historians who wrote uncritical eulogies of 1688, regarding the fall of the Stuarts as manifest destiny. He is also the writer most responsible for the belief that the Bill of Rights forced the monarch to accept the civil contract as a binding pledge to rule with responsibility to his people. In point of fact the contract clause was omitted from the Bill of Rights when it became law. Nonetheless Trevelyan succeeded as no one before him in relating the Revolution of 1688 to the development of democratic nationalism.

Professor William Sachse places the Revolution in the context of national mass action. It was indeed a respectable revolution, but that should not blind us to the fact that it came about amid a swirl of public protest perhaps unmatched in England's turbulent history. Unlike Trevelyan, Sachse would not call the mob's support indicative of emergent democracy, but he does support the contention that the Revolution was a national experience.

Part I closes with an essay by this writer on the Revolution's meaning to those who lived with its consequences. In the eighteenth century, 1688 quickly became the "year one," the year of genesis. But only a few Englishmen came to realize that once a revolution, no matter how properly conducted, becomes a cherished part of national tradition, the need to relive it will sooner or later return. The philosopher Edmund Burke, writing a hundred years after 1688, had difficulty accepting this. To Burke a revolution need happen but once to a nation (somewhat the same understanding most Americans and Russians entertain regarding the destruction of their old regimes). But this essay suggests that the Glorious Revolution bequeathed a legacy of perpetual revolution to the Western world.

Part II, "The Revolution, the Constitution, and the Crown," concentrates on the legal and constitutional achievements of 1688, which are perhaps the Revolution's most prominent features. It opens with the famous Bill of Rights, which, for a statute, is one of the most enigmatic documents in English history, implying much more than it actually states. Hammered out in the early months of William III's first Parliament, it was supposed to provide the nation with an official, if not quite reasonable, explanation of what had taken place in 1688. As such it is necessarily an indictment of the previous king's rule, but, interestingly, it does not state that King James should be tried for his offenses—or that he *could* be tried. Instead the bill declares that James "abdicated," leaving Parliament no recourse but to recognize William and Mary as the new monarchs. Finally, the bill contains a program committing England to religious toleration, abolition of standing armies, parliamentary control over law and taxation, civil liberty, and a Protestant monarchy. Yet a careful reading reveals that the bill is vaguely like a declaration of independence and a constitution, as well as being an indictment and a program for future action. Perhaps the success of the Revolution of 1688 can be attributed to the fact that the Bill of Rights could mean most things to most men.

The two readings following the Bill of Rights, John Locke's famed *Second Treatise of Government* and the modern scholar Peter Laslett's commentary on it, place the Revolution in the broader context of the era of the Exclusionists, who began the attack against James a decade before 1688. Though Laslett, in an intriguing example of scholarly detective work, shows that Locke did not write to justify the Revolution after the fact, Locke's work nonetheless remains the era's great ideological statement. The ideas he articulated—the right of revolution based on property, inalienable liberty, and government as a trust—remain as closely associated with the Glorious Revolution as are the legalities of the Bill of Rights.

The great institutional historian, David Ogg, has most thoughtfully related the Revolution constitution to the whole fabric of medieval and modern English history. His sense of continuity makes the reader aware that the Revolution concentrated within itself all the major tendencies of English public life. Resolving medieval contradictions about notions of sovereignty, at the same time it created new opportunities for the future.

While Ogg stands in the tradition of Trevelyan, the next three essays, by this writer, and Professors Pinkham and Baxter, revive the lost royalist dimensions of the Revolution. It was once supposed that because William accepted a parliamentary title to the throne, no one could any longer believe in the divine right of kingship, the bulwark of Stuart despotism. Yet, as shown in the first article in this group, William's Revolution was of necessity accepted on divine-right terms, for most Englishmen could not dissociate divinity from monarchy. Pious Anglicans made adroit modifications in their thinking about divine right so that they could continue to believe that William's crown was as sacredly bestowed as James II's.

Pinkham's article (and the book from which it is taken), represents one of the most daring reappraisals of the Revolution. Traditionally the Prince of Orange has been seen as a passive participant in the nation's and Parliament's plan, desiring only an alliance to protect his native Netherlands from France. But in Pinkham's analysis William appears as a clever and powerful usurper, and the Revolution becomes little more than an old-fashioned act of conquest.

This section is concluded by Stephen Baxter's study of William's conquest of England. Though he seems not to share Pinkham's notion that William wanted the throne for its own sake, his extraordinary reconstruction of William's role in the Revolution leaves no doubt that William was the master designer. At this point in the readings it becomes difficult to accept Trevelyan's thesis of national unity as the cause for the fall of James II.

The final section, Part III, "The Revolution and the Emergence of

Party Politics," reflects a recent trend in studies about the Revolution of 1688: preoccupation with the supposed growth of a two-party system during the Revolution era. It opens, however, with a glance at a third party, the Jacobites (from *Jacobus,* Latin for James), whose dogged allegiance to the deprived James II plagued English politics well into George II's reign. The Jacobites, shocked that Parliament should so quickly have set aside any possible deliberations with King James in France in favor of a hasty transference of the crown to William and Mary, appeared during the deliberations over the Bill of Rights. Of the Jacobite pamphlets condemning the settlement, one of the abler attacks is reprinted here.

George L. Cherry's article defending the Jacobite position appears next. His is a refreshing new view that the Jacobites were an intelligent major part of the political fabric during the Revolution, not merely a grumpy group of malcontents blindly devoted to a lost cause.

The article by Henry Horwitz serves to introduce the current debate over the rise of parties during the era. The issue is based largely on whether "Namierism" (for Lewis B. Namier, the great scholar whose work explained much of the politics of George III's time) can be applied to the research about William and Queen Anne's reigns. The Namier method is based on the assumption that English politics, at least throughout the eighteenth century, are power politics played by factions and individuals for their own immediate benefit. It downgrades the role of ideology and consequently the ideology of a Whig or Tory party. It emphasizes the need to study the whims and predilections of individuals through minute biographical research, statistical voting patterns in Parliament, and the deployment of patronage. The Namierite believes it possible, in other words, to study English politics without reference to either Whig or Tory parties, which he would consider literary fictions.

Namier's leading exponent in the last thirty years has been Robert Walcott, Jr., who announced his stand in a now famous paper in 1941. The excerpt here is drawn from his full analysis published in 1956. Though it focuses on Queen Anne's reign, Walcott felt it necessary to push his inquiry back to the Revolution, since ideological differences might have dominated party contests in the aftermath of the Revolution. But Walcott finds little, even in the decade after 1688, to justify the usage of two-party terminology. Beyond the contemporary convenience these terms gave to orators and pamphle-teers, he claims, Whigs and Tories did not exist.

By way of rejoinder, J. H. Plumb's selection attempts to retrieve from oblivion the older interpretation that Whigs and Tories actually existed and that they indeed fought as parties over their respective interpretations of policy. Much of Plumb's evidence, to match Wal-cott's approach, is necessarily statistical, but at the forefront of his analysis is the conviction that *ideas* motivated the politicians of William's reign, as much as interest. Above all Plumb feels that to focus merely on power plays runs the risk of ignoring the reason the Revolution took place. Men had to chose between two philosophies of government in 1688, and their choices determined their party loyalties more than unprincipled self-interest.

The many meanings of the Glorious Revolution have yet to be synthesized. Perhaps they never can be. At this stage, however, scholars seem to sense that the Revolution's significance lies out-side the immediate events of 1688–1689. The Revolution may only have been a symptom of something greater that transpired within the whole framework of English public life. It may only have been a breakdown in royal policy, perhaps an ideological transition, or it may have been a stage in the development of party politics. But in any case the Revolution Settlement is no longer the idol of con-stitutional perfection it was in Trevelyan's day, an immutable decree stipulating rank and degree to monarchs, lords, politicians, and people. It is considered, instead, a token that Englishmen would not retreat to a time of Tudor, Stuart, or Cromwellian paternalism.

I THE REVOLUTION AND THE NATION

John Evelyn
THE CONFUSION OF EVENTS, MAY, 1688–FEBRUARY, 1689

While many of Evelyn's works were concerned chiefly with gardening, he is particularly remembered today for his diary, kept from 1640 to his death in 1706. It is an extremely valuable document because Evelyn's place in society allowed him intimacy with many of the great figures of the century. His pacific nature would not allow him to defend Charles I during the civil wars, but in his loyalties he remained a staunch monarchist and served in a number of minor posts under Charles II. His is the outlook of the moderate Tory element that supported the Revolution with lukewarm enthusiasm.

[May 1688] 18th. The King enjoining the ministers to read his Declaration for giving liberty of conscience (as it was styled) in all the churches of England, this evening, six Bishops, Bath and Wells, Peterborough, Ely, Chichester, St. Asaph, and Bristol, in the name of all the rest of the Bishops, came to his Majesty to petition him, that he would not impose the reading of it to the several congregations within their dioceses; not that they were averse to the publishing it for want of due tenderness towards Dissenters, in relation to whom they should be willing to come to such a temper as should be thought fit, when that matter might be considered and settled in Parliament and Convocation; but that, the Declaration being founded on such a dispensing power as might at pleasure set aside all laws ecclesiastical and civil, it appeared to them illegal, as it had done to the Parliament in 1661 and 1672, and that it was a point of such consequence, that they could not so far make themselves parties to it, as the reading of it in church in time of Divine Service amounted to.

The King was so far incensed at this address, that he with threatening expressions commanded them to obey him in reading it at their perils, and so dismissed them. . . .

25th. All the discourse now was about the Bishops refusing to read the injunction for the abolition of the Test, &c. It seems the injunction came so crudely from the Secretary's office, that it was neither sealed nor signed in form, nor had any lawyer been consulted,

From the book *Diary* by John Evelyn. Ed. by William Bray. Everyman's Library edition. Published by E. P. Dutton & Co., Inc. Used with their permission, and by permission of J. M. Dent & Sons Ltd.

so as the Bishops, who took all imaginable advice, put the Court to
great difficulties how to proceed against them. Great were the con-
sults, and a proclamation was expected all this day; but nothing was
done. The action of the Bishops was universally applauded, and
reconciled many adverse parties, Papists only excepted, who were
now exceedingly perplexed, and violent courses were every moment
expected. Report was, that the Protestant secular Lords and Nobility
would abet the Clergy. . . .

8th June. This day, the Archbishop of Canterbury, with the Bishops
of Ely, Chichester, St. Asaph, Bristol, Peterborough, and Bath and
Wells, were sent from the Privy Council prisoners to the Tower, for
refusing to give bail for their appearance, on their not reading the
Declaration for liberty of conscience; they refused to give bail, as it
would have prejudiced their peerage. The concern of the people for
them was wonderful, infinite crowds on their knees begging their
blessing, and praying for them, as they passed out of the barge along
the Tower-wharf.

10th. A *young Prince* born, which will cause disputes.

About two o'clock, we heard the Tower-ordnance discharged, and
the bells ring for the birth of a Prince of Wales. This was very surprising, it having been universally given out that her Majesty did not
look till the next month. . . .

15th. Being the first day of Term, the Bishops were brought to
Westminster on Habeas Corpus, when the indictment was read, and
they were called on to plead; their Counsel objected that the warrant
was illegal; but, after long debate, it was over-ruled, and they
pleaded. The Court then offered to take bail for their appearance;
but this they refused, and at last were dismissed on their own recog-
nizances to appear that day fortnight; the Archbishop in £200, the
Bishops £100 each. . . .

29th. They appeared; the trial lasted from nine in the morning to
past six in the evening, when the Jury retired to consider of their
verdict, and the Court adjourned to nine the next morning. The Jury
were locked up till that time, eleven of them being for an acquittal;
but one (Arnold, a brewer) would not consent. At length he agreed
with the others. The Chief Justice, Wright, behaved with great moderation and civility to the Bishops. Alibone, a Papist, was strongly
against them; but Holloway and Powell being of opinion in their

favor, they were acquitted. When this was heard, there was great rejoicing; and there was a lane of people from the King's Bench to the waterside, on their knees, as the Bishops passed and repassed, to beg their blessing. Bonfires were made that night, and bells rung, which was taken very ill at Court, and an appearance of nearly sixty Earls and Lords, &c., were all along full of comfort and cheerful.

Note, they denied to pay the Lieutenant of the Tower (Hales, who used them very surlily) any fees, alleging that none were due.

The night was solemnized with bonfires, and other fireworks, &c. . . .

12th July. The camp now began at Hounslow,[1] but the nation was in high discontent.

Colonel Titus, Sir Henry Vane (son of him who was executed for his treason), and some other of the Presbyterians and Independent party, were sworn of the Privy Council, from hopes of thereby diverting that party from going over to the Bishops and Church of England, which now they began to do, foreseeing the design of the Papists to descend and take in their most hateful of heretics (as they at other times expressed them to be) to effect their own ends, now evident; the utter extirpation of the Church of England first, and then the rest would follow. . . .

10th August. Dr. Tenison now told me there would suddenly be some great thing discovered. This was the Prince of Orange intending to come over. . . .

23rd August. . . . Dr. Sprat, Bishop of Rochester, wrote a very honest and handsome letter to the Commissioners Ecclesiastical, excusing himself from sitting any longer among them, he by no means approving of their prosecuting the Clergy who refused to read the Declaration for liberty of conscience, in prejudice of the Church of England.

The Dutch make extraordinary preparations both at sea and land, which with the no small progress Popery makes among us, puts us to many difficulties. The Popish Irish soldiers commit many murders and insults; the whole nation disaffected, and in apprehension. . . .

18th September. I went to London, where I found the Court in the utmost consternation on report of the Prince of Orange's landing;

---

[1] The army encampment set up by James outside of London, officered by Catholics, to discourage popular demonstrations against his policies.—Ed.

which put Whitehall into so panic a fear, that I could hardly believe it possible to find such a change.

Writs were issued in order to a Parliament, and a declaration to back the good order of elections, with great professions of maintaining the Church of England, but without giving any sort of satisfaction to the people, who showed their high discontent at several things in the Government.

30th. The Court in so extraordinary a consternation, on assurance of the Prince of Orange's intention to land, that the writs sent forth for a Parliament were recalled. . . .

7th October. . . . Hourly expectation of the Prince of Orange's invasion heightened to that degree, that his Majesty thought fit to abrogate the Commission for the dispensing Power (but retaining his own right still to dispense with all laws) and restore the ejected Fellows of Magdalen College, Oxford. In the meantime, he called over 5,000 Irish, and 4,000 Scots, and continued to remove Protestants and put in Papists at Portsmouth and other places of trust, and retained the Jesuits about him, increasing the universal discontent. It brought people to so desperate a pass, that they seemed passionately to long for and desire the landing of that Prince, whom they looked on to be their deliverer from Popish tyranny, praying incessantly for an east wind, which was said to be the only hindrance of his expedition with a numerous army ready to make a descent. To such a strange temper, and unheard-of in former times, was this poor nation reduced, and of which I was an eyewitness. The apprehension was (and with reason) that his Majesty's forces would neither at land nor sea oppose them with that vigor requisite to repel invaders.

The late imprisoned Bishops were now called to reconcile matters, and the Jesuits hard at work to foment confusion among the Protestants by their usual tricks. A letter was sent to the Archbishop of Canterbury, informing him, from good hands, of what was contriving by them. A paper of what the Bishops advised his Majesty was published. The Bishops were enjoined to prepare a form of prayer against the feared invasion. A pardon published. Soldiers and mariners daily pressed.

14th. The King's Birthday. No guns from the Tower as usual. The sun eclipsed at its rising. This day signal for the victory of William the Conqueror against Harold, near Battel, in Sussex. The wind, which had been hitherto west, was east all this day. Wonderful ex-

FIGURE 1. James II, king of England, Scotland and Ireland from 1685-1688. (*The Granger Collection*)

pectation of the Dutch fleet. Public prayers ordered to be read in the churches against invasion.

28th. A tumult in London on the rabble demolishing a Popish chapel that had been set up in the City.

29th. Lady Sunderland acquainted me with his Majesty's taking away the Seals from Lord Sunderland, and of her being with the

Queen to intercede for him. It is conceived that he had of late grown remiss in pursuing the interest of the Jesuitical counsels; some reported one thing, some another; but there was doubtless some secret betrayed, which time may discover.

There was a Council called, to which were summoned the Archbishop of Canterbury, the Judges, the Lord Mayor, &c. The Queen Dowager, and all the ladies and lords who were present at the Queen Consort's labor, were to give their testimony upon oath of the Prince of Wales's birth, recorded both at the Council-Board and at the Chancery a day or two after. This procedure was censured by some as below his Majesty to condescend to, on the talk of the people. It was remarkable that on this occasion the Archbishop, Marquis of Halifax, the Earls of Clarendon and Nottingham, refused to sit at the Council-table amongst Papists, and their bold telling his Majesty that whatever was done whilst such sat amongst them was unlawful and incurred *praemunire;*[2]—at least, if what I heard be true. . . .

1st November. Dined with Lord Preston, with other company, at Sir Stephen Fox's. Continual alarms of the Prince of Orange, but no certainty. Reports of his great losses of horse in the storm, but without any assurance. A man was taken with diverse papers and printed manifestos, and carried to Newgate, after examination at the Cabinet-Council. There was likewise a Declaration of the States for satisfaction of all Public Ministers at the Hague, except to the English and the French. There was in that of the Prince's an expression, as if the Lords both Spiritual and Temporal had invited him over, with a deduction of the causes of his enterprise. This made his Majesty convene my Lord of Canterbury and the other Bishops now in town, to give an account of what was in the manifesto, and to enjoin them to clear themselves by some public writing of this disloyal charge. . . .

4th. Fresh reports of the Prince being landed somewhere about Portsmouth, or the Isle of Wight, whereas it was thought it would have been northward. The Court in great hurry.

5th. I went to London; heard the news of the Prince having landed at Torbay, coming with a fleet of near 700 sail, passing through the Channel with so favorable a wind, that our navy could not intercept,

---

[2] *Praemunire* refers to the fourteenth-century law against sending legislative and judicial appeals to the papal court at Rome. The council here felt that the mere presence of papists constituted a breach of that law.—Ed.

or molest them. This put the King and Court into great consternation, they were now employed in forming an army to stop their further progress, for they were got into Exeter, and the season and ways very improper for his Majesty's forces to march so great a distance.

The Archbishop of Canterbury and some few of the other Bishops and Lords in London, were sent for to Whitehall, and required to set forth their abhorrence of this invasion. They assured his Majesty they had never invited any of the Prince's party, or were in the least privy to it, and would be ready to show all testimony of their loyalty; but, as to a public declaration, being so few, they desired that his Majesty would call the rest of their brethren and Peers, that they might consult what was fit to be done on this occasion, not thinking it right to publish anything without them, and till they had themselves seen the Prince's Manifesto, in which it was pretended he was invited in by the Lords Spiritual and Temporal. This did not please the King; so they departed.

A Declaration was published, prohibiting all persons to see or read the Prince's Manifesto, in which was set forth at large the cause of his expedition, as there had been one before from the States.

These are the beginnings of sorrow, unless God in His mercy prevent it by some happy reconciliation of all dissensions among us. This, in all likelihood, nothing can effect except a free Parliament; but this we cannot hope to see, whilst there are any forces on either side. . . .

14th. The Prince increases every day in force. Several Lords go in to him. Lord Cornbury carries some regiments, and marches to Honiton, the Prince's headquarters. The City of London in disorder; the rabble pulled down the nunnery newly bought by the Papists of Lord Berkeley, at St. John's. The Queen prepares to go to Portsmouth for safety, to attend the issue of this commotion, which has a dreadful aspect.

18th. It was now a very hard frost. The King goes to Salisbury to rendezvous the army, and return to London. Lord Delamere appears for the Prince in Cheshire. The nobility meet in Yorkshire. The Archbishop of Canterbury and some Bishops, and such Peers as were in London, address his Majesty to call a Parliament. . . .

2nd December. Dr. Tenison preached at St. Martin's on Psalm xxxvi. 5, 6, 7, concerning Providence. I received the blessed Sacrament. Afterwards, visited my Lord Godolphin, then going with the Marquis of Halifax and Earl of Nottingham as Commissioners to the Prince of Orange; he told me they had little power. Plymouth declared for the Prince. Bath, York, Hull, Bristol, and all the eminent nobility and persons of quality through England, declare for the Protestant religion and laws, and go to meet the Prince, who every day set forth new Declarations against the Papists. The great favorites at Court, Priests and Jesuits, fly or abscond. Every thing, till now concealed, flies abroad in public print, and is cried about the streets. Expectation of the Prince coming to Oxford. The Prince of Wales and great treasure sent privily to Portsmouth, the Earl of Dover being Governor. Address from the Fleet not grateful to his Majesty. The Papists in offices lay down their commissions, and fly. Universal consternation amongst them; it looks like a revolution. . . .

9th. Lord Sunderland meditates flight. The rabble demolished all Popish chapels, and several Papist lords' and gentlemen's houses, especially that of the Spanish Ambassador, which they pillaged, and burnt his library.

13th. The King flies to sea, puts in at Feversham for ballast; is rudely treated by the people; comes back to Whitehall.

The Prince of Orange is advanced to Windsor, is invited by the King to St. James's, the messenger sent was the Earl of Feversham, the General of the Forces, who going without trumpet, or passport, is detained prisoner by the Prince, who accepts the invitation, but requires his Majesty to retire to some distant place, that his own guards may be quartered about the Palace and City. This is taken heinously, and the King goes privately to Rochester; is persuaded to come back; comes on the Sunday; goes to mass, and dines in public, a Jesuit saying grace (I was present).

17th. That night was a Council; his Majesty refuses to assent to all the proposals; goes away again to Rochester.

18th. I saw the King take barge to Gravesend at twelve o'clock— a sad sight! The Prince comes to St. James's, and fills Whitehall with Dutch guards. A Council of Peers meet about an expedient to call a Parliament; adjourn to the House of Lords. The Chancellor, Earl of Peterborough, and diverse others taken. The Earl of Sunderland flies; Sir Edward Hales, Walker, and others, taken and secured.

All the world go to see the Prince at St. James's, where there is a great Court. There I saw him, and several of my acquaintance who came over with him. He is very stately, serious, and reserved. The English soldiers sent out of town to disband them; not well pleased.

24th. The King passes into France, whither the Queen and child were gone a few days before.

26th. The Peers and such Commoners as were members of the Parliament at Oxford, being the last of Charles II meeting, desire the Prince of Orange to take on him the disposal of the public revenue till a convention of Lords and Commons should meet in full body, appointed by his circular letters to the shires and boroughs, 22nd January. I had now quartered upon me a Lieutenant-Colonel and eight horses. . . .

1689. 15th January. I visited the Archbishop of Canterbury, where I found the Bishops of St. Asaph, Ely, Bath and Wells, Peterborough, and Chichester, the Earls of Aylesbury and Clarendon, Sir George Mackenzie Lord-Advocate of Scotland, and then came in a Scotch Archbishop, &c. After prayers and dinner, diverse serious matters were discoursed, concerning the present state of the Public, and sorry I was to find there was as yet no accord in the judgments of those of the Lords and Commons who were to convene; some would have the Princess made Queen without any more dispute, others were for a Regency; there was a Tory party (then so called), who were for inviting his Majesty again upon conditions; and there were Republicans who would make the Prince of Orange like a Stadt-holder. The Romanists were busy among these several parties to bring them into confusion: most for ambition or other interest, few for conscience and moderate resolutions. I found nothing of all this in this assembly of Bishops, who were pleased to admit me into their discourses; they were all for a Regency, thereby to salve their oaths, and so all public matters to proceed in his Majesty's name, by that to facilitate the calling of a Parliament, according to the laws in being. Such was the result of this meeting. . . .

The great convention being assembled the day before, falling upon the question about the Government, resolved that King James having by the advice of the Jesuits and other wicked persons endeavored to subvert the laws of Church and State, and deserted the kingdom, carrying away the seals, &c., without any care for the management of the government, had by demise abdicated himself and wholly vacated his right; they did therefore desire the Lords' concurrence to their vote, to place the crown on the next heir, the Prince of Orange, for his life, then to the Princess, his wife, and if she died without issue, to the Princess of Denmark, and she failing, to the heirs of the Prince, excluding forever all possibility of admitting a Roman Catholic. . . .

29th. The votes of the House of Commons being carried up by Mr. Hampden, their chairman, to the Lords, I got a station by the Prince's lodgings at the door of the lobby to the House, and heard much of the debate, which lasted very long. Lord Derby was in the chair (for the House was resolved into a grand committee of the whole House); after all had spoken, it came to the question, which was carried by three voices against a Regency, which 51 were for, 54 against; the minority alleging the danger of dethroning Kings, and scrupling many passages and expressions in the vote of the Commons, too long to set down particularly. Some were for sending to his Majesty with conditions: others that the King could do no wrong, and that the maladministration was chargeable on his ministers. There were not more than eight or nine bishops, and but two against the Regency; the archbishop was absent, and the clergy now began to change their note, both in pulpit and discourse, on their old passive obedience, so as people began to talk of the bishops being cast out of the House. In short, things tended to dissatisfaction on both sides; add to this, the morose temper of the Prince of Orange, who showed little countenance to the noblemen and others, who expected a more gracious and cheerful reception when they made their court. The English army also was not so in order, and firm to his interest, nor so weakened but that it might give interruption. Ireland was in an ill posture as well as Scotland. Nothing was yet done towards a settlement. God of His infinite mercy compose these things, that we may be at last a Nation and a Church under some fixed and sober establishment. . . .

6th February. . . . The Convention of the Lords and Commons now declare the Prince and Princess of Orange King and Queen of England, France, and Ireland (Scotland being an independent kingdom), the Prince and Princess being to enjoy it jointly during their lives; but the executive authority to be vested in the Prince during life, though all proceedings to run in both names, and that it should descend to their issue, and for want of such, to the Princess Anne of Denmark and her issue, and in want of such, to the heirs of the body of the Prince, if he survive, and that failing, to devolve to the Parliament, as they should think fit. These produced a conference with the Lords, when also there was presented heads of such new laws as were to be enacted. It is thought on these conditions they will be proclaimed.

There was much contest about the King's abdication, and whether he had vacated the government. The Earl of Nottingham and about twenty Lords, and many Bishops, entered their protests, but the concurrence was great against them.

The Princess hourly expected. Forces sending to Ireland, that kingdom being in great danger by the Earl of Tyrconnel's army, and expectations from France coming to assist them, but that King was busy in invading Flanders, and encountering the German Princes. It is likely that this will be the most remarkable summer for action, which has happened in many years.

21st. . . . I saw the *new Queen* and *King* proclaimed the very next day after her coming to Whitehall, Wednesday, 13th February, with great acclamation and general good reception. Bonfires, bells, guns, &c. It was believed that both, especially the Princess, would have showed some (seeming) reluctance at least, of assuming her father's Crown, and made some apology, testifying by her regret that he should by his mismanagement necessitate the Nation to so extraordinary a proceeding, which would have showed very handsomely to the world, and according to the character given of her piety; consonant also to her husband's first declaration, that there was no intention of deposing the King, but of succoring the Nation; but nothing of all this appeared; she came into Whitehall laughing and jolly, as to a wedding, so as to seem quite transported. She rose early the next morning, and in her undress, as it was reported, before her women were up, went about from room to room to see the convenience of Whitehall; lay in the same bed and apartment where the late Queen lay, and within a night or two sat down to play at basset, as the Queen her predecessor used to do. She smiled upon and talked to everybody, so that no change seemed to have taken place at Court since her last going away, save that infinite crowds of people thronged to see her, and that she went to our prayers. This carriage was censured by many. She seems to be of a good nature, and that she takes nothing to heart: whilst the Prince her husband has a thoughtful countenance, is wonderful serious and silent, and seems to treat all persons alike gravely, and to be very intent on affairs: Holland, Ireland, and France calling for his care.

Diverse Bishops and Noblemen are not at all satisfied with this so sudden assumption of the Crown, without any previous sending, and offering some conditions to the absent King; or, on his not returning, or not assenting to those conditions, to have proclaimed him Regent; but the major part of both Houses prevailed to make them King and Queen immediately, and a crown was tempting. . . .

The Archbishop of Canterbury and some of the rest, on scruple of conscience and to salve the oaths they had taken, entered their protests and hung off, especially the Archbishop, who had not all this while so much appeared out of Lambeth. This occasioned the wonder of many who observed with what zeal they contributed to the Prince's expedition, and all the while also rejecting any proposals of sending again to the absent King; that they should now raise scruples, and such as created much division among the people, greatly rejoicing the old courtiers, and especially the Papists.

Another objection was, the invalidity of what was done by a Convention only, and the as yet unabrogated laws; this drew them to make themselves on the 22nd [February] a Parliament, the new King passing the Act with the crown on his head. The lawyers disputed, but necessity prevailed, the Government requiring a speedy settlement.

George Macaulay Trevelyan

THE REVOLUTION AS A MOVEMENT FOR DEMOCRATIC UNIFICATION

George Macaulay Trevelyan, born in 1876, is one of the greatest of Britain's modern historians. Before his retirement in 1951, he was Regius Professor of Modern History at Cambridge (1927), and later Master of Trinity College (1940). He is noted for his respect for the Whig tradition, his belief that scholarship and literary excellence should be united, and his interest in social history. He died in 1962 at the age of eighty-eight.

Why do historians regard the Revolution of 1688 as important? And did it deserve the title of "glorious" which was long its distinctive epithet? "The Sensible Revolution" would perhaps have been a more appropriate title and certainly would have distinguished it more clearly as among other revolutions.

But insofar as it was indeed "glorious," in what does its "glory" consist? It is not the Napoleonic brand of glory. It is not to be sought in the glamor of its events, the drama of its scenes, and the heroism of its actors, though these also rouse the imagination and stir the blood. The Seven Bishops passing to the Tower through the kneeling throngs; William's fleet floating into Torbay before the Protestant wind; the flight of James II, following his wife and infant son to France, none of them ever to return—doubtless these are romantic scenes, that live in memory. Such also are the events that followed more bloodily in Scotland and in Ireland—the roaring pass of Killie-crankie, the haggard watch on Londonderry walls, and Boyne water bristling with musket and pike. Yet all these are not, like the fall of the Bastille or Napoleon's Empire, a new birth of time, a new shape of terror. They are spirited variations on themes invented forty years before by a more heroic, creative and imprudent generation.

The Seven Bishops whom James II prosecuted were milder and more conservative men than the Five Members whom Charles I attempted to arrest, yet the second story reads much like a repetition of the first: in both cases the king rashly attacks popular leaders who are protected by the law, and by the mass opinion of the capital.

From G. M. Trevelyan, *The English Revolution, 1688–1689* (Oxford, 1938). Reprinted by permission of the Oxford University Press.

In both cases the king's downfall shortly follows. Much else indeed is very different: there is no English Civil War on the second occasion, for in 1688 even the Cavaliers (renamed Tories) were against the king. But the men of the Revolution, James and William, Danby, Halifax, Sancroft, Dundee, are manipulating forces, parties and ideas which had first been evoked in the days of Laud, Strafford, Pym, Hampden, Hyde, Cromwell, Rupert, Milton and Montrose. In the later Revolution there are no new ideas, for even toleration had been eagerly discussed round Cromwell's camp-fires. But in 1688 there is a very different grouping of the old parties, and a new and happier turn is given to the old issues, in England though not in Ireland, by compromise, agreement and toleration. An heroic age raises questions, but it takes a sensible age to solve them. Roundheads and Cavaliers, high in hope, had broken up the soil, but the Whigs and Tories soberly garnered the harvest.

A certain amount of disillusionment helps to make men wise, and by 1688 men had been doubly disillusioned, first by the rule of the Saints under Cromwell, and then by the rule of the Lord's Anointed under James. Above all, taught by experience, men shrank from another civil war. The burned child fears the fire. The merit of this Revolution lay not in the shouting and the tumult, but in the still, small voice of prudence and wisdom that prevailed through all the din.

The true "glory" of the Revolution lies not in the minimum of violence which was necessary for its success, but in the way of escape from violence which the Revolution Settlement found for future generations of Englishmen. There is nothing specially glorious in the victory which our ancestors managed to win, with the aid of foreign arms, over an ill-advised king who forced an issue with nine-tenths of his English subjects on the fundamentals of law, politics and religion. To have been beaten at such odds would have been national ignominy indeed. The "glory" of that brief and bloodless campaign lies with William, who laid deep and complicated plans and took great risks in coming over at all, rather than with the English who had only to throw up their caps for him with sufficient unanimity when once he and his troops had landed. But it is England's true glory that the cataclysm of James's overthrow was not accompanied by the shedding of English blood either on the field or on the scaffold. The political instincts of our people appeared in the avoidance of a second civil war, for which all the elements were present. Our enemy Louis XIV of France had confidently expected that another long period of confusion and strife would ensue in our factious island if William should land there; if he had thought otherwise, he could have threatened the frontiers of Holland, and so prevented his rival from setting sail at all.

But the Convention Parliament of February 1689, by uniting England, baffled the policy of France. By wise compromise it stanched forever the blood feud of Roundhead and Cavalier, of Anglican and Puritan, which had broken out first at Edgehill and Naseby, and bled afresh only four years back at Sedgemoor. Whig and Tory, having risen together in rebellion against James, seized the fleeting moment of their union to fix a new-old form of government, known in history as the Revolution Settlement. Under it, England has lived at peace within herself ever since. The Revolution Settlement in church and state proved to have the quality of permanence. It stood almost unaltered until the era of the Reform Bill of 1832. And throughout the successive stages of rapid change that have followed, its fundamentals have remained to bear the weight of the vast democratic superstructure which the nineteenth and twentieth centuries have raised upon its sure foundation. Here, seen at long range, is "glory," burning steadily for 250 years: it is not the fierce, short, destructive blaze of *la gloire.*

The expulsion of James was a revolutionary act, but otherwise the spirit of this strange Revolution was the opposite of revolutionary. It came not to overthrow the law but to confirm it against a law-breaking king. It came not to coerce people into one pattern of opinion in politics or religion, but to give them freedom under and by the law. It was at once liberal and conservative; most revolutions are neither one nor the other, but overthrow the laws, and then tolerate no way of thinking save one. But in our Revolution the two great parties in church and state united to save the laws of the land from destruction by James; having done so, and having thereby become jointly and severally masters of the situation in February 1689, neither the Whig nor the Tory party would suffer its clients to be any longer subject to persecution, either by the royal power or by the opposite party in the state. Under these circumstances the keynote of the Revolution Settlement was personal freedom under the law, both in religion and in politics. The most conservative of all revolutions in history was also the most liberal. If James had been overthrown either by the Whigs alone or by the Tories alone, the settlement that followed his downfall would not have been so liberal, or so permanent.

In the realm of thought and religion, individual liberty was secured by the abandonment of the cherished idea that all subjects of the state must also be members of the state church. The Toleration Act of 1689 granted the right of religious worship, though not complete political equality, to Protestant dissenters; and so strong was the latitudinarian and tolerant spirit of the age ushered in by the Revolution, that these privileges were soon extended in practice though not in law to the Roman Catholics, against whom the Revolution had in one aspect been specially directed.

The political freedom of the individual was secured in a like spirit, by the abolition of the Censorship (1695), by the milder and less partial administration of political justice, and by the balance of power between the Whig and Tory parties, under whose rival banners almost everyone in some sort found shelter. In these ways the distinctively English idea of the freedom of opinion and the rights of the individual were immensely enhanced by the peculiar character of this Revolution.

James had tried to put the king above Parliament and above the law. The Revolution, while leaving the king the source of executive authority, subjected him to the law, which was henceforth to be interpreted by independent and irremovable judges, and could only be altered by act of Parliament. At the same time, by the annual Mutiny Act that made the army dependent of Parliament, and by the refusal to grant to William for life the supplies that had been granted for the lives of Charles and James II, the House of Commons obtained a power of bargaining with government that rendered it even more important than the House of Lords; indeed, from the Revolution onwards the Commons gradually gained a control even over the executive power of the king, through the cabinet system which grew up step by step under William, Anne and the first two Georges. All this was not foreseen by the men of 1689, whose intention was only to subject the kingly power to the bounds of law as defined by the parliamentary lawyers. But the Hanoverian constitution of Walpole and the Pitts grew straight out of the Revolution Settlement by the logic of experience.

The Revolution has been branded as aristocratic. It was effected by the whole nation, by a union of all classes; but in a society still mainly agricultural, where the economic and social structure rendered the landlords the natural and accepted leaders of the countryside, noblemen and squires like the Tories Danby and Seymour, the Whigs Devonshire and Shrewsbury took the lead when resistance to government had to be improvised. The nation indeed recognized no other chiefs through whom it could act in such an emergency. A similar aristocratic and squirearchical leadership of the country had organized both the Roundhead and Cavalier armies at the beginning of the Civil War; it had, indeed, been partially eclipsed during the rule of Cromwell's military saints, but had been fully re-established at the Restoration of 1660. It continued after 1689 as before, and would in any case have continued until the Industrial Revolution gradually raised up a new social order. Even despotism, if James had succeeded in setting it up, must in that age have governed through nobles and squires. James attempted to use the lords and country gentlemen who were the Lieutenants and J.P.'s of their counties as the instruments of his Catholicizing policy, but they, like everyone else, turned against him. Having no other bureaucracy through which to work, he fell.

So far, the Revolution was indeed a demonstration of the power of the landlord classes, Whig and Tory alike. They were politically powerful because in the then formation of English society they were indispensable. Any form of English government must in those days have worked through them.

The Revolution did quite as much for the legal, mercantile and popular elements in our national life as for the aristocratic or squirearchical. The worst permanent result of the Revolution was not the alleged increase in the power of the aristocracy but the undue conservatism that continued throughout the whole eighteenth century. The result of the reaction against James II's innovations was to put too great a stress, for many years to come, on the perpetuation of institutions in their existing form. James, in the interest of Roman Catholicism and despotism, had remodelled the town corporations, invaded the liberties of the universities and of the Church, and attempted to pack the House of Commons. In the rebound, the ministries and Parliaments of the eighteenth century feared to reform the corporations, universities, Church benefices and Parliamentary Constituencies, even in the interest of purer and more efficient government. James had treated charters as waste paper, so the men of the eighteenth century regarded the sheepskin with superstitious reverence. They held that whatever is is right—if it can show a charter. The hundred and fifty years that followed the Revolution are the most conservative in our annals though by no means the least free, happy or prosperous.

The Whig governments before Burke, and the Tory governments after him, all had too much reverence for the letter of the Revolution Settlement. It became a flag of ultraconservatism, first Whig, then Tory. To Walpole, Blackstone, Burke, Eldon and the anti-Jacobin Tories of the early nineteenth century, the year 1689 seemed the last year of creation, when God looked upon England and saw that it was good.

But when this ultraconservative mood at length passed away, the bases of the Revolution Settlement still remained as the foundations of the new era of rapid reform, in which we are still living after more than a hundred years. The relation of the Crown to Parliament and to the law; the independence of judges; the annual meeting of Parliament; the financial supremacy of the Commons; the position of the Church of England; the toleration of religious dissent; freedom of political speech and writing subject to no control but the opinion of a jury; in short a constitutional monarchy for a free people, these are the bases of our polity and they were well and truly laid by the Whigs and Tories, the nobles, squires, lawyers, merchants and populace who rose up against James II.

But unless strength upholds the free, freedom cannot live. And the Revolution Settlement gave us strength as well as freedom. The Marlborough wars soon demonstrated that; and England was never so safe and so powerful as in the eighteenth century, especially after the Parliamentary Union with Scotland, made in 1707, had united the whole island of Britain "on a Revolution basis."

Between the death of Elizabeth and the Revolution of 1688, the constant struggle between Parliament and king had rendered England weak in the face of the world, except during the few years when Cromwell had given her strength at a heavy price. Our civil broils had occupied our energies and attention; sometimes both the king and the statesmen of the opposition were pensioners of France; always Parliament had been chary of supply to governments whose policy they could not continuously control. In the reigns of the Jameses and Charleses, foreign countries had regarded our Parliament as a source of weakness, hampering the executive power: the constitution of England was contemptuously compared to that of Poland.

But after the Revolution the world began to see that our parliamentary government, when fully established, was capable of becoming a source of national strength. Supplies that had been refused to kings whom the Commons could not trust, were lavished on ministries that had the confidence of the House. The money must be voted afresh annually, not granted for the king's life; and the Commons must see to its appropriation. On these strict conditions, the governments of William, Anne and the Georges had the run of the national purse such as their predecessors had not enjoyed. Moreover, the "Revolution Governments" had the confidence of the City as well as of Parliament. The system of loans based on taxes gave England the key to power. It was "Revolution finance" and Revolution policy that enabled Marlborough to defeat the Grand Monarch, when free government and religious toleration triumphed over the revoker of the Edict of Nantes. As a result of that victory, the European philosophers of the eighteenth century turned against political despotism and religious intolerance as causes of national weakness, and proclaimed to the world the peculiar merits of England's "happy constitution in church and state."

Speaking of the wars of William and Anne, and more generally of the eighteenth century, Professor G. N. Clark writes:

> In France and Prussia and almost everywhere militarism and autocracy went hand in hand, but what enabled Britain to deploy its strength was the Revolution Settlement. The main lines of policy were laid down by a small gathering of ministers who had at their disposal full departmental information about foreign affairs, finance, military and naval preparations and trade. By means of Parliament the ministers brought into the service of that policy the wealth and manpower of the nation. . . . Parliament was a meeting-place where divergent economic interests were reconciled and combined so as to provide an adequate body of support for the government of the day.

In this way Britain obtained, not only political and religious liberty, but national power, greater than that of the unlimited monarchy of France. Such are the reasons why modern historians regard the

Revolution a turning point in the history of our country and of the world. . . .

The liberal-conservative character of the Revolution Settlement must be sought in the character of the House of Commons elected in January 1689. How and in what spirit was that House chosen? What, if any, were the instructions given to its members by their constituents?

The elections to the Convention Parliament took place under abnormal conditions. There was no king and no regular government. The country was in the greatest danger of internal convulsion and foreign conquest, and the national crisis loomed larger in men's minds than the usual Whig and Tory nonsense. An anxious, sober patriotism was the spirit of the hour. Moreover, the Whigs and Tories had for some time past been acting together as one party against James and had not yet had time to fly asunder and resume their old quarrels. . . .

The first business of the Convention was to decide who should fill the throne, and on that issue the new Whig and the new Tory parties came into existence. Yet the differences of parties on the dynastic question arose from a difference of theory rather than of practice. Both sides desired William to stay in England as head of the administration. The question in dispute was by what right and with what title he should bear rule.

The Tory politicians and the Anglican clergy in Charles II's reign had pledged themselves repeatedly to the theory of divine hereditary right of kings and nonresistance of subjects. They had since been compelled to resist James II, in spite of all their theories, because they were men. But also because they were men, they could not all of them at once abandon the whole set of associated ideas in which they had been brought up. They could not, as quickly as the Vicar of Bray, treat "passive obedience as a jest" and make "a joke of nonresistance." They set themselves therefore to explain away the Revolution while reaping its fruits in practice. They desired to make such a settlement of the Crown as would not be in too obvious contradiction of the doctrines which they had all so recently proclaimed, and which many of them still loved and reverenced. They asserted, to begin with, that James had never been driven away, but that he had voluntarily deserted his functions. They had risen against him in arms, meaning only to bring him to reason, and he had, instead of submitting, fled oversea to the national enemy. The blessed word "abdicate" would save his subjects from the sin of having deposed him. James had "abdicated" the government. And further, the Tories hoped that a little ingenuity could surely be used to avoid a breach in the divinely appointed order of hereditary succession.

Such was the nature of Tory anxieties when the Convention met in January 1689.

The Whigs, on the other hand, thought that a slight change in the order of succession would be a good thing in itself, because it would kill the Stuart theory of divine hereditary right. It would make the title to the Crown a parliamentary title, to the same extent as in Plantagenet and Tudor days, when Parliament had several times disposed of the Crown, not always to the nearest of kin. The Whigs believed that such another parliamentary gift of the Crown would establish their own theory of the contract between king and people, involving the forfeiture of the Crown in case of breach of that contract. Only so, thought the Whigs, could the limited nature of the monarchy be secured for all time. No doubt the Tories of 1689, like the Cavaliers of 1640 and 1660, wished the powers of the Crown to be limited in practice. But was such a constitutional practice consonant with a theory suited only to despotism? For if the king continued, in the eyes of half his subjects, to hold a quasi-divine office by inheritance, how was a mere earthly Parliament to limit his supernatural rights whenever he chose to insist on them? A divine monarchy must always override a mere human Parliament. Since monarchy and Parliament could not both be divine in men's eyes, let them both, said the Whigs, be human, and here is our great opportunity to make them so. . . .

One important concession was made to the Tory view. James was declared to have "abdicated" the government by his voluntary flight. He was not declared to have been "deposed," nor to have "forfaulted," that is "forfeited," the Crown as the Scottish Convention at Edinburgh pronounced, in its more thoroughgoing Whig manner. . . .

The Commons' formula, to which the Lords finally agreed, ran as follows:

That King James the Second, having endeavored to subvert the Constitution of the Kingdom, by breaking the Original Contract *between King and people [a Whig remark], and by the advice of Jesuits and other wicked persons having violated the fundamental laws and withdrawn himself out of the Kingdom, hath* abdicated *the government [a concession to the Tories] and that* the throne is thereby vacant *[a Whig conclusion]*. . . .

William and Mary were not made king and queen without conditions. The instrument by which the Convention raised them to the throne was the famous Declaration of Right. It made a long recital of the various illegal acts of James, more especially his claim to suspend the laws by prerogative; it declared all these actions to have been illegal, and it required the acceptance of these limitations of the royal power by the new sovereigns as a condition of their elevation to the throne.

. . . An agreed contract was freely made between Crown and people which prevented for all time to come a repetition of the tragedies of the Stuart kings. The pendulum-swing of alternate violence of rebels and royalists was slowed down to the gentler oscillation of rival parliamentary parties. And what the Crown lost in power it gained in security. The Republican movement was buried, not to revive in England in any formidable manner either at the time of the French Revolution, or with the coming of social democracy in the nineteenth and twentieth centuries. England had acquired the outline of a constitution in which she could work out her remoter destinies.

. . .

The fundamental question at issue in 1688 had been this—Is the law above the king, or is the king above the law? The interest of Parliament was identified with that of the law, because, undoubtedly, Parliament could alter the law. It followed that, if law stood above the king's will, yet remained alterable by Parliament, Parliament would be the supreme power in the state.

James II attempted to make the law alterable wholesale by the king. This, if it had been permitted, must have made the king supreme over Parliament, and, in fact, a despot. The events of the winter of 1688–1689 gave the victory to the opposition idea, which Chief Justice Coke and Selden had enunciated early in the century, that the king was the chief servant of the law, but not its master; the executant of the law, not its source; the laws should only be alterable by Parliament—kings, Lords and Commons together. It is this that makes the Revolution the decisive event in the history of the English constitution. It was decisive because it was never undone, as most of the work of the Cromwellian Revolution had been undone.

It is true that the first Civil War had been fought partly on this same issue: the Common Law in league with Parliament had, on the field of Naseby, triumphed over the king in the struggle for the supreme place in the constitution. But the victory of law and Parliament had, on that occasion, been won only because Puritanism, the strongest religious passion of the hour, had supplied the fighting force. And religious passion very soon confused the constitutional issue. Puritanism burst the legal bounds and, coupled with militarism, overthrew law and Parliament as well as king. Hence the necessity of the restoration in 1660 of king, law and parliament together, without any clear definition of their ultimate mutual relations.

Now, in this second crisis of 1688, law and Parliament had on their side not only the Puritan passion, which had greatly declined, but the whole force of Protestant-Anglicanism, which was then at its height, and the rising influence of Latitudinarian scepticism—all arrayed against the weak Roman Catholic interest to which James had attached the political fortunes of the royal cause. The ultimate victor of the seventeenth-century struggle was not Pym or Cromwell, with their Puritan ideals, but Coke and Selden with their secular idea of the supremacy of law. In 1689 the Puritans had to be content with a bare toleration. But law triumphed, and therefore the law-making Parliament triumphed finally over the king. . . .

The ultimate view that we take of the Revolution of 1688 must be determined by our preference either for royal absolutism or for parliamentary government. James II forced England to choose once for all between these two: he refused to inhabit any halfway house. It was as well that the choice had to be made so decisively and so soon; for the compromise system of the Restoration, though very useful in its day, had led to weakness abroad and constant strife at home.

The system of government by discussion has its disadvantages, under which in new forms we are laboring today, in face of absolutist governments of a new and more formidable type than those of Europe of the *ancien régime*. But if, on the balance, we prefer the path on which our feet are planted, we must commend the choice that was made once for all at the English Revolution.

William L. Sachse

MASS MOVEMENT BEHIND THE REVOLUTION

Professor William L. Sachse, born in Illinois in 1912, studied at Yale under Wallace Notestein, and was a Rhodes Scholar from 1935 to 1937. He has been at the University of Wisconsin since 1938, serving as chairman of the History Department from 1958 to 1961. His works cover a wide range of English and American colonial studies.

Among the major political upheavals which have been called revolutions, the English Revolution of 1688 is generally recognized as extraordinary. Long accepted among moderate Englishmen as "glorious," a revolution to end revolutions, in more radical quarters it has not been regarded as constituting a true revolution. Contemporary Russian opinion, for example, refuses to bestow upon it this accolade, regarding it as a mere coup d'état. Its conservatism, its legalism, its bloodlessness, the absence of zeal to be found among its protagonists: all contribute to this point of view. That these are characteristics of the Glorious Revolution cannot be denied. More precisely, they characterize the actions of the leaders of the Revolution—of the councilors and legislators and soldiers whose names are known. Of popular opinion and aspiration much less is known, and it is probable that little can be discovered in the surviving evidence. But they can be assessed, to some degree, by following the actions of the mob—or, more accurately, the mobs—as they erupted in London and other parts of the kingdom.

Mob disturbances, like the plague, were more or less endemic in Stuart England. Roger North, in his *Examen,* asserts that "the Rabble first changed their Title, and were called *the mob*" in the gatherings of the Green Ribbon Club. Regardless of when the term was first used, seventeenth-century Englishmen were well acquainted with various manifestations of mob activity. England's growing urban population augmented the mob, and before Shaftesbury, Pym had demonstrated that he was aware of the existence of this popular force and of the uses to which it could be put.

From W. L. Sachse, "The Mob and the Revolution of 1688," *Journal of British Studies* 4 (November, 1964): 23–40. Reprinted by permission.

In the years before his accession, James II had ample opportunity to observe the mob in action, for the exclusion controversy had evoked one protest after the other. Contemporary accounts abound with references to attacks on Catholic chapels, demonstrations against unpopular figures, millings and crowdings and jostlings at which volatile throngs were stimulated by polemics and indictments. Although the last years of Charles's reign (with the city muzzled, Parliament in abeyance, and the Tories ascendent) were comparatively quiet, the mob was still in being. With Charles on his deathbed, the fear of popular disturbance (if it had ever really subsided) revived. On February 2, orders went forth from Whitehall to Lieutenants and Deputy-Lieutenants, calling upon them to prevent any disorders that might happen "upon any false reports or by any seditious practices" at this critical time.

Although James succeeded without immediate incident, and was blessed with an almost unprecedentedly cooperative Parliament, he soon had occasion to issue similar orders. In May there was turbulence when Titus Oates stood in the pillory, and the following month the Lord Mayor was called upon to be extraordinarily watchful for fear of ill practices among the disaffected party. James could scarcely have been ignorant of his subjects' ill will toward his Catholic policies. So tumultuously was Guy Fawkes Day celebrated in 1685 that on the following day the Council decreed that no bonfires or fireworks should be permitted without official license; in this way it was hoped that the disaffected folk who "commonly make use of such occasions to turne those Meetings into Riotts and Tumults" might be thwarted. The following May, the Bishop of Durham took it upon himself to counsel the king to withdraw his protection from "Romish" chapels in London. These, he said, were "daily made the occasion of so much Disturbance and Mischief here, and if continued any longer, I fear, will unavoidably endanger the Peace and Safety of Your great City, and consequently of Your whole Kingdom." Evidence of popular outbursts against Catholic houses of worship was about the same time forthcoming from another source. Van Citters, the Dutch Minister, commented upon the effects of riots caused by the creation of such chapels, pointing in particular to economic repercussions. According to him, the Commissioners of the Customs had reported that, in the month following the opening of the chapel in Lime Street, "the receipt in the port of the Thames had fallen off by some thousands of pounds." The business of the Royal Exchange, he told his government, was "at a stand."

The arrest and trial of the seven bishops was the occasion of popular disturbances, not only in the capital but in outlying communities. On June 1 the Royalist Lord Mayor, Shorter, reported to Sunderland, Lord President of the Council, that despite his efforts to prevent bonfires, several outrages had been committed the previous night by the "ordinary rabble." It appears that many people mistook the release of the bishops on bail for a full acquittal, and sought here and there to celebrate the turn of events; in Lichfield, where some had attempted to interfere, there had been "a very great Ryot." The actual trial attracted a large assemblage, and Van Citters, commenting upon the enthusiasm shown on this occasion for the bishops, found it surprising that "under so great a concourse of people so very much affected for the Bishops, a general insurrection did not take place." The people, rejoicing in the outcome of the trial, were averted from violent courses; the mob would wait until the end of the year to show what it could do. But they were restless and sensitive: when the magistrates of Lichfield tried to prevent fireworks on the liberation of the bishops, a mob beat some of them with sticks.

With the coming of autumn it became common knowledge that the Prince of Orange had assumed the role of a deliverer and was projecting an invasion of the kingdom, and early in November word passed from village to village that he stood with his army upon English soil. The alarm had long since been sounded by the government; Englishmen were called upon to close ranks in defense of their anointed sovereign. That these rallying attempts were ineffective is well known. The mistrust in which James was held vitiated such efforts. According to Van Citters, writing late in September, the perturbation of the court was not reflected in either urban or rural attitudes. Many suspected a made-to-order crisis, which would serve as a pretext for the king to augment his troops and introduce French forces. An ill-defined element continued to regard James's regime as a threat to civil liberties and the Protestant cause. Nor did James, despite some last-ditch attempts to improve what today would be called his public image, succeed in counteracting these opinions. In the last days of October, he was still in a mood to "catechize" the magistrates of London for not taking adequate steps to prevent recent outrages on Catholic chapels. He was fearful of what the mob might do on the anniversary of the Gunpowder Plot, and urged the municipal authorities to take the necessary precautions. The latter appear to have responded energetically, for it seems that the Lord Mayor, in addition to mustering all constables, had ten companies under arms. Perhaps because of these measures, perhaps because the people were pleased by the removal of Irish troops from the metropolis, the holiday passed by peacefully enough.

The government was now concerned with the possibility of rioting on November 17. This was the anniversary of the accession of Queen Elizabeth, an occasion popularly celebrated until well into the eighteenth century. It was reported that, in addition to the customary burning of an effigy of the Pope, the people, including the apprentices, had elected three colonels from among themselves, and had made three standards, bearing such legends as "No Pope, No Popists," and the like. This is the nearest they came to anything resembling a project for military organization among the people, and it is unlikely that it represents much more than a device for dramatizing agitation. But it is worthy of note that the Dutch minister, reporting these events, refers to the presence of five thousand troops in London, by which it was hoped that "apprehended mischief" might be checked. And it is clear, from the same source, that moderate men were afraid that "wonderfull occurances might take place in Town" if the king departed, which was obviously necessary if he were to deal with the invader. Actually, the departure of James for Salisbury took place on this very day, November 17, and sparked no particular reaction. His defection a few weeks later would be a very different matter.

Throughout the autumn there was a steadily mounting crescendo of anti-Catholic incidents and outrages, ranging from isolated harassments of unpopular individuals and attacks on chapels to the full-scale destruction and near anarchy of the night of December 11. The people were still gripped by an obsession. It was, after all, but a decade since the hysterical days of the Oates Plot. Late in September, the Jesuit Charles Petre, a brother of James's father confessor, attracted the attention of a mob by preaching in disparagement of the King James Version; according to Evelyn, "they pulled him out of the Pulpit, & treated him very coursely, insomuch as it was like to create a very greate disturbance in the City." From other sources it appears that this was not the first time that Petre had offended in this respect; that the Lord Mayor and his officers were forced to appease the mob, which pulled down the pulpit and damaged the altar; and that Petre saved himself from death only by flight. That the place of worship was the Elector Palatine's chapel in Lime Street seems to have made no difference. Doubtless the preacher suffered to some extent for his brother's sake, for he was held in popular detestation. Toward the end of the following month, on the occasion of the Lord Mayor's show, the mob in a somewhat bolder gesture demolished and publicly burned the altar furnishings of the Carmelite chapel in Bucklersbury; the trained bands and constables were ineffective though the priest was saved by the City guard. Only the intervention of the sheriffs prevented a similar outrage at the Lime Street chapel. Two weeks later the chapel at St. John's, Clerkenwell, was, in effect, sacked, the apprentices seizing and burning two cartloads of furniture which priests were "prudently" attempting to remove. Evelyn speaks of this establishment as a nunnery, but he probably errs, as the inmates appear to have been men. A contemporary newsletter refers to it as an abbey, and says that a "rabble" attacked it believing that within it were stored "Gridirons Long Knives & Caldrons to destroy the Protestants." In this case the forces of law and order, if not more successful were at least more aggressive, and the episode may have provided the mob's first martyrs; "the Horse and Footguards came & shot and killed some, wounded a great many, & took some prisoners"—so goes the newsletter.

From elsewhere in the country came similar accounts. In Norwich a mob of over a thousand (though for the most part made up of boys), threatening a Catholic chapel, was dispersed by the mayor and sheriffs. The priest was reported "very ill used." A "mass-house" in Newcastle was sacked and used by "Jack Pudding and his brethren for a Play-House." A chapel in York was destroyed. Early in December Cambridge priests were attacked by a mob, and at Sidney Sussex College paraphernalia of Catholic worship, including vestments, were destroyed. About the same time attacks were made on the houses of "papists" at Bristol, and an anti-Catholic riot occurred at Oxford.

As a result of the Clerkenwell incident, all Catholic places of worship in the capital were closed, save for those maintained by the royal family and representatives of foreign governments. To the doughtiest of Catholics, the signs of the times must now have been clear. An inquest held in connection with the slain demonstrators at Clerkenwell, under the usual jury procedure, proclaimed the victims to have been public-spirited persons wilfully done to death by the soldiery while opposing the activities of traitors. But, open or shut, the Catholic establishments were yet to experience the worst excesses of the mob. On December 10 the king, who had abandoned the field to his Dutch adversary, foresook his capital. Into the political vacuum thus created the energies of the mob poured with terrifying abandon, and, for a brief time, virtually without check.

According to the *English Courant,* "no sooner was the King's withdrawing known, but the Mobile consulted to wreak their vengeance on Papists and Popery." Chapels, embassies, and private residences, hitherto protected in some degree by royal or municipal authority, felt the full impact of mob violence. The Franciscans' new establishment in Lincoln's Inn Fields was pulled to pieces and set ablaze by "a prodigious Number." Nearby Wild (or Weld) House, the official residence of the Spanish ambassador, Ronquillo, was next seized upon; there they "ransackt, destroy'd and burnt all the Ornamental and Inside Part of the Chappel," leaving not even the wainscoting intact. The attacks upon the chapels in Bucklersbury and Lime Street were renewed; the rioters also returned to the charge at St. John's, Clerkenwell, and "demolisht it quite." Perhaps the destruction was not so complete as the newsbooks would have it believed—it was acknowledged at the time that accounts of the fate of chapels and Catholic houses differed—but there can be no doubt that it was a wild night, in which motley throngs inspired by a variety of motives indulged their passions, vandalistic instincts, and greed.

The attacks upon the embassies point up the absence of control. According to the *Universal Intelligence,* the mob broke into the residences of the representatives of Florence and Venice, as well as Spain, "and whilst some pluck'd down and threw out all the Pictures, Goods, and Furniture out of the Windows, others without and below set them on fire," so that "the whole Town seem'd in a Flame." Wild House certainly suffered in this way. In addition to ravaging the chapel, the mob destroyed "some Cartloads" of books and manuscripts, and included money, plate, and jewels in their plunder. James himself was a loser here, for among the loot was the plate of the Chapel Royal. This was not the only treasure deposited for safekeeping by apprehensive Catholics; one "Gentlewoman," it is said, lost a trunk containing £800 in cash and a large quantity of plate. According to Van Citters, Wild House was singled out as the principal place where the Mass was attended, but he adds that Ronquillo was unpopular because of debts which he owed widely. He goes on to say that the house of Barillon, the French ambassador, which was located in St. James's Square, though entered and searched for arms and priests, suffered no further molestation. Its happier fate reveals no predilection for the French, but appears to have resulted from the personal popularity of the ambassador (who had a reputation for liberality), from his foresight in obtaining a guard of soldiers, and from "the Neighborhood of some Noblemen, who caused their own Houses to be guarded." The abode of the Resident of Venice was also protected by soldiery, but the establishments of the Florentine Envoy and the Resident of the Elector Palatine were overrun. According to one account, the apprentices had designs on the Papal Nuncio's house, but finding on it a sign, "This house to be let," desisted.

With such treatment meted out, or at least threatened, to the embassies, with the guards forced to defend even the Royal Chapel at St. James's Palace, the property of private citizens must have been precariously held. Prudent tradesmen having establishments bearing such unpopular signs as the Cardinal's Hat, Nun's Head, or Pope's Head, removed them. There were threats to "pull down all Papists Houses" in the City, and several were pillaged and destroyed. Perhaps the most damage was suffered by Henry Hill, the king's printer. As the publisher, for three years, of various works in support of the Catholic religion, he was a marked man. A month earlier, upon complaint that a mob numbering over a thousand had broken his windows and threatened more mischief, the government had ordered the Lord Mayor to provide a sufficient guard for his protection. But there was no security now; his printing house was destroyed, with the equipment of his trade, including two or three hundred reams of paper, printed and unprinted, which went up in smoke. So fanatical was the multitude, as it roamed the city, that it even threatened the house at Newgate Market, "for no other reason, but that one Burdet, a Papist, was one of the Farmers of the Market."

As far as the capital was concerned, the night of December 11 marked the peak of mob violence and destruction. Not since the conflagration of 1666 had the London skies been so brightly lighted. There followed the "Irish Night" of December 12, when the citizens were alarmed to the point of panic by rumors that disbanded Irish soldiers, numbering many thousands, were "burning Towns, massacring the people, and marching directly for London to put the like in execution here." But though the tocsin was sounded and, according to one source, a hundred thousand "were presently at their weapons," little is heard of rioting and pillaging, and the following day, which brought news of the groundlessness of such fears, found the people in a soberer mood. In the meantime, such authorities as continued to function took steps to curb the repetition of lawless acts.

Throughout December, and even later, outbreaks were reported from widely scattered localities in the kingdom. On December 11 the *Universal Intelligence* noted that Protestants had demolished all "Popish Chapels" in and near York, Bristol, Gloucester, Worcester, Shrewsbury, Stafford, Wolverhampton, Birmingham, Cambridge, and Bury St. Edmunds. Perhaps some allowance should be made for journalistic exaggeration; on the other hand, one can add similar instances of mob depredations at other places, such as Hull, Newcastle, and Northamptonshire. Some of these chapels can be precisely identified. At Clevely Park, Lord Dover's seat near Cambridge, a mob from that town "tore down all the Furniture of the Romish Chappel and burnt it." Dover was prominently associated with James's Catholic retinue; he was a Commissioner of the Treasury and at the Revolution was entrusted with the infant Prince of Wales. Similarly visited was Peterborough House, near Northampton, whose master, Henry Mordaunt (the second Earl), had been suspected of complicity in the Popish Plot and was a recent convert to the Roman faith. Here, as in some other cases, the mob, having despoiled the chapel, made a search for arms; according to the newsbooks, the Earl's steward, intimidated by threats of being burned alive, revealed "Arms for about 150 Persons, and about 260 Weight of Gunpowder," which had been hidden in one of the fishponds. Another Catholic house near Northampton, that of Mr. Hinds, was reported destroyed. In Hertfordshire the "Country Mobile," on information that Lord Aston had "stor'd up great quantities of Provisions" at his seat at Standen, descended upon it and demolished the house and furnishings. An

attempt to do likewise at Hatfield House, whose owner, the fourth
Earl of Salisbury, would soon be imprisoned as a Catholic, was
"prevented by the Militia that happened to be then there." These
are but some of the more newsworthy acts of lawlessness; there were
undoubtedly many instances of lesser vandalism.

Clerics identified with Roman Catholicism or regarded as sympathetic to it were sometimes singled out for rough treatment. At
Nantwich, Dr. James Arderne, the Dean of Chester and onetime
chaplain to Charles II, was seized while taking refreshment at an
alehouse. He appears to have served as a consolation prize; the
mob would have preferred his Bishop, Dr. Cartwright, who, as an
ecclesiastical commissioner and chief visitor to Magdalen College,
was recognized as one of James's principal aides. As it was, Arderne
was charged with applying to Father Petre "to intercede for part
of the Quire to be appropriated to Popist Worship," and was saved
from the pillory, or something like it, only by the protestations of
"more moderate Persons." In Balsham, Cambridgeshire, a mob from
Cambridge, apparently augmented by like-minded men from Bury
St. Edmunds, discovered Dr. Thomas Watson, the Bishop of St.
Davids, another strong supporter of King James and a well-known
opponent of the succeeding regime. Watson's disguise was to no
avail; he was seized and "mounted upon a paultry Horse, without
Saddle or Bridle, and so led in a triumphant Manner to Cambridge,"
where the magistrates were obliged to secure him in the castle. At
one village the people threatened the parson that "in case he ever
hereafter did pray for Queen Mary, or her supposed Child, they would
make him be glad to eat up his words."

Watson was but one of the figures prominently associated with
the beleaguered regime who fell into the clutches of a mob, or
suffered narrow escapes, or sustained damage to their property.
Perhaps the best known, and certainly one of the most detested,
was Lord Chancellor Jeffreys, notorious for his drastic decrees on
the "Bloody Assizes" and as the backbone of the Ecclesiastical Commission. Jeffreys was recognized while lying low in Wapping, in
the disguise of a common seaman. He was with difficulty rescued
by a company of trained bands from a raging mob, which was
"ready to pull him to peces before he be brought to public justice."
Indeed, some believed that Jeffreys's death, which occurred soon
afterwards, was occasioned by injuries received at the hands of the

populace. Actually, he was conveyed, well guarded, in a hackney coach "accompanied by a vast Crowd and loud Shouts to the Lord Mayors, where the Multitude cry'd out for Justice." Thence, primarily for his own protection, he was committed by order of the Lords at Whitehall to the Tower, his progress being marked (in the words of one observer) "with such a din of the rabble as the writer never heard before." Another well-known figure who was forced into prison by the mob was Sir Roger L'Estrange, the official licenser of the press. Long unpopular because of his rejection of the evidence for the Oates Plot, and for his journalistic attacks on Dissenters and Whigs, he was sent to Newgate by the Court of Aldermen when the people continued "dis-satisfied" after an earlier dismissal by a Tory magistrate, Sir John Moore. In Lincoln's Inn Fields the town house of Lord Powis, the leader of the Catholic nobility imprisoned in connection with the Oates Plot, and a commissioner for the regulation of corporations, escaped pillage when the mob learned that it was to be occupied by Lord Delamere, who had been charged with complicity in Monmouth's Rebellion and was a well-known adherent of the Prince of Orange. The crowds showed their anger toward two men significantly associated with the king's use of the dispensing power. Sir Thomas Jenner, who, as Baron of the Exchequer, had supported the royal position in his judgment in Hales's case, had his lodging in Serjeant's Inn ransacked and lost £400. Hales himself was apprehended in the company of the King at Faversham, on James's first flight; there "the Rabble . . . got together, and would not be satisfied till Sir Edward Hales was taken from the King's Presence, and secured in the Prison of that Town." In the meantime another mob, hearing that Hales was in custody, assaulted his house in Kent, "entirely destroying his great Library, and all else that was Valuable." Others who were stopped and in some cases robbed, presumably while fleeing London, were Obadiah Walker, the Catholic Master of University College; John Leyburn, the first Vicar Apostolic of the London district; and "Lord Arundel's Son and Grandson." Jenner, too, was so affronted.

The most valuable prize to fall into the hands of a mob was, of course, James himself. The story of how the king, having fled his capital, was awaiting a favorable tide off Faversham in order to flee his realm, and was there seized by a band of local fishermen, needs no retelling. That he was at first not recognized (being in disguise and taken for a Jesuit) detracts from the revolutionary implications of the episode: it was not the royal purse that was consciously rifled, or the royal person that was consciously searched and addressed with such expressions as "old rogue, ugly, lean-jawed, hatchet-faced Jesuit, popish dog, etc." Nonetheless, after he had been taken to the Arms of England at Faversham, and his identity made known, he was still kept a close prisoner; his demands to be allowed to continue his journey were refused, his privacy was not respected, and he was not spared the affront of a reading of William's manifesto beneath his windows. And it is significant that the provisional government in London found it expedient to send to Faversham 120 guards and 50 grenadiers to attend him and secure him "from the Insolence of the numbers of People who may presse to come neer Him upon this occasion."

Even without such an escort, James would probably have been secure from attacks upon his person. With it he was assured of an orderly return to his capital, for the rank and file were not as a rule sufficiently bold and well armed to challenge a military contingent. Here and there, however, there were encounters. Early in November some "inhabitants of Sherburne" are said to have fallen upon a party of soldiers and wounded some of them; the king ordered an investigation of this outrage. In December, Dover Castle was seized and, according to a newsbook, the "mobile" at Norwich dared bid defiance to the trained bands as well as the civil magistrates. From more than one source comes evidence that the soldiery sometimes sympathized with the mob. At Bury St. Edmunds, upon "Rumour of some Irish approaching with Fire and Sword," over five hundred inhabitants armed themselves and fortified the town gates and streets. The fears being proved groundless, the "rabble" turned to indiscriminate plunder and mischief; but when a company of the militia was ordered to disperse them, they "turned their Musquets, knocked out their Ball, and forced the Colonel to declar for a free Booty, and so joyned with the Rabble." In Maidstone five grenadiers, "with some of the Youth of this Town," robbed a local Catholic of money and spoiled his goods. And when Lord Langdale, the Catholic Governor of Hull (one of the strongest garrisons in England), was ousted in a military coup led by the Deputy-Governor, the latter "raised the Town to his Assistance; so that the Rabble presently fell upon the Masshouse and all the Houses of the Papists in Town,"

Langdale being "guarded out of Town to prevent the Destruction threatned him by the Mobilee."

Of mob organization or leadership little is known, probably because there is little to be known. Even in London the mob was a faceless thing, drifting and shifting, lacking cohesion and, apart from antipathy toward Catholicism, a strong, binding purpose. That women as well as men filled its ranks cannot be doubted. At Bury St. Edmunds "the Female was reputed to do the most mischief"— at least so the undoubtedly masculine reporter for the *London Courant* averred, pointing out that "they burnt all manner of Goods which they found in Papists houses, they ript up Featherbeds, and scattered the Feathers abroad, and have given superabundant testimony of the ill consequences of a popular fury." It is obvious that mob demonstrations and attacks cloaked and abetted many a crime and misdeameanor on the part of the London underworld, and of like-minded folk elsewhere, and doubtless many an "honest" citizen, convinced that he was furthering Protestantism by sacking a Catholic establishment, did not surrender all his loot to the flames. As for leadership, two or three figures emerge, though without much substantiating evidence. Hugh Speke, in his *Secret History of the Revolution,* published in 1715, claimed that it was he who forged a printed declaration which set the mob upon the Catholics. He had been in King James's bad books since at least 1683, when he produced a pamphlet reflecting upon James (then Duke of York) in connection with the alleged suicide of the Earl of Essex; in the same year Jeffreys sent him to prison for three years for sedition. Speke, an accomplished liar, was writing in hope of reward for services to the revolutionary regime, but there is no evidence to disprove his claim. Apart from this, almost nothing is heard of specific acts of agitation. Two aristrocrats, both connected with the abortive Rye House Plot of 1683, may deserve some scrutiny. Lord Grey of Warke, a zealous exclusionist who commanded Monmouth's horse at Sedgemoor, was rash and lawless enough for any mob; indeed, he had been found guilty, along with others, of committing a riot in the City in 1687. The other is John, third Baron Lovelace. That he was at least in contact with mob elements is demonstrated by the fact that he drew up a petition in support of William's candidacy for the throne, which was presented to the Houses of Parliament on February 12 by "ten of the mobile, each deputed to this by 5000 of the like." One may well suspect this pair; yet there is not enough, even in the way of circumstantial evidence, for an indictment, much less a conviction.

From all the principal sources of administrative authority—from James II, the Prince of Orange, the lords of the Interregnum, the magistrates of London and other places—flowed directives aimed at curbing and punishing the excesses of the mob. Not since the Revolt of 1381, it would seem, had so many Englishmen of substance, so widely scattered over the country, been so alarmed by the latent passions and energies of the masses. There was concern, too, lest Englishmen and English interests in "papist" lands might suffer by way of retaliation. Thus a contemporary pamphleteer was afraid that the recent excesses, representing only the "Fury of an Ungovernable Rabble" might be looked upon as "the Act of a whole City," and resented as such, to the detriment of English factories beyond the seas. Rumors of all kinds abounded. It was reported that Englishmen in France were being held as hostages until James II's chaplains could safely make their way to that country; that Englishmen in Calais had been threatened with attack upon the arrival of Mary of Modena; that the Earl of Essex was confined to the Bastille, and that other English Protestants in France were ill used. From Falmouth came word that the French were attacking English shipping. It was necessary to sooth diplomatic sensibilities. The acting government moved speedily to provide the Spanish ambassador with lodgings and entertainment at Whitehall, and ordered that £6,000 be paid him for the losses he had sustained. A reward was offered for the recovery of his effects; goods removed from his premises were to be brought to Sir Henry Firebrace, Chief Clerk of the Green Cloth, under threat of prosecution. A similar order applied to the losses of the Florentine Resident. Some "pilfering Villains," caught with goods stolen from Wild House on their persons, were committed to Newgate; these, the *London Courant* advised, would be "treated by the Justices of the Nation as the worst of Thieves."

On December 12 the peers who had constituted themselves an emergency administrative committee issued a proclamation prohibiting further assaults on private property (particularly the residences of foreign ministers). In addition, they called upon the sheriffs of London, Middlesex, and Surrey, as well as justices of the peace and other magistrates, to summon the militia and *posse comitatus,* if necessary, to suppress riots and tumults. The following night, when the citizenry was inflamed by the Irish rumors, they instructed the trained bands of the Tower Hamlets to fire with bullet, if necessary, upon rioters, and ordered that "the footguards should stand to their arms in St. James's Park, and the horse guards the same." They also commanded that cannon should be "planted in the Park, Charing Cross, at the entrance into Piccadilly from Hyde Park side, and other proper places." A special order was directed to the Earl of Craven, Lord Lieutenant of Middlesex, to call together the militia of Middlesex, Westminster, and Southwark "for the preventing any disorders which might hapen in the suburbs of London." The Dowager Queen requested that thirty horse be drawn up before her residence at Somerset House to disperse any mobs, and that Lord Faversham be permitted to remain there to defend her. The lords were concerned about their own safety, and Dartmouth's regiment, commanded by Sir Henry Shere, was called upon to protect them "from the rage of the rabble." Lord Lucas was made Governor of the Tower of London in place of the detested Hales, and Catholic soldiers were disarmed and cashiered. Catholic houses were searched and arms found within them seized; as early as December 7 the Lord Mayor had enjoined the individual aldermen to conduct searches in their wards for papists and suspicious persons, in response to popular fears that Catholics were resorting to the City in great numbers and were preparing to launch an attack. On the thirteenth, the Prince of Orange issued a proclamation from Henley, requiring the soldiery to be kept under discipline in the interest of the public peace, which had been disturbed by their dispersal, and a few days later, upon King James's brief return to his capital, the hapless monarch issued orders in council requiring all civil officers to "prevent and suppress" the disorders of the mob, "as also all Roietous and Tumultuous Assemblies whatsoever." What may be regarded as the culminating counterstroke came near the end of December, when William, acting "upon the Trusts and Powers reposed in him by the Lords Spritual and Temporal, and Commons late assembled at Westminster," issued a declaration calling upon various Protestant magistrates to execute the duties of their offices, to suppress "all Riots, Routs, and tumultuous Assemblies," and to keep the peace.

These measures appear to have been successful in stemming what many must have feared might swell to an engulfing tide of lawlessness. It should be remembered, however, that outside the capital

England had no adequate military force, and repression was sometimes approached in a gingerly fashion. Late in November, before
the worst manifestations of popular unrest had unfolded, the king
had rejected Sir Edward Hales's suggestion that mortars be mounted
in Bristol, even in case of disorders there, "since they could not
destroy the Riotters but the City it selfe in which principally consists
the wealth & strength of the nation, & consequently his own"; it
might, moreover, so exasperate the people throughout the realm "as
to cause a Generall defection." In piecemeal manner, with such resources as were ready to hand, the guardians of law and order had
to deal with local situations as they saw fit. At Bury St. Edmunds,
Sir John Cordel, an "active Gentleman in this County," took matters
into his own hands, raising two troops of horse, "being 120 Gentlemen Volanteers, well Accoutred." At Gloucester the mob was quieted
by one Esquire Cook, by whose authority most of its plunder was
recovered. On the other hand, Lord Dover's country house was saved
from destruction only by bribing the assailants. It appears to have
taken some months for the country to quiet down. Even while the
Convention was deliberating, the mob, as has been noted, assembled
tumultuously to present petitions for settling the Prince and Princess
of Orange upon the throne. Nor did formal recognition of this pair
as joint sovereigns put a stop to sporadic disorder. There was a
mutiny in Ipswich in April 1689; in February and May riotous mobs
caused concern in Shropshire, and the same may be said for North-
hamptonshire in April and for Worcestershire later in the spring.
Nearly six months after James had fled his kingdom, rioters in Newcastle sought to destroy a statue of that monarch. The new sovereigns must have been acceptable to the great majority of the
turbulent masses, but it took time to reestablish the king's peace;
to travel the highways to London in the aftermath of revolution was,
it was said, "to court personal risks."

It is unlikely that the tumultuous and lawless acts described above
—even when as frightening and destructive as the London riots of
mid-December—had any appreciable effect upon the outcome of the
Revolution. It still presents the aspect of a conservative and prop-
ertied movement, both as to implementation and settlement. The mob
was never politically minded enough, or sufficiently well led and
organized, to present a people's charter; the closest, it seems, that
it came to political negotiation was in the presentation of the petitions

on behalf of William and Mary. There appears to be no evidence that any advantages, directly affecting the various turbulent bands, followed upon their demonstrations and ravagings. Rather, where possible, they were proceeded against as criminals or miscreants.

But there are lessons to be learned from these events. They point to the ease with which, in the days before the maintenance of an adequate police force, riotous propensities could be fanned into flame. They underscore the deep-seated and pervasive hostility toward Roman Catholicism. And they help to explain the readiness with which the Prince of Orange was accepted, even by some whose political convictions kept them out of step with the march of events. "All the Lords and city have invited the Prince of Orange, which we all pray may come quickly that a stop may be put to the fury of the rabble who have done great mischief"—so commented a Londoner on December 13. Without the rioting and mobbing, it might have taken considerably longer to convince the peers and the magistrates of London that it was in their best interest to support William as a provisional governor, or to induce the burghers to advance private funds to him, in lieu of taxation, more than a month before he was formally tendered the crown. The Convention, with its divided Tory majority, might have bogged down in the search for an acceptable compromise. To men of property and moderation, to those who remembered with abhorrence the drastic dislocations which had followed the defeat of Charles I, these turbulent manifestations of popular restlessness, bigotry, and discontent can only have emphasized the urgency of a speedy and practical settlement.

Gerald M. Straka

THE NATION CONTEMPLATES ITS REVOLUTION, 1689–1789

*Professor Gerald M. Straka was born in Milwaukee, Wisconsin, in 1931,
and received his education at the Universities of Virginia and Wisconsin and
as a Fulbright Scholar at the London School of Economics. As a teacher at
the University of Delaware, he specializes in English political thought.*

Within a few months the religious and constitutional tensions introduced by the later Stuarts were relaxed by an astonishing sequence —the invasion of William of Orange, the flight of James II to France, the quiet assemblage of the "Convention Parliament," the recognition of a collateral Stuart line in the joint reign of William and Mary —that has since been called the Glorious Revolution of 1688. After a tortuous period of national debate over the constitutional legitimacy of the Settlement, over religious toleration, and over the increased military expenditures required by two mammoth wars with France, the Hanoverian succession of 1714 brought to England a rapid acquiescence to the Settlement. Having once digested the Revolution, eighteenth-century gentlemen came to praise what they had been forced to swallow.

Both extremes—Bolingbroke, the Tory idealist, and Hume, the Whig skeptic—united in praising the Settlement of 1689, the former asserting that "the Revolution is looked upon by all sides as a new era. . . . On this foundation all the reasonable Whigs and Tories unite. . . . If this creed were made a test of political orthodoxy, there would appear at this time but very few heretics amongst us." And Hume concurred that "the Revolution forms a new epoch in the constitution. . . . We in this island have ever since enjoyed, if not the best system of government, at least the most perfect system of liberty, that ever was known amongst mankind."

Since these eighteenth-century pronouncements, nothing has been written to diminish the glory of the Revolution, and little has been

Reprinted by permission from *Studies in Eighteenth-Century Culture,* Volume 1:
The Modernity of the Eighteenth Century, edited by Louis T. Milic (Cleveland: The
Press of Case Western Reserve University, 1971), copyright © 1971 by The Press of
Case Western Reserve University, Cleveland, Ohio 44106.

done to define its precise nature. Extremes from parliamentary supremacy to popular right are said to have been established in 1688, as well as the cabinet system, a national debt, political parties, mercantilism, international prestige, imperialism—even, as the great Lecky observed, the English compulsion for trimming trees and hedges, and the love of good cupboard china. . . .

The hundreds of pamphlets and volumes contributed by such familiar names as Defoe, Steele, Hoadly, Warburton, Bolingbroke, Hume, Blackstone, and Burke, among others, hardly need delineation, though it might be well to be reminded that both of the above concepts—hereditary Protestant monarchialism and the Revolution Settlement statutes—were complementary. The eighteenth-century Englishman believed in the reigning House of Hanover because it acted as guarantor of the Settlement; the Settlement, conversely, was the guarantee of Protestant religious freedom, the regularization of parliamentary sittings, and due process. The dual character of this arrangement was accented by the belief that Catholicism throve on arbitrary rule and the consequent suspension of prescriptive and declaratory law, and that Catholic life (as depicted on the continent) was nasty, brutish, and short, while Protestantism encouraged arts, letters, science, and the blessings of trade.

David Hume, who in many respects is more the clarion of the Revolution than is John Locke, eulogized 1688 in just this way:

> . . . during these last sixty years [since 1688] when a parliamentary establishment has taken place; whatever factions may have prevailed either among the people or in public assemblies, the whole force of our constitution has always fallen to one side, and an uninterrupted harmony has been preserved between our princes and our parliaments. Public liberty, with internal peace and order, has flourished almost without interruption: Trade and manufactures, and agriculture, have encreased: The arts, and sciences, and philosophy, have been cultivated. Even religious parties have been necessitated to lay aside their mutual rancour: And the glory of the nation has spread itself all over Europe; derived equally from our progress in the arts of peace, and from valor and success in war. So long and so glorious a period no nation almost can boast of: Nor is there another instance in the whole of mankind, that so many millions of people have, during such a space of time, been held together, in a manner so free, so rational, and so suitable to the dignity of human nature. . . .

It is through these commonplace views that the Revolution of 1688 became the Year One in eighteenth-century thought, for as one orator asked, "Shall I call this our Birth-day? or rather the day of our Resurrection?" Sixteen eighty-eight was "our wonderful deliverance" from popery and slavery. November the fifth, celebrated in the Church throughout the seventeenth century as "Gunpowder Treason Day," was celebrated in the eighteenth for the landing of William of Orange at Torbay. Nonconformists cherished the Revolution for its toleration, under which they had gained open worship. Four of the nation's major public debates—the Sacheverell trial, the Bangorian controversy, the American Revolution, and the Price-Burke-Paine controversy—centered on explaining in what ways 1688 constituted a genesis. Historians began or concluded their chronicles with the Revolution and were universally struck by the national enterprise displayed, contrasting it with medieval revolts of the "turbulent and barbarous aristocracy, plunging headlong from the extremes of one faction into those of another." Writers extolled the freedom of the press engendered by the lapse of the Licensing Act, attributing the greater liberality to the Revolution. Even Bolingbroke, who was accused by some of being a Jacobitical betrayer of the Settlement, reinforced the custom of referring to the Revolution as an age of founding fathers in his attack on the Septennial Act:

> *If it had been foretold to those patriots at the Revolution who remembered long parliaments, . . . who struggled hard for annual, and obtained with much difficulty . . . triennial parliaments, that a time would come, when . . . a parliament, chosen for three years, would choose itself for four more . . . and that it would be brought about, while our government continued on the foundations they had then so newly laid . . . it would have appeared improbable and monstrous to the friends of the Revolution.*

Legists and constitutional historians were dispensing with the customary reference to "fundamental and ancient constitutions," and using the Revolution as the ultimate precedent. In the 1784 case of the Dean of St. Asaph, accused of but exonerated from the charge of seditious libel for having published a tract advocating parliamentary reform, Chief Justice Mansfield based his decision on "the uniform judicial practice since the Revolution." The Revolution had already reached its most promising legal eminence as early as 1765 on the question of the legality of general warrants. The crown's plaintiff, Carrington, had raided one Entick's establishment on a general warrant for whatever seditious material he could confiscate, but the court threatened to disqualify the evidence because of the unlawful seizure. The crown based its defense on the grounds that general warrants were "the practice since the Revolution, . . . an usage tolerated from the era of liberty, and continued downwards to this time through the best ages of the constitution." Therefore, the Revolution was a proper precedent for "legal commencement." Here was a clear attempt to link the Revolution with the great germinal ages of England's constitutional past—Magna Carta, Edward I, the later fourteenth century. Had it been allowed by the court as a properly established age of legal precedent, the Revolution would have been elevated from the realm of patriotic rhetoric to that of legal citation. Perhaps even Burke's plea for adherence to the Revolution's principles would have been obviated, for the precepts of 1688 would have already been enshrined as fundamental law. Everything done in the Revolution's name could have frozen parliamentary reform for two hundred years. As it was, mere respect for the political world which created the Settlement, though it nonetheless congealed the thinking of men like Burke, who conceived of 1688 as the Year One, was not enough to cause it to be cited as binding precedent. Chief Justice Camden decided that the Revolution

> can have no place in the question made by this plea. . . . If the practice [of employing general warrants for arbitrary search and seizure] began then, it began too late to be law now. If it was more ancient, the Revolution is not to answer for it; and I could have wished that upon this occasion the Revolution had not been considered as the only basis of our liberty. . . .

At the very least, however, the Revolution did come to be accepted as commencing the "best ages of the constitution" and the "era of liberty," even if it was not to be usable as a point of law.

The Glorious Revolution of 1688 was truly a year of creation to the gentlemen of the English Enlightenment, though not in the same sense for which the children of later revolutions—the American, French, or Russian—were taught to cherish and cultivate their rebellions. The difference in attitudes can be detected in two contrasting remarks. The Englishman Sir Joseph Jekyll, speaking for the Revolution during the trial of Henry Sacheverell, said that "the constitution was wholly lost before, and recovered by the Restoration [of 1660]

. . . and before the Revolution, it is known how popery and absolute power had invaded the constitution. . . . In both these great events were the regal power and the rights of the people recovered"; a French deputy, speaking before the French National Assembly in 1790, said, "Let us destroy everything, yes, everything, for everything has to be remade."

To the English, the Revolution of 1688 was the apotheosis of their ancestors' genius for freedom, the recovery of a valued past; to the French, the Revolution of 1789 became the remedy for their ancestors' propensity for servility, a remedy effective only through destruction and regeneration. In this aspect, if in no other, Burke was correct when he admonished the French that by "respecting your forefathers, you would have been taught to respect yourselves. You would not have chosen to consider the French as a people of yesterday, as a nation of low-born servile wretches until the emancipating year of 1789." Thus was 1688 the year of creation, of resurrection, but only in an unchangeable, irrevocable sense. "It is finished," was its message. . . .

Thus when one searches for the effects of the Revolution on the eighteenth century, one finds precious little that has to do with the principles involved in the Revolution. Sixteen eighty-eight closed the door on medieval English history, freeing future generations to pursue new avenues of institutional development heretofore barely brushed: a workable party system, a ministerial system alloying Parliament with the crown, a professional fiscal mechanism, an imperial policy, a humane and practicable criminal code, reform of public manners, improved labor conditions, better education, parliamentary redistricting, and implementation of democratic aspirations. True, there were to be some holdovers in the matter of the Jacobites or of Catholic emancipation, but in most respects the Revolution of 1688, perhaps unlike any other revolution, had been self-terminating and conclusive—except regarding one matter, the issue of violent overthrow of legitimate authority.

The eighteenth-century Englishman remained uneasy over the brazen methods employed to unseat a king. Talk as he might about the bloodlessness, the decency of it all, he was haunted by the thought that, though the Revolution had escaped bloodshed, it might possibly have been by nothing more than sheer luck. As for its victim,

James II, one Jacobite approached the truth when he accused England of implicit regicide.

> 'Tis such a jest, such a banter, to say, we did take up arms, but we did not kill him: Bless us, kill our king, we would not have hurt a hair of his head! Why, every bullet shot at the battle of the Boyne was a killing the king; for if you did not, 'twas because you could not hit him.

This was overstatement, no doubt, but nonetheless it was true that the renowned doctrines of passive obedience and nonresistance had been trampled underfoot as naked power triumphed in 1688. Furthermore, the portrayal of the Revolution as an unconventional popular power play in the press gradually displaced the image of the Revolution as a mundane constitutional compendium. Slowly it dawned on the English that the techniques involved in revolution could be used by any group seeking redress, permitting not only the right to resist a tyrant, but resistance on points of policy having neither justice nor public opinion behind them.

The earliest recognition of power politics as an adjunct to 1688 came with Lord Halifax's conclusion that sovereignty invariably means the right to use power, regardless of right.

> I lay down . . . as fundamental—first, that in every constitution there is some power which neither will nor ought to be bounded. . . . If the Common Law is supreme, then those are so who judge what is the Common Law; and if none but the Parliament can judge so, there is an end of the controversy; there is no fundamental, for the Parliament may judge as they please—that is, they have the authority. But they may judge against right—their power is good, though their act is ill; no good man will outwardly resist the one, or inwardly approve the other.
>
> There is, then, no other fundamental but that every supreme power must be arbitrary.

Halifax, who had observed the occurrences of 1688 with some discretion, believed that Parliament had gained such a revolutionary power that none could gainsay it, though he seemed partly aware of the popular base upon which even crown and Parliament rested: "If kings are only answerable to God, that doth not secure them even in this world," he said in his "Political Thoughts," "since if God upon the appeal thinkith fit not to stay, He maketh the people His instruments"; and he adds that "kings assuming prerogative teach the people to do so too."

The disparity between sovereign right and revolutionary might called attention to itself in a dramatic gust of acrimonious discussion during the Sacheverell trial of 1710. The Anglican divine Dr. Henry Sacheverell, popular and respected preacher at St. Paul's, audaciously indicted the Revolution before the Lord Mayor and aldermen of London with a typically Jacobitical argument that "the necessary means used to bring about the said Happy Revolution were odious and unjustifiable." The cause of the outburst is difficult to pin down, though it might have resulted from the long and costly War of the Spanish Succession in which England was then engaged and which the good doctor felt would not have been entered into had it not been for the Revolution. For the first time the methods used to carry out the Revolution were publicly questioned. Sir Joseph Jekyll, testifying for the prosecution, stated incredulously that "the Commons cannot but think it hard, that in this assembly . . . they should now, after more than twenty years' enjoyment of the benefits arising by the Revolution . . . be forced to plead in vindication of the justice of that Revolution." The present trial, said prosecutor Sir John Holland, "depend[s] upon the lawfulness of the resistance at the Revolution," that is, whether revolutionary tactics can be used even in the most dire circumstances. The prosecution might have been better off had it left that branch of the inquiry alone and built its case on the irrelevance of Sacheverell's sermon by maintaining that 1688 had witnessed little more than a nation reconstituting itself in the exigency of a defaulted monarch, which was a commonly used and quite acceptable argument. The Bill of Rights, after all, contained no claims to justification by violent overthrow, no "When in the course of human events . . ." But Sir John Holland weakened his case in this fashion: "that there was a resistance is most plain, if taking up arms in Yorkshire, Nottinghamshire, Cheshire and almost all the counties of England . . . and turning [these] arms against their sovereign be resistance." Other Revolution adherents leapt into the same defense. Sir John Eyre unwittingly admitted that "people are to be the judges, when and how far they are to obey" and that "necessity always make[s] a justifiable exception." Robert Walpole, then treasurer of the Navy, drew the grand conclusion that only commonwealthsmen had heretofore suggested, that "the very being of our present government, is the resistance that was necessarily used at the Revolution," as if questions of justice were secondary. A few vague speculations that Halifax had entertained only in his study—that sovereign right is based on power, that power is necessity, and that popular revolutionary power was used in 1688—now became the basis of Parliament's argument and a matter for public record. Of course, no one then could have conceived that such an argument might be used, as Tom Paine was to do, against the Revolution Settlement, since few believed that an exigency could again arise that might cause public opinion to entertain revolutionary tactics to achieve redress. Even Daniel Defoe, the crypto-republican, said that democratic revolution might never again rear its head in England, because

> *the genius of this nation has always appeared to tend to a monarchy, a legal limited monarchy, and having had in the late Revolution a full and uninterrupted liberty, to cast themselves into what form of government they pleased: there was not discovered the least inclination in any party towards a commonwealth. . . .*
>
> *A commonwealth can never be introduced, but by such invasions of right, as must make our constituted government impracticable: the reason is, because men never willingly change for the worst; and the people of England enjoy more freedom in our regal, than any people in the world can do in a popular government.*

A small quarter of the populace, however, particularly among the Nonconformist clergy, quietly cherished the popular revolutionary appeal to violence they thought implicit in the Revolution, an appeal which their more respectable Anglican brethren dignified by the word "resistance." While they refrained from calling attention to themselves, these descendants of the Puritans looked back to the Civil Wars and to the Commonwealth and Protectorate for their ideals, states Professor Caroline Robbins. Most of them were angered by the appellations of "rebel" and "regicide." They were mollified with the Toleration Act of 1689, but still approved the cause that lay behind the revolution of 1641.

This was eminently true of the Reverend Robert Fleming, a royal chaplain to William III and a London Presbyterian preacher, whose *Divine Right of the Revolution* first appeared in 1706. In an interesting comparison he found William and the Biblical King David to be "revolution-kings," leading popular insurrectionary wars against

King Saul and James II for the liberty of their subjects. In a number of other works Fleming elaborated his theory that history progresses through revolutionary violence, that even Moses, having broken the normal succession of the Hebrew tribes, had set up a constitution which "was a revolution-erection founded on new laws and regulations." His works were republished with startling regularity throughout the eighteenth and nineteenth centuries, and in a Philadelphia edition of 1794 the editor added an assertion that God's design in history

> *is to effect revolutions as well in nations and communities as in the affairs of families and individuals. The world subsists by revolutions. Good men, indeed should be cautious of promoting such as are needless and may tremble at the most necessary: but if the voice from heaven cry, "Revolution!" in vain would all the powers upon earth attempt to arrest the motions of these wheels.*

But all in all Fleming and the Nonconformist contingent generally seemed to have read more into the Glorious Revolution than its supporters at Sacheverell's trial would have considered proper.

For the most part, ideas of resistance and civil disobedience were deemphasized throughout the eighteenth century. Outcries for reform abounded, and many were the attacks against corruption and deceit. But these were aimed by political cliques against governmental cliques and never were elevated to extreme appeals to revolution. Yet the memory and understanding of such an appeal remained, if only in off-hand remarks made by detached savants. Bolingbroke's aversion to the Whig preponderance in Parliament led him at one point to paraphrase Locke's warning against an overweening legislature: "Who hath the right and the means to resist the supreme legislative power? The whole nation hath the right; and a people who deserve to enjoy liberty will find the means." At any point when the lawmakers override the crown and the nation, the "bargain" between the legislature and the people is broken and the people may then "return to their original, their natural right, the right of restoring the same constitution or of making a new one." Bolingbroke was no revolutionary, however, and it may only have given him satisfaction to recite the slogans of '88 before the faces of his bumptious, borough-mongering Whig adversaries.

Nor was David Hume a revolutionary, but, like Halifax, he was struck by revolutionary power politics. He found the writings of Locke, Sydney, and Hoadly to be "compositions the most despicable both for style and matter"; though displaying "a regard to liberty, . . . a laudable passion," liberty "ought commonly to be subordinate to a reverence for established government." In his judgment the real flaw with Lockean ideas, however, was that they confuse the observer into thinking that ideology was a motivating force:

> *Let not the establishment at the Revolution deceive us, or make us so much in love with a philosophical origin to government. . . . Even that event was far from corresponding to these refined ideas. It was only the succession, and that only in the regal part of the government, which was then changed: And it was only the majority of seven hundred, who determined that change for near ten millions. I doubt not, indeed, but the bulk of those ten millions acquiesced willingly in the determination: But was the matter left, in the least, to their choice?*

The Revolution was an act of will rather than of ideology. Its physical shock to regality was such that the English monarchy never recovered, and because "the mere name of king [now] commands little respect," Hume concluded that if the Revolution had occurred in his century the monarchy probably would have been altogether abolished. As a result of the crown's declining powers, England could expect more revolutions if future sovereigns attempted to reassert their slipping prerogatives. . . .

Sir William Blackstone was as much perturbed by the legal questions created by the Revolution as was Hume over the political issues. Though impressed by the Revolution's legal establishment, he was cautious lest its tactical amorality become an equally binding precedent for future revolutionaries. On the one hand, he felt that Locke and the Revolution theorists had been right in asserting the people's natural liberty against the Stuarts' legal tyranny, but, "we cannot adopt [this view], nor argue from it, under any dispensation of government at present actually existing." In other words, the appeal to revolution had no place in due process. But while the Revolution remedy is not the cure for a future legal tyranny, "future generations, whenever necessity and the safety of the whole shall require it," will exert "those inherent (though latent) powers of society which no climate, no time, no constitution, no contract, can ever destroy or diminish."

On the eve of the American revolt, then, there emerged a tentative recognition of the method of revolution, though the impressive stability of the eighteenth-century constitution seemed to have obviated forever the need for its application. Of particular interest is that, on the rare occasions when revolutionary methods were discussed, the subject was broached by representatives and spokesmen of the establishment, not by malcontents or commonwealthsmen. The radicals, for all their discussion of popular rights and royal absolutism, seldom if ever raised the spectre of a second 1688. When they occasionally spoke of revolutionary recourse, they flashed such a collection of Whig clichés as to obscure the thrust of their arguments. John Trenchard is a case in point, for while he thunders that "no society of men will groan under oppressions longer than they know how to throw them off," and that "upon this principle of people's judging for themselves, and resisting lawless force, stands our late happy Revolution," he quickly camouflages his veiled threat by adding, "and with [the Revolution] the just and rightful title of our most excellent sovereign King George, to the scepter of these realms; a scepter which he has, and I doubt not will ever sway, to his honor, and the honor, protection, and prosperity of us his people." This is an argument far less awesome than even John Locke's or Bishop Hoadly's.

Furthermore, until the American Revolution made the subject one of more general discussion, only gentlemen of Bolingbroke's, Blackstone's, or Hume's stature spoke of revolution in the context of necessity. Back in the seventeenth century, whenever the painful subject of resistance was broached, it was, of course, decried as the resort of insane zeal, misguided theology, or untrammeled ambition—witness Clarendon's famous description of the causes of the Great Rebellion. In the Enlightenment it became common to discuss resistance, though cautiously, as a proper last resort. It lost its tie with the satanic ambition attributed to Essex or Cromwell, and became linked with righteous mass protest and natural right. Though everyone supposed the conditions preceding 1688 could never be repeated, no one could safely assume that the revolutionary pathway to reform, now that it had been blazed, would never have to be trod again. Boswell once confessed that his blood was stirred by the "pitch of fancied resistance, the possibility of which I am glad to keep in mind, but to which I trust I never shall be forced."

After 1760 the restive Americans made much of the unshared gains of the Glorious Revolution, and though their brothers in London chuckled at their antiquated use of Locke's contract theory, the appeal to arms was well understood under their Declaration: "When in the course of human events it becomes *necessary. . . .*" The rhetoric unleashed at home during the prolonged "Wilkes and Liberty" crusade, though rarely of a revolutionary nature, slowly brought to the fore the possibility of a future 1688. Revolution was now coming to be regarded as an active agent in national regeneration. It was not enough for "'Junius" to warn in 1769 that

> *the name of Stuart, of itself, is only contemptible; armed with the sovereign authority, their principles are formidable. The prince who imitates their conduct should be warned by their example; and while he plumes himself upon the security of his title to the crown, should remember that, as it was acquired by one revolution, it may be lost by another.*

Nor was it enough in 1779 for Charles Fox to compare George III with Henry VI and then conclude, "it was not a secret to [the House of Commons] that the present sovereign's claim to the throne of this country was founded only upon the delinquency of the Stuart family—a circumstance which should never be one moment out of his majesty's recollection." By 1789 the mere threat was expressed as a more active principle by the Reverend Dr. Richard Price:

> *Let us . . . take care not to forget the principles of the Revolution. . . . First: The right to liberty of conscience. . . . Secondly: The right to resist power when abused. And, Thirdly: The right to choose our own governors; to cashier them for misconduct; and to frame a government for ourselves. . . . Were it not true that liberty of conscience is a sacred right, that power abused justifies resistance, and that civil authority is a delegation from the people—were not, I say, all this true—the Revolution would have been not an assertion, but an invasion of rights; not a revolution, but a rebellion. . . . Tremble all ye oppressors of the world! Take warning all ye supporters of slavish hierarchies! Call no more (absurdly and wickedly) reformation, innovation. You cannot now hold the world in darkness. Struggle no longer against increasing light and liberality. Restore to mankind their rights; and consent to the correction of abuses before they and you are destroyed together.*

Price brought the doctrine of necessity forward a great step: from revolution as a last resort against kings to a justifiable and only resort. The apologists for necessity at Henry Sacheverell's trial had regarded the causes of the Revolution as unique. Do not call reform by the misnomer innovation, Price urged; in so doing, he conveyed his understanding that revolution should be the regular, not the irregular, rule for future change.

In 1796, in the trial of Sir John Reeves for publishing a seditious libel, this transformation of the Revolution of 1688 from an immutable monument to a transmutable tool for achieving change reached full bloom. As the defense summarized the charges against Reeves, the point gradually emerged that

> *"They [the republicans, Presbyterians, and Sectaries] invented"—you see with what truth and accuracy in the history of this country this is stated—"they invented the term revolution, to blind and mislead:" They invented it!—"and they have never ceased repeating it, that they may put the people in mind of making another." Gentlemen, those who have used it, in the most solemn proceedings in this country, . . . have used it, for the very purpose . . . of not putting the people in mind of making another, but of putting the people in mind, that by the transactions of that day [1688], both with respect to the regal government of the country, and the interest of the people in their rights and liberties, as well in the one view of the constitution as in the other, they were then restored, and for ever inviolably to be preserved. He says, he fears that those, who recur so much to this period [the Revolution era], and make so much of this term, are not so fond of what was then transacted, as they are of "Revolutions in the abstract," and that they wish to lay hold of the term, to make it a precedent for any future revolution they may please to project. They are fond of the term and cling to the term; and that sole reason, it is, that he quarrels with the term, and endeavors to show, that this event is no proper precedent for a revolution that does not come up to the case in point; and that the case in point, however termed a revolution, was improperly so termed, being in truth only a reestablishment of what was the law before.*

There is a letter by Bishop Gilbert Burnet in the Public Record Office, written shortly after the Glorious Revolution, in which he reveals awareness that the precedent of violence and popular right may not be eternally laid to rest, saying that

> *upon the whole matter [of the Revolution] I do not think that now, when we are at quiet, it is convenient to write much upon this subject of proving the right of the people's defending themselves when the whole constitution is in danger of being overturned. That is a question fit to be laid to sleep; for in quiet times there is no occasion to dispute it, and when-*

soever a new occasion is given by the violence of the government to examine it, authors and matter will be found to support it.

"Quiet times" had perhaps come to an end in George III's reign. At any rate, this letter is evidence that one who had such an influential hand in conducting the Revolution perceived that its activistic spirit might be needed again against "the violence of the government." The trial of John Reeves bears witness that the idea of revolutionary solutions had become common coin.

The man whose reflections most give us insight into the Revolution's influence on the eighteenth century is, of course, Edmund Burke. His monumental *Reflections on the French Revolution* was the quintessential presentation of the Revolution as immemorial law contrasted to its supposed creation of a right to "revolutions in the abstract:"

> *The Revolution was made to preserve our ancient indisputable laws and liberties, and that ancient constitution of government which is our only security for law and liberty. . . . The very idea of the fabrication of a new government is enough to fill us with disgust and horror. We wished at the period of the Revolution, and do now wish, to derive all we possess as an inheritance from our forefathers.*

This is the classic Burke, standing among the monuments of England's great age of constitutional creation. Sixteen eighty-eight was truly, for him, the Year One, eminently so, not because Burke was an antiquarian or a sentimentalist—though he may have been these things, they determined his rhetoric more than his thought—but because he believed in a stratified society which would forever make democracy and democratic revolutionary challenges impossible. In his view earlier revolutions had been conducted by a *noblesse* exceedingly well trained in a natural law of subordination and the duties of privilege. His "permanent body composed of transitory parts" was a paean to the wisdom of God and man for having created an unchangeable social chain of obligatory relations from king to peasant.

Though Burke was partisan to the *ancien régime,* he did not blind himself to the strength of the revolutionary's appeal against tyranny. He understood through careful study of the transcripts of Sacheverell's trial how liberty must at times be vindicated by what Locke had called "an appeal to heaven." But because the appeal to arms must be made in an unequivocally good cause, he detested the crasser aspects of the Glorious Revolution, the influences that were purely monetary. The cant of the social compact had degenerated into "nothing better than a partnership agreement in a trade of pepper and coffee, calico, or tobacco."

Burke understood the doctrine of necessity behind the present revolutionary appeal, however, more clearly than most of his contemporaries, and he was much less hostile to revolutionary methodology than his modern critics have supposed. In a dozen qualifications, all militating against rebellion, he admits that when at last the moment for revolution comes,

> *it is the first and supreme necessity only, a necessity that is not chosen but chooses, a necessity paramount to deliberation, that admits no discussion and demands no evidence, which alone can justify a resort to anarchy. This necessity is no exception to the rule, because this necessity itself is a part, too, of that moral and physical disposition of things to which man must be obedient by consent or force.*

Out of context Burke's portrayal of the revolutionary imperative would fit well in the mouth of Maximilien Robespierre, who claimed that "the [French] revolutionary government . . . is based on the most sacred of all laws, on the general weal and on the ironclad law of necessity!" This comparison is not meant to place Burke in a revolutionary ethos, but to display the depth of his grasp of the revolutionary imperative. Still, Burke attributed the same motive to the English revolutionaries of 1688:

> *Laws are commanded to hold their tongues amongst arms, and tribunals fall to the ground with the peace they are no longer able to uphold. The Revolution of 1688 was obtained by a just war [not that Burke here is willing to concede that 1688 was an implied act of civil insurrection], in the only case in which any war, and much more a civil war, can be just. "Justa bella quibus necessaria" ["Wars are just to whom they are necessary"—Livy]. . . . The speculative line of demarcation where obedience ought to end and resistance must begin is faint, obscure, and not easily definable. It is not a single act, or a single event, which determines it. Governments must be abused and deranged, indeed, before it can be thought of; and the prospect of the future must be as bad as the experience of the past. . . . Times and occasions and provocations will teach their own lessons. The wise will determine from the gravity of the case; the irritable, from sensibility to oppression; the high-minded, from dis-*

dain and indignation at abusive power in unworthy hands; the brave and bold, from the love of honorable danger in a generous cause; but, with or without right, a revolution will be the very last resource of the thinking and the good.

In principle, then, there may be nothing more separating Burke from his radical contemporaries than "the speculative line . . . where obedience ought to end and resistance must begin," for Burke here recognizes an imperative beyond reason and right, just as did Dr. Price and Tom Paine. That Burke could find no militating preconditions justifying the French Revolution made him opposed to Paine on specific, perhaps more than on general, propositions governing revolutionary causation. He is certainly less the unqualified defender of the old order in these statements than in most traditional representations.

In his later "Appeal from the New to the Old Whigs," Burke develops his argument further:

It is not worth our while to discuss, like sophisters, whether in no case some evil for the sake of some benefit is to be tolerated. Nothing universal can be rationally affirmed on any moral or any political subject. . . . The lines of morality are not like the ideal lines of mathematics. . . . They admit of exceptions; they demand modifications. . . . Without attempting, therefore, to define, what never can be defined, the case of a revolution in government, this, I think, may be safely affirmed—that a sore and pressing evil is to be removed, and that a good, great in its amount and unequivocal in its nature, must be probable almost to certainty, before the inestimable price of our own morals and the well-being of a number of our fellow-citizens is paid for a revolution.

He accuses the French revolutionaries of not telling the world of France's grievances. Instead of "prattling about the Bastile," they ought to have established the rightness of their cause beyond doubt and revealed the monstrosity of the French crown in order to justify their actions. Though he remained unconvinced that a parallel between the house of Bourbon and the house of Stuart existed, Burke could see exigencies that require revolutionary departures. Had they established these exigencies, Burke might have been sympathetic, for if the principles of the French Revolution were "beneficial to the human race, . . . the English Constitution ought no more to stand against it than the ancient Constitution of the kingdom in which the new system prevails."

As we pass to Tom Paine's generation of reformers (though he was but eight years younger than Burke), the issue of the revolutionary right raised by the Glorious Revolution gradually becomes academic. Paine had little to say about 1688, dismissing all earlier politics as being under the control of a self-serving crown and aristocracy. The Bill of Rights was the "Bill of Wrongs," in that it had done nothing to extend political power to the people. When in 1797 Paine published his *Agrarian Justice,* he began to see that no civil equality could be established without equality in property. From that point in the development of English revolutionary thought, the purely civil issues raised by the English Revolution were displaced by growing demands for economic justice. The age of proletarian revolution had begun.

So, too, for the followers of Jeremy Bentham, who launched a new wave of reformism based on utilitarian principles which ignored historical legacies. In the corpus of Bentham's writings there is no reference to the Glorious Revolution. Thus nineteenth-century reformers and the revolutionaries alike went their ways ignoring the work done by the fundamentalists of 1688.

Perhaps this is an indication that the framers of the Revolution Settlement had done their job too well. They had striven for a conclusive governmental statement defining a civilized political arena within which future generations could solve their problems without having everlastingly to recreate the mechanism for their solution. King, lords, commons, civil liberty, and the Protestant religion, being carefully defined, need then only be defended and articulated. Purely civil revolutions need not again distract England. The only open-ended question, that of social reform, would be left for another day, for in any event no one in 1688 believed that it was the government's duty to tamper with problems of private wealth or private misery. The eighteenth-century state was not omnicompetent; it could only define itself, and this the Glorious Revolution had achieved for it.

The single living issue regarding the Revolution that then remained a source for continued deliberation in the eighteenth century was the process of revolutionary protest itself. The methods by which the government had changed in 1688 continued to intrigue and frighten. That respectable men could conduct a respectable revolution no doubt took much of the sting out of the older curse of irresponsible rebellion lingering from the Civil War years. But that the multitude might claim a 1688 precedent for violent protest introduced the ingredient of fear. Happily, no such appeal was to be made in eighteenth-century England, because democratic leaders were generally convinced that the constitutional establishment of 1688 actually had successfully safeguarded their liberties and that only corrupt politicians kept them from enjoying the Revolution's full fruits. Not until 1832 was the radical mind to be thoroughly disillusioned with the Revolution constitution and to entertain prospects for another major governmental overhaul.

Though by 1800 the Glorious Revolution was becoming as remote an episode in the nation's life as the Petition of Right and Magna Carta, a middle-class revolution tradition survived, which, like all traditions, became something to cherish but seldom to utilize. It was a decorative tradition too, like an ancient musket over the mantel or a suit of armor in the hall, a souvenir of a brave, if chaotic, past. But to flaunt such a revolution before destitute neighbors, to say, "Look what we have made; the first revolution in modern history based on true political and religious principles," was perhaps the very reason why England never underwent the experience again; it would have been tantamount to recognizing one's own national fallibility.

The tradition of an appeal to revolutionary methods greatly enhanced the Englishman's sense of his own stature, of his shrewdness in never letting the rascals in government get away with a thing, and of his power to create change in the nation's history—a power once reserved to kings alone. Even the irascible old Tory Dr. Johnson, though he deplored "what we did at the Revolution," muttered that it was necessary even though "it broke our constitution," and boasted that if any ruler abused the people again, "nature will rise up, and claiming her original rights, overturn a corrupt political system." In a lighter vein, Englishmen taught themselves to live with the expectation of revolutionary change. One man who had lived through the Revolution "enjoined his relations to bury him with his face downward, saying, that in a short time the world would be turned upside-down, and then he should be the only person who lay decently in his grave . . . there has been a considerable revolution." Finally, on a grander scale, Henry Thomas Buckle, composing his *History of Civilization in England* in the mid-nineteenth century, displayed the degree to which the English mind was committed to revolutionary improvement in declaring that

> *since the sixteenth century, local insurrections, provoked by immediate injustice, are diminishing, and are being superseded by revolutions, which strike at once at the source from whence the injustice proceeds. There can be no doubt that this change is beneficial; partly because it is always good to rise from effects to causes, and partly because revolutions being less frequent than insurrections, the peace of society would be more rarely disturbed, if men confined themselves entirely to the larger remedy. At the same time, insurrections are generally wrong; revolutions are always right. An insurrection is too often the mad and passionate effort of ignorant persons, who are impatient under some immediate injury, and never stop to investigate its remote and general causes. But a revolution, when it is the work of the nation itself, is a splendid and imposing spectacle, because to the moral quality of indignation produced by the presence of evil, it adds the intellectual qualities of foresight and combination; and uniting in the same act some of the highest properties of our nature, it achieves a double purpose, not only punishing the oppressor, but also relieving the oppressed.*

The Revolution of 1688 had bequeathed, as its most particular legacy, a revolutionary spirit with which generations since have had to live. While twentieth-century youth is growing and learning under the tensions of revolutionary expectation, and our institutions yearly receive revolutionary challenges, it is increasingly necessary that we understand the ideological antecedents which sprang from the shock of revolutionary recognition when the English Enlightenment discovered what awesome precedent had been set by the Glorious Revolution of 1688.

II THE REVOLUTION, THE CONSTITUTION, AND THE CROWN

The Bill of Rights
THE REVOLUTION AS A CONSTITUTIONAL PROGRAM

Throughout the end of January and early February of 1689 Parliament debated the Declaration of Rights, attempting to establish those fundamental political rights of Parliament and the people. The Declaration was later, after much revision, embodied in the final Bill of Rights (October, 1689), the fundamental constitutional guide to the relationship of the crown and the nation still in effect today.

An act for declaring the rights and liberties of the subject and settling the succession of the crown.

Whereas the lords spiritual and temporal, and commons, assembled at Westminster, lawfully, fully, and freely representing all the estates of the people of this realm, did upon the thirteenth day of February, in the year of our Lord one thousand six hundred eighty-eight, present unto their Majesties, then called and known by the names and stile of William and Mary, prince and princess of Orange, being present in their proper persons, a certain declaration in writing, made by the said lords and commons, in the words following: viz.

Whereas the late King James The Second, by the assistance of divers evil counselors, judges, and ministers employed by him, did endeavor to subvert and extirpate the protestant religion, and the laws and liberties of this kingdom.

By assuming and exercising a power of dispensing with and suspending of laws, and the execution of laws, without consent of parliament.

By committing and prosecuting divers worthy prelates, for humbly petitioning to be excused concurring to the said assumed power.

By issuing and causing to be executed a commission under the great seal for erecting a court called, The court of commissioners for ecclesiastical causes.

By levying money for and to the use of the crown, by pretence of

From *The Statutes at Large,* edited by D. Pickering (Cambridge, 1762–1806), vol. 9, item 67.

prerogative, for other time, and in other manner, than the same was granted by parliament.

By raising and keeping a standing army within this kingdom in time of peace, without consent of parliament, and quartering soldiers contrary to law.

By causing several good subjects, being protestants, to be disarmed, at the same time when papists were both armed and employed, contrary to law.

By violating the freedom of election of members to serve in parliament.

By prosecutions in the court of King's bench, for matters and causes cognizable only in parliament; and by divers other arbitrary and illegal courses.

And whereas of late years, partial, corrupt, and unqualified persons have been returned and served on juries in trials and particularly divers jurors in trials for high treason, which were not freeholders.

And excessive bail hath been required of persons committed in criminal cases, to elude the benefit of the laws made for the liberty of the subjects.

And excessive fines have been imposed; and illegal and cruel punishments inflicted.

And several grants and promises made of fines and forfeitures, before any conviction or judgment against the persons, upon whom the same were to be levied.

All which are utterly and directly contrary to the known laws and statutes, and freedom of this realm.

And whereas the said late King James the Second having abdicated the government, and the throne being thereby vacant, his highness the Prince of Orange (whom it hath pleased Almighty God to make the glorious instrument of delivering this kingdom from popery and arbitrary power) did (by the advice of the lords spiritual and temporal, and divers principal persons of the commons) cause letters to be written to the lords spiritual and temporal, being protestants; and other letters to the several counties, cities, universities, boroughs, and cinque-ports, for the choosing of such persons to represent them, as were of right to be sent to parliament, to meet and sit at Westminster upon the two and twentieth day of January, in this year one thousand six hundred eighty-eight, in order to such an establishment, as that their religion, laws, and liberties might not again be in danger of being subverted: upon which letters, elections have been accordingly made.

And thereupon the said lords spiritual and temporal, and commons, pursuant to their respective letters and elections, being now assembled in a full and free representative of this nation, taking into their most serious consideration the best means for attaining the ends aforesaid; do in the first place (as their ancestors in like case have usually done) for the vindicating and asserting their ancient rights and liberties, declare:

That the pretended power of suspending of laws, or the execution of laws, by regal authority, without consent of parliament, is illegal.

That the pretended power of dispensing with laws, or the execution of laws, by regal authority, as it hath been assumed and exercised of late, is illegal.

That the commission for erecting the late court of commissioners for ecclesiastical causes, and all other commissions and courts of like nature are illegal and pernicious.

That levying money for or to the use of the crown, by pretense of prerogative, without grant of parliament, for longer time, or in other manner than the same is or shall be granted, is illegal.

That it is the right of the subjects to petition the King, and all commitments and prosecutions for such petitioning are illegal.

That the raising or keeping a standing army within the kingdom in time of peace, unless it be with consent of parliament, is against law.

That the subjects which are protestants, may have arms of their defense suitable to their conditions, and as allowed by law.

That election of members of parliament ought to be free.

That the freedom of speech, and debates or proceedings in parliament, ought not to be impeached or questioned in any court or place out of parliament.

That excessive bail ought not to be required, nor excessive fines imposed; nor cruel and unusual punishments inflicted.

That jurors ought to be duly impaneled and returned, and jurors which pass upon men in trials for high treason ought to be freeholders.

That all grants and promises of fines and forfeitures of particular persons before conviction, are illegal and void.

And that for redress of all grievances, and for the amending, strengthening and preserving of the laws, parliaments ought to be held frequently.

And they do claim, demand, and insist upon all and singular the premises, as their undoubted rights and liberties; and that no declarations, judgments, doings or proceedings, to the prejudice of the people in any of the said premises, ought in any wise to be drawn hereafter into consequence or example.

To which demand for their rights they are particularly encouraged by the declaration of his highness the prince of Orange, as being the only means for obtaining a full redress and remedy therein.

Having therefore an entire confidence, That his said highness the Prince of Orange will perfect the deliverance so far advanced by him, and will still preserve them from the violation of their rights, which they have here asserted, and from all other attempts upon their religion, rights, and liberties.

The said lords spiritual and temporal, and commons, assembled at Westminster, do resolve, That William and Mary prince and princess of Orange be, and be declared, King and Queen of England, France and Ireland, and the dominions thereunto belonging, to hold the crown and royal dignity of the said kingdoms and dominions to them the said prince and princess during their lives, and the life of the survivor of them; and that the sole and full exercise of the regal power be only in, and executed by the said prince of Orange, in the names of the said prince and princess, during their joint lives; and after their deceases, the said crown and royal dignity of the said kingdoms and dominions to be to the heirs of the body of the said princess; and for default of such issue to the princess Anne of Denmark and the heirs of her body; and for default of such issue to the heirs of the body of the said prince of Orange. And the lords spiritual and temporal, and commons, do pray the said prince and princess to accept the same accordingly.

And that the oaths hereafter mentioned be taken by all persons of whom the oaths of allegiance and supremacy might be required by law, instead of them; and that said oaths of allegiance and supremacy may be abrogated.

I A.B. do sincerely promise and swear, That I will be faithful, and bear true allegiance, to their Majesties King William and Queen Mary:

So help me God.

I A.B. do swear, That I do from my heart, abhor, detest, and abjure as impious and heretical, that damnable doctrine and position, That princes excommunicated or deprived by the pope, or any authority of the see of Rome, may be deposed or murdered by their subjects, or any other whatsoever. And I do declare, That no foreign prince, person, prelate, state, or potentate hath, or ought to have any jurisdiction, power, superiority, pre-eminence, or authority, ecclesiastical or spiritual, within this realm:

So help me God.

Upon which their said Majesties did accept the crown and royal dignity of the kingdoms of England, France, and Ireland, and the dominions thereunto belonging, according to the resolution and desire of the said lords and commons contained in the said declaration.

And thereupon their Majesties were pleased. That the said lords spiritual and temporal, and commons, being the two houses of parliament, should continue to sit, and with their Majesties royal concurrence make effectual provision for the settlement of the religion, laws and liberties of this kingdom, so that the same for the future might not be in danger again of being subverted; to which the said lords spiritual and temporal, and commons, did agree and proceed to act accordingly.

Now in pursuance of the premises, the said lords spiritual and temporal, and commons, in parliament assembled, for the ratifying, confirming and establishing the said declaration, and the articles, clauses, matters, and things therein contained, by the force of a law made in due form by authority of parliament, do pray that it may be declared and enacted, That all and singular the rights and liberties asserted and claimed in the said declaration, are the true, ancient, and indubitable rights and liberties of the people of this kingdom, and so shall be esteemed, allowed, adjudged, deemed, and taken to be, and that all and every the particulars aforesaid shall be firmly and strictly holden and observed, as they are expressed in the said declaration; and all officers and ministers whatsoever shall serve their Majesties and their successors according to the same in all times to come.

And the said lords spiritual and temporal, and commons, seriously considering how it hath pleased Almighty God, in his marvellous providence, and merciful goodness to this nation, to provide and preserve their said Majesties' royal persons most happily to reign over us upon the throne of their ancestors, for which they render unto him from the bottom of their hearts their humblest thanks and praises, do truly, firmly, assuredly, and in the sincerity of their hearts think, and do hereby recognize, acknowledge and declare, That King James the Second having abdicated the government, and their Majesties having accepted the crown and royal dignity as aforesaid, their said Majesties did become, were, are, and of right ought to be, by the laws of this realm, our sovereign liege and lady, King and Queen of England, France, and Ireland, and the dominions thereunto belonging, in and to whose princely persons the royal state, crown, and dignity of the said realms, with all honors, stiles, titles, regalities, prerogatives, powers, jurisdictions and authorities to the same belonging and appertaining, are most fully, rightfully, and entirely invested and incorporated, united and annexed.

And for preventing all questions and divisions in this realm, by reason of any pretended titles to the crown, and for preserving a certainty in the succession thereof, in and upon which the unity, peace, tranquility, and safety of this nation doth, under God, wholly consist and depend, The said lords spiritual and temporal, and commons, do beseech their Majesties that it may be enacted, established and declared, That the crown and regal government of the said kingdoms and dominions, with all and singular the premises thereunto belonging and appertaining, shall be and continue to their said Majesties, and the survivor of them, during their lives, and the life of the survivor of them; And that the entire, perfect, and full exercise of the regal power and government be only in, and executed by his Majesty, in the names of both their Majesties during their joint lives; and after their deceases the said crown and premises shall be and remain to the heirs of the body of her Majesty; and for default of such issue, to her royal highness the princess Anne of Denmark, and the heirs of her body; and for default of such issue, to the heirs of the body of his said Majesty; And thereunto the said lords spiritual and temporal, and commons do, in the name of all the people aforesaid, most humbly and faithfully submit themselves, their heirs and posterities for ever; and do faithfully promise, That they will stand to, maintain, and defend their said Majesties, and also the limitation and succession of the crown herein specified and contained, to the utmost of their powers, with their lives and estates against all persons whatsoever, that shall attempt any thing to the contrary.

And whereas it hath been found by experience, that it is inconsistent with the safety and welfare of this protestant kingdom, to be governed by a popish prince, or by any King or Queen marrying a papist; the said lords spiritual and temporal, and commons, do further pray that it may be enacted, That all and every person and persons that is, are or shall be reconciled to, or shall hold communion with, the see or church of Rome, or shall profess the popish religion, or shall marry a papist, shall be excluded, and be for ever incapable to inherit, possess, or enjoy the crown and government of this realm, and Ireland, and the dominions thereunto belonging, or any part of the same, or to have, use, or exercise any regal power, authority, or jurisdiction within the same; and in all and every such case or cases the people of these realms shall be, and are hereby absolved of their allegiance; and the said crown and government shall from time to time descend to, and be enjoyed by such person or persons, being protestants, as should have inherited and enjoyed the same, in case the said person or persons so reconciled, holding communion, or professing, or marrying as aforesaid, were naturally dead.

And that every King and Queen of this realm, who at any time hereafter shall come to and succeed in the imperial crown of this kingdom, shall on the first day of the meeting of the first parliament, next after his or her coming to the crown, sitting in his or her throne in the house of peers, in the presence of the lords and commons therein assembled, or at his or her coronation, before such person or persons who shall administer the coronation oath to him or her, at the time of his or her taking the said oath (which shall first happen) make, subscribe, and audibly repeat the declaration mentioned in the statute made in the thirtieth year of the reign of King Charles the Second, entitled, *An act for the more effectual preserving the King's person and government, by disabling papists from sitting in either house of parliament.* But if it shall happen, that such King or Queen, upon his or her succession to the crown of this realm, shall be under the age of twelve years, then every such King or Queen shall make, subscribe, and audibly repeat the said declaration at his or her coronation, or the first day of the meeting of the first parliament as aforesaid, which shall first happen after such King or Queen shall have attained the said age of twelve years.

All which their Majesties are contented and pleased shall be declared, enacted, and established by authority of this present parliament, and shall stand, remain, and be the law of this realm for ever; and the same are by their said Majesties, by and with the advice and consent of the lords spiritual and temporal, and commons, in parliament assembled, and by the authority of the same, declared, enacted, and established accordingly.

And be it further declared and enacted by the authority aforesaid, That from and after this present session of parliament, no dispensation by *non obstante* of or to any statute, or any part thereof, shall be allowed, but that the same shall be held void and of no effect, except a dispensation be allowed of in such statute, and except in such cases as shall be specially provided for by one or more bill or bills to be passed during this present session of parliament.

Provided that no charter, or grant, or pardon, granted before the three and twentieth day of October in the year of our Lord one thousand six hundred eighty-nine shall be any ways impeached or invalidated by this act, but that the same shall be and remain of the same force and effect in law, and no other than as if this act had never been made.

John Locke
REVOLUTION AND THE NATURAL RIGHT OF REBELLION

John Locke, born in 1632, became famous only in the last years of his life. He had been a prominent member of Shaftesbury's household, contributing much to Whig political philosophy. He shared his master's exile after the Oxford Parliament, during which time he preoccupied himself with the nature of political sovereignty. The product of his thinking appeared in print when he returned to England with the Revolution. His vast philosophical contributions affected the fields of government, psychology, religion, education, and economics. He served in a number of posts under William and Mary until his death in 1704.

To understand political power aright, and derive it from its original, we must consider what state all men are naturally in, and that is a state of perfect freedom to order their actions and dispose of their possessions and persons as they think fit, within the bounds of the law of nature, without asking leave, or depending upon the will of any other man.

A state also of equality, wherein all the power and jurisdiction is reciprocal, no one having more than another; there being nothing more evident than that creatures of the same species and rank, promiscuously born to all the same advantages of nature, and the use of the same faculties, should also be equal one amongst another without subordination or subjection, unless the Lord and Master of them all should by any manifest declaration of His will set one above another, and confer on him by an evident and clear appointment an undoubted right to dominion and sovereignty. . . .

But though this be a state of liberty, yet it is not a state of license; though man in that state have an uncontrollable liberty to dispose of his person or possessions, yet he has not liberty to destroy himself, or so much as any creature in his possession, but where some nobler use than its bare preservation calls for it. The state of nature has a law of nature to govern it, which obliges every one; and reason, which is that law, teaches all mankind who will but consult it,

From John Locke, *Treatise of Civil Government and a Letter Concerning Toleration,* ed. by Charles L. Sherman (New York, 1937). Copyright, 1937, D. Appleton-Century Company, Inc.

that, being all equal and independent, no one ought to harm another in his life, health, liberty, or possessions. For men being all the workmanship of one omnipotent and infinitely wise Maker —all the servants of one sovereign Master, sent into the world by His order, and about His business—they are His property, whose workmanship they are, made to last during His, not one another's pleasure; and being furnished with like faculties, sharing all in one community of nature, there cannot be supposed any such subordination among us, that may authorize us to destroy one another, as if we were made for one another's uses, as the inferior ranks of creatures are for ours. Every one, as he is bound to preserve himself, and not to quit his station willfully, so, by the like reason, when his own preservation comes not in competition, ought he, as much as he can, to preserve the rest of mankind, and not, unless it be to justice on an offender, take away or impair the life, or what tends to the preservation of the life, the liberty, health, limb, or goods of another. . . .

God, who hath given the world to men in common, hath also given them reason to make use of it to the best advantage of life and convenience. The earth and all that is therein is given to men for the support and comfort of their being. And though all the fruits it naturally produces, and beasts it feeds, belong to mankind in common, as they are produced by the spontaneous hand of nature; and nobody has originally a private dominion exclusive of the rest of mankind in any of them as they are thus in their natural state; yet being given for the use of men, there must of necessity be a means to appropriate them some way or other before they can be of any use or at all beneficial to any particular man. The fruit or venison which nourishes the wild Indian, who knows no enclosure, and is still a tenant in common, must be his, and so his, i.e., a part of him, that another can no longer have any right to it, before it can do any good for the support of his life.

Though the earth and all inferior creatures be common to all men, yet every man has a property in his own person; this nobody has any right to but himself. The labor of his body and the work of his hands we may say are properly his. Whatsoever, then, he removes out of the state that nature hath provided and left it in, he hath mixed his labor with, and joined to it something that is his own, and thereby makes it his property. It being by him removed from the common state nature placed it in, it hath by this labor something annexed to it that excludes the common right of other men. For this labor being the unquestionable property of the laborer, no man but he can have a right to what that is once joined to, at least where there is enough, and as good left in common for others. . . .

Man being born, as has been proved, with a title to perfect freedom, and an uncontrolled enjoyment of all the rights and privileges of the law of nature equally with any other man or number of men in the world, hath by nature a power not only to preserve his property—that is, his life, liberty, and estate—against the injuries and attempts of other men, but to judge of and punish the breaches of that law in others as he is persuaded the offense deserves, even with death itself, in crimes where the heinousness of the fact in his opinion requires it. But because no political society can be nor subsist without having in itself the power to preserve the property, and, in order thereunto, punish the offenses of all those of that society, there, and there only, is political society, where every one of the members hath quitted this natural power, resigned it up into the hands of the community in all cases that exclude him not from appealing for protection to the law established by it; and thus all private judgment of every particular member being excluded, the community comes to be umpire; and by understanding indifferent rules and men authorized by the community for their execution, decides all the differences that may happen between any members of that society concerning any matter of right, and punishes those offenses which any member hath committed against the society with such penalties as the law has established; whereby it is easy to discern who are and who are not in political society together. Those who are united into one body, and have a common established law and judicature to appeal to, with authority to decide controversies between them and punish offenders, are in civil society one with another; but those who have no such common appeal—I mean on earth—are still in the state of nature, each being, where there is no other, judge for himself and executioner, which is, as I have before shown it, the perfect state of nature.

And thus the commonwealth comes by a power to set down what punishment shall belong to the several transgressions which they think worthy of it committed amongst the members of that society, which is the power of making laws, as well as it has the

FIGURE 2. John Locke. (*The Granger Collection*)

power to punish any injury done unto any of its members by anyone that is not of it, which is the power of war and peace; and
all this for the preservation of the property of all the members of that
society as far as is possible. But though every man entered into civil
society, has quitted his power to punish offenses against the law of

nature in prosecution of his own private judgment, yet with the judgment of offenses, which he has given up to the legislative in all cases where he can appeal to the magistrate, he has given a right to the commonwealth to employ his force for the execution of the judgments of the commonwealth whenever he shall be called to it; which, indeed, are his own judgments, they being made by himself or his representative. And herein we have the original of the legislative and executive power of civil society, which is to judge by standing laws how far offenses are to be punished when committed within the commonwealth, and also by occasional judgments founded on the present circumstances of the fact, how far injuries from without are to be vindicated; and in both these to employ all the force of all the members when there shall be need.

Wherever, therefore, any number of men so unite into one society, as to quit every one his executive power of the law of nature, and to resign it to the public, there, and there only, is a political, or civil society. And this is done wherever any number of men, in the state of nature, enter into society to make one people one body politic, under one supreme government, or else when anyone joins himself to, and incorporates with, any government already made. For hereby he authorizes the society, or, which is all one, the legislative thereof, to make laws for him, as the public good of the society shall require, to the execution whereof his own assistance (as to his own decrees) is due. And this puts men out of a state of nature into that of a commonwealth, by setting up a judge on earth with authority to determine all the controversies and redress the injuries that may happen to any member of the commonwealth; which judge is the legislative, or magistrates appointed by it. And wherever there are any number of men, however associated, that have no such decisive power to appeal to, there they are still in the state of nature. . . .

If man in the state of nature be so free, as has been said, if he be absolute lord of his own person and possessions, equal to the greatest, and subject to nobody, why will he part with his freedom, this empire, and subject himself to the dominion and control of any other power? To which, it is obvious to answer, that though in the state of nature he hath such a right, yet the enjoyment of it is very uncertain, and constantly exposed to the invasions of others. For all being kings as much as he, every man his equal, and the greater part no strict observers of equity and justice, the enjoyment of the property he has in this state is very unsafe, very unsecure. This makes him willing to quit this condition, which, however free, is full of fears and continual dangers; and it is not without reason that he seeks out and is willing to join in society with others, who are already united, or have a mind to unite, for the mutual preservation of their lives, liberties, and estates, which I call by the general name, property.

The great and chief end, therefore, of men's uniting into commonwealths, and putting themselves under government, is the preservation of their property; to which in the state of nature there are many things wanting. . . .

Thus mankind, notwithstanding all the privileges of the state of nature, being but in an ill condition, while they remain in it, are quickly driven into society. Hence it comes to pass that we seldom find any number of men live any time together in this state. The inconveniences that they are therein exposed to by the irregular and uncertain exercise of the power every man has of punishing the transgressions of others, make them take sanctuary under the established laws of government, and therein seek the preservation of their property. It is this makes them so willingly give up every one his single power of punishing, to be exercised by such alone, as shall be appointed to it amongst them; and by such rules as the community, or those authorized by them to that purpose, shall agree on. And in this we have the original right and rise of both the legislative and executive power, as well as of the governments and societies themselves. . . .

But though men when they enter into society give up the equality, liberty and executive power they had in the state of nature into the hands of the society, to be so far disposed of by the legislative as the good of the society shall require; yet it being only with an intention in every one the better to preserve himself, his liberty and property (for no rational creature can be supposed to change his condition with an intention to be worse), the power of the society, or legislative constituted by them, can never be supposed to extend farther than the common good, but is obliged to secure every one's property by providing against those . . . defects above-mentioned that made the state of nature so unsafe and uneasy. And so whoever has the legislative or supreme power of any commonwealth is bound to govern by established standing laws, promulgated and known to the people, and not by extemporary degrees; by indifferent and upright judges, who are to decide controversies by those laws; and to employ the force of the community at home only in the execution of such laws, or abroad, to prevent or redress foreign injuries, and secure the community from inroads and invasion. And all this to be directed to no other end but the peace, safety, and public good of the people. . . .

The great end of men's entering into society being the enjoyment of their properties in peace and safety, and the great instrument and means of that being the laws established in that society: the first and fundamental positive law of all commonwealths, is the establishing of the legislative power; as the first and fundamental natural law, which is to govern even the legislative itself, is the preservation of the society, and (as far as will consist with the public good) of every person in it. This legislative is not only the supreme power of the commonwealth, but sacred and unalterable in the hands where the community have once placed it; nor can any edict of anybody else, in what form soever conceived, or by what power soever backed, have the force and obligation of a law, which has not its sanction from that legislative which the public has chosen and appointed. For without this the law could not have that, which is absolutely necessary to its being a law, the consent of the society over whom nobody can have a power to make laws; but by their own consent, and by authority received from them; and therefore all the obedience, which by the most solemn ties anyone can be obliged to pay, ultimately terminates in this supreme power, and is directed by those laws which it enacts; nor can any oaths to any foreign power whatsoever, or any domestic subordinate power discharge any member of the society from his obedience to the legislative, acting pursuant to their trust; nor oblige him to any obedience contrary to the laws so enacted, or farther than they do allow; it being ridiculous to imagine one can be tied ultimately to obey any power in the society which is not the supreme. . . .

. . . Civil society being a state of peace amongst those who are of it, from whom the state of war is excluded by the umpirage which they have provided in their legislative for the ending all differences that may arise amongst any of them, it is in their legislative that the members of a commonwealth are united and combined together in one coherent living body. This is the soul that gives form, life, and unity to the commonwealth. From hence the several members have their mutual influence, sympathy, and connection. And, therefore, when the legislative is broken or dissolved, dissolution and death follow. For the essence and union of the society consisting in having one will, the legislative, when once established by the majority, has the declaring and, as it were, keeping of, that will. The constitution of the legislative is the first and fundamental act of the society, whereby provision is made for the continuation of their union, under the direction of persons and bonds of laws made by persons authorized thereunto by the consent and appointment of the people, without which no one man or number of men amongst them can have authority of making laws that shall be binding to the rest. When any one or more shall take upon them to make laws, whom the people have not appointed so to do, they make laws without authority, which the people are not therefore bound to obey; by which means they come again to be out of subjection, and may constitute to themselves a new legislative, as they think best, being in full liberty to resist the force of those who without authority would impose anything upon them. Everyone is at the disposure of his own will when those who had by the delegation of the society the declaring of the public will, are excluded from it, and others usurp the place who have no such authority or delegation.

This being usually brought about by such in the commonwealth who misuse the power they have, it is hard to consider it aright, and know at whose door to lay it, without knowing the form of government in which it happens. Let us suppose, then, the legislative placed in the concurrence of three distinct persons.

1. A single hereditary person having the constant supreme executive power, and with it the power of convoking and dissolving the other two within certain periods of time.

2. An assembly of hereditary nobility.

3. An assembly of representatives chosen *pro tempore* by the people. Such a form of government supposed, it is evident,

First, That when such a single person or prince sets up his own arbitrary will in place of the laws which are the will of the society, declared by the legislative, then the legislative is changed. For that being in effect the legislative whose rules and laws are put in execution and required to be obeyed when other laws are set up, and other rules pretended and enforced, than what the legislative constituted by the society have enacted, it is plain that the legislative is changed. Whoever introduces new laws, not being thereunto authorized by the fundamental appointment of the society, or subverts the old, disowns and overturns the power by which they were made, and so sets up a new legislative.

Secondly, When the prince hinders the legislative from assembling in its due time, or from acting freely, pursuant to those ends for which it was constituted, the legislative is altered. For it is not a certain number of men, no, nor their meeting, unless they have also freedom of debating and leisure of perfecting what is for the good of the society, wherein the legislative consists. When these are taken away or altered so as to deprive the society of the due exercise of their power, the legislative is truly altered. For it is not names that constitute governments, but the use and exercise of those powers that were intended to acompany them; so that he who takes away the freedom, or hinders the acting of the legislative in its due seasons, in effect takes away the legislative, and puts an end to the government.

Thirdly, When, by the arbitrary power of the prince, the electors or ways of elections are altered, without the consent and contrary to the common interest of the people, there also the legislative is altered. For if others than those whom the society hath authorized thereunto, do choose, or in another way than what the society hath prescribed, those chosen are not the legislative appointed by the people.

Fourthly, The delivery also of the people into the subjection of foreign power, either by the prince, or by the legislative, is certainly a change of the legislative, and so a dissolution of the government. For the end why people entered into society being to be preserved one entire, free, independent society, to be governed by its own laws, this is lost whenever they are given up into the power of another.

Why in such a constitution as this the dissolution of the government in these cases is to be imputed to the prince, is evident; because he, having the force, treasure, and offices of the state to employ, and often persuading himself, or being flattered by others, that, as supreme magistrate he is incapable of control, he alone is in a condition to make great advances towards such changes, under pretense of lawful authority, and has it in his hands to terrify or suppress opposers, as factious, seditious, and enemies to the government. Whereas no other part of the legislative or people is capable by themselves to attempt any alteration of the legislative, without open and visible rebellion, apt enough to be taken notice of, which, when it prevails, produces effects very little different from foreign conquest. Besides, the prince in such a form of government, having the power of dissolving the other parts of the legislative, and thereby rendering them private persons, they can never, in opposition to him, or without his concurrence, alter the legislative by a law, his consent being necessary to give any of their decrees that sanction. But yet so far as the other parts of the legislative any way contribute to any attempt upon the government, and do either promote, or not, what lies in them, hinder such designs, they are guilty, and partake in this, which is certainly the greatest crime men can be guilty of one towards another.

There is one way more whereby such a government may be dissolved, and that is, when he who has the supreme executive power neglects and abandons that charge, so that the laws already made can no longer be put in execution. This is demonstratively to reduce all to anarchy, and so effectually to dissolve the government. For laws not being made for themselves, but to be by their execution the bonds of the society, to keep every part of the body politic, in its due place and function, when that totally ceases, the government visibly ceases, and the people become a confused multitude without order or connection. Where there is no longer the administration of justice, for the securing of men's rights, nor any remaining power within the community to direct the force, or provide for the necessities of the public, there certainly is no government left. Where the laws cannot be executed, it is all one as if there were no laws; and a government without laws is, I suppose, a mystery in politics, inconceivable to human capacity, and inconsistent with human society.

In these and the like cases, when the government is dissolved, the people are at liberty to provide for themselves by erecting a new legislative, differing from the other, by the change of persons, or form, or both, as they shall find it most for their safety and good. For the society can never, by the fault of another, lose the native and original right it has to preserve itself, which can only be done by a settled legislative, and a fair and impartial execution of the laws made by it. But the state of mankind is not so miserable that they are not capable of using this remedy, till it be too late to look for any. To tell people they may provide for themselves by erecting a new legislative, when by oppression, artifice, or being delivered over to a foreign power, their old one is gone, is only to tell them they may expect relief when it is too late, and the evil is past cure. This is in effect no more than to bid them first be slaves, and then to take care of their liberty; and when their chains are on tell them they may act like free men. This, if barely so, is rather mockery than relief; and men can never be secure from tyranny if there be no means to escape it till they are perfectly under it. And therefore it is that they have not only a right to get out of it, but to prevent it. . . .

If a controversy arise betwixt a prince and some of the people in a matter where the law is silent or doubtful, and the thing be of great consequence, I should think the proper umpire in such a case should be the body of the people; for in cases where the prince hath a trust reposed in him, and is dispensed from the common ordinary rules of the law; there, if any men find themselves aggrieved, and think the prince acts contrary to or beyond that trust, who so proper to judge as the body of the people (who at first lodged that trust in him) how far they meant it should extend? But if the prince or whoever they be in the administration decline that way of determination, the appeal then lies nowhere but to heaven; force between either persons who have no known superior on earth, or which permits no appeal to a judge on earth, being properly a state of war, wherein the appeal lies only to heaven, and in that state the injured party must judge for himself when he will think fit to make use of that appeal and put himself upon it.

To conclude, the power that every individual gave the society when he entered into it, can never revert to the individuals again as long as the society lasts, but will always remain in the community, because without this there can be no community, no commonwealth, which is contrary to the original agreement; so also when the society hath placed the legislative in any assembly of men to continue in them and their successors, with direction and authority for providing such successors, the legislative can never revert to the people whilst that government lasts, because having provided a legislative with power to continue forever, they have given up their political power to the legislative and cannot resume it. But if they have set limits to the duration of their legislative, and made this supreme power in any person or assembly only temporary; or else when by the miscarriages of those in authority it is forfeited; upon the forfeiture, or at the determination of the time set, it reverts to the sociey, and the people have a right to act as supreme, and continue the legislative in themselves; or place it in a new form, or new hands as they think good. . . .

Peter Laslett

REAPPRAISAL OF JOHN LOCKE'S RELATION TO REVOLUTION THEORY

Peter Laslett, born in 1915, a Fellow of Trinity College, Cambridge, has edited the definitive edition of John Locke's Second Treatise of Government. *He has since left the field of political philosophy for social analysis as director of the Cambridge Group for the History of Population and Social Structure. His current fame rests on a study of preindustrial Western society,* The World We Have Lost.

John Locke received the following letter from the Hague on 31 January 1689, whilst he was waiting in Rotterdam for a ship to take him home, now that his exile in Holland could come to an end after the Revolution:

> *I have been very ill this fortnight. The beginning was what is called the disease of one's country, impatience to be there, but it ended yesterday with violence, as all great things do but kings. Ours went out like a farthing candle, and has given us by this Convention an occasion not only of mending the Government but of melting it down and making all new, which makes me wish you were there to give them a right scheme of government, having been infected by the great man Lord Shaftesbury.*

The writer was the wife of Locke's friend, Lord Mordaunt, one of those who had been in Holland helping to bring the Revolution about. Mordaunt himself was now in England with William, Stadtholder of Holland, who was already in military and political control of the country. The "Convention" she mentions, the Convention Parliament, was

From Peter Laslett, "The English Revolution and Locke's 'Two Treatises of Government,'" *Cambridge Historical Journal,* vol. 12, no. 1 (1956). Reprinted by permission of Curtis Brown Ltd.

working out the constitutional future of England after James II had spluttered out. By 11 February Locke was in London: on the 12th the Declaration of Right was completed: on the 13th William and Mary were offered the crown.

This letter, except perhaps for its last phrase, aptly expressed the traditional view of the reasons why Locke sat down to write *Two Treatises of Government.* The book has 1690 on its title page. The year 1689 had been one of wavering in the face of a dangerous reaction, which threatened to make of the first Revolution in the history of the modern world just another dynastic usurpation accompanied by an appeal to the turbulent Estates. What was wanted was an argument, along with a scheme of government, an argument deep in its analysis and theoretical, even philosophical, in its premises, but cogent and convincing in its expression. *Two Treatises* presents along with its constitutional scheme an argument of precisely this type. The object of its author and the occasion of his authorship are set out just as might be expected in its Preface. He wrote to "establish the Throne of our Great Restorer, Our present King William; to make good his Title, in the Consent of the People, and justifie to the World, the People of *England,* whose love of their Just and Natural Rights, with their Resolution to preserve them, saved the Nation when it was on the very brink of Slavery and Ruine."

The traditional case, then, for supposing that the composition of this work belongs wholly and indissolubly to 1688, the year of the Glorious Revolution, is superficially convincing. The book contains passages which refer unmistakably to the political events of the eighteen months between the change of the seat of power and the time of its publication, and one statement which dates itself. It is a wonderfully effective justification of what the people of England had done in the year before its appearance, and of what they were going to do in the years to come, indeed of their political behavior for the following century and more. It gave coherence to their new constitution, it crystalized their social and political beliefs, it rationalized their Revolution then as it rationalized the American and French Revolutions which came after. Statements like these are a standard feature of all the history books and the works on political theory, for Locke on the English Revolution is the supreme example of the way in which political event interplays with political thinking. This belief has never been seriously doubted there since his book appeared, and it is far too deeply engrained, far, far too useful, to be easily abandoned. Nevertheless, it is quite untrue.

Untrue, that is to say, in its most useful form. What Locke wrote did justify "the Whig Revolution of 1688," if that phrase can be permitted at all. It is quite correct to assume that some of the text was written in 1689 to apply to the political situation then. What cannot be maintained is that the original conception of the book was to justify a revolution which had already been consummated. A detailed examination of the text and of all the evidence bearing on it goes to show that it cannot have been the events of 1688 which fastened Locke's attention on the fundamental nature of society and politics, political personality and property, the sacred rights of the individual and the ethical imperatives of government. The conjunction of affairs which set his mind working on these problems must be sought at an earlier period. *Two Treatises* in fact turns out to be not the rationalization of a revolution in need of defense, but a demand for a revolution yet to be brought about.

This is the view of its historical occasion which will be presented here, and an attempt will be made to establish its connection with the years 1679–1681, when a Revolution, an abortive Revolution of the peculiarly English, constitutional sort, was being contemplated. Some of the evidence will be taken from the papers of Locke, only recently made available, in the Lovelace Collection in the Bodleian Library, supplemented by the study of what remains of Locke's library, books from which the present writer has been able to examine and borrow. But much of it comes from the content of the book itself and from historical circumstances which have both alike been always open to investigation.

It must be said at once that the fallacy we have attacked is not supported by Locke's biographers. H. R. Fox Bourne published the longest and still the most authoritative *Life* as long ago as 1876 and made the following assertions on this subject:

> *It is probable that in 1681 or 1682 Locke prepared the first of the* Two Treatises *published in 1690, and more than he then published. Though what is now the second essay may possibly have been prepared in England in 1689, its tone and method seem to suggest that it was composed before, instead of after, King William's accession. . . . On these grounds, supported by some minor considerations which hardly need here be set*

forth, it may be fairly assumed that the whole work was substantially completed during the last year of Locke's residence in Holland.

It is a pity that he did not go into his minor considerations, but it seems clear that the men who have so glibly repeated the traditional account of the occasion of the book, have done so without consulting the standard biography.

This account focuses attention on two features which the superficial student has little reason to notice, because he practically never sees the book in anything like its original form. They are these: that it consists of two separate books, the first of which breaks off unfinished in the middle of a sentence, and that Locke wrote a Preface stating that over half of what he had originally composed had been lost. The first book has only once been reprinted since 1884, and that in the most unsatisfactory of all editions, though the most used. Even this edition omits Locke's Preface, which, though it is indispensable for the proper appreciation of the occasion of the work, has never appeared in any edition at all since the year 1824. When we treat what we are pleased to call our great political classics like this, there can be little wonder that a minor mythology should have grown up around one of them.

I have quoted from the Preface the words in which Locke expresses the hope that the book would serve to justify the Revolution, but he is mainly concerned there with the writings, the influence and person of Sir Robert Filmer, a figure of wonderful obscurity and doltishness, or so he deftly suggests. He tells us that the *First Treatise,* described on the title page as a refutation of Filmer, had originally been much longer, twice as long again. Nothing he says refers directly to the time at which the work was composed, but, since he goes on to explain why it would not be worth his while to rewrite the work at its original length, we may take him to imply that the polemic against Filmer had been written some time before, and was not so much a thing of the moment when the Preface was composed. This fits the chronology. Filmer's great vogue had been seven or eight years earlier and only the lingering attachment to his principles of the passive obedience party in the Church justified the appearance between the same covers of the *First* and *Second Treatise.*

This evidence, reinforced perhaps by allusions in the text and tiny

scraps in Locke's papers, evidently led Fox Bourne to the view of the
date or dates of composition which we have mentioned. Recent
specialist students of Locke have followed him. They have freely
granted that the *First Treatise* was written before his Dutch exile
began late in 1683, and they explain the fact that it contains the only
statement which incontrovertibly belongs after the events of 1688
(the reference to Judge Jeffries) as an insertion of 1689. But the
second book, they seem to agree, must be much later, and can belong only to the months immediately before and the months immediately after the Revolution, though, with certain exceptions, it is
not easy to see which passages preceded or succeeded it. They have
noticed that the very few books which Locke directly refers to were
all in print before 1683. But in the absence of any complete knowledge of the editions and copies which Locke actually used for the
purpose of the *Second Treatise* and in general, they have not interpreted this fact as pointing to an earlier date for the second book.
They see nothing impossible in supposing that Locke wrote this
second book in its entirety between February and August 1689, when
it must have been complete for the Licenser's stamp on 23 August,
except that the drift of his statements makes it look as if the Revolution was yet to come. Their general position seems to be that to
press for too definite an occasion for the writing of the book is to
detract from its perennial value as political philosophy. It would
seem that if it cannot be shown to have been occasioned by the
English Revolution, it must not be allowed to have an occasion at all.

After this there is very little left of the traditional view. But before
it is abandoned, it should be pointed out that there is evidence in its
favor which has never been brought forward. In some ways it pro-
vides a far better explanation than the one just summarized. If the
wording of Locke's Preface is considered carefully, it will be seen
that he refers to the work as a whole; he does not imply that it was
written in two parts and on two different occasions, separated by
some years. It is "a Discourse concerning Government," with a
beginning, a middle (now missing) and an end, not two disparate
essays, one a fragment, brought together for common publication.
His cross-references within the text tend to confirm that this was his
view of it. They all occur in the first book, which is an interesting
point to which we shall have to return. In §66 he talks of something
he will examine "in its due place," which turns out to be the second

book §§52–76: in §87 he talks of acquiring Property, "which how he could do will be shown in another place," namely in the *Second Treatise,* Ch. 5: in §100 he says "for which I refer my Reader to the Second Book." The first words of the second book are "It having been shewn in the foregoing Discourse," which means the preceding part of the work in progress, not an earlier and separate "discourse," for that word is reserved for the complete work.

These points may look overrefined, but the fine details of Locke's own references to his own writing are important in view of Dr. Gerritsen's very interesting discovery, made by the exact use of the subtle methods of analytical bibliography. He has shown that the title page to the second book was a later insertion in the course of printing, which may imply that the title page to the whole, printed later, was brought into line with it. It follows from this that Locke may not originally have thought of his volume as in two parts at all, any more than any work divided into two "books." The word "Treatise," the expression "Two Treatises," the title "An essay of Civil Government" applied to the second book, were all afterthoughts, appearing on the title pages, and not used in the text, even in the cross-references. What Locke thought he was writing was a whole Discourse, presented for his own literary purposes in two books.

Now the general difficulty of this discussion is its unreality. No one can tell how long a "historical occasion" lasts, and it does not make sense to question historians about it. The phrase "The English Revolution" is already commonly used to cover the years after 1688 up to 1714, and to cover many other things as well as periods of time. If we permit ourselves this sort of latitude, there is no difficulty in making the occasion of the "Revolution" which gave rise to Locke's political philosophy include the years 1679–1687 also. The recognition, then, that the span of time taken up in the actual composition of *Two Treatises* was relatively short makes very little difference to the general issue. But it does make possible an exact chronological argument about the work Locke put into it, the work of original creation that is to say, as distinct from addition and revision. If it can be shown that any considerable part of it can belong only to the situation of a few particular months, then the whole belongs to those months.

A straightforward demonstration that the complete book was composed between 1679 and 1681, or 1683 at latest, can be made from the obvious connection of the *First Treatise* with the controversy over the republication of the works of Sir Robert Filmer. It is well known that the ability of the Monarchy and the Monarchists, or Tories as they were beginning to be called, to withstand the attacks of the Exclusionists, or Whigs, was due to their superior journalism and propaganda. Dryden, L'Estrange and the Tory pamphleteers won a striking victory over Shaftesbury and the Green Ribbon Club. The most successful move which they made was undoubtedly the resurrection of the works of this forgotten Royalist knight, who had published absolutist, patriarchal tracts between 1648 and 1652, and who had left his *pièce de résistance,* the *Patriarcha,* in manuscript. I have tried to show elsewhere how rapidly the collected works of Filmer became the *ipsissima verba* of the established order after their republication in 1679, *Patriarcha* being added to them in 1680, when there was a second issue of the tracts.[1] Locke's *First Treatise,* as we have seen, is a sentence-by-sentence refutation of the whole body of Filmer's works. Moreover, the exhaustive contradiction of patriarchalism runs right through the *Second Treatise* too. This is perhaps the most important result of editing it critically. If the *First Treatise* belongs to these earlier years, and if the *Second Treatise* is part and parcel of it, then the whole work was written before 1683, and there is an end of it.

Though a simple proof of this sort carries conviction to an editor of the book, there are points at which it can easily be attacked. The impression that the book was written as a whole, and is not the result of two separate impulses from historical circumstance, is a matter of critical opinion. It might be granted that the whole work was completed in some form as early as this, but maintained that it was so modified later as to be in fact a book of dual or multiple composition; moreover, Locke's practice with his other works could be used to confirm this view. It could be asserted that Filmer and Filmerism were not issues confined to the early 1680's, but were still very much alive in 1688 and 1689, and even later. If so, the argument could be that the book was composed as a whole, but at this later period, or (for an author in a hurry could certainly have done it) between February and August 1689.

These possible objections make it necessary to go further into

[1] Laslett, "Sir Robert Filmer," in *William and Mary Quarterly,* 3rd series, V, no. 4 (October, 1948); and Filmer, *Patriarcha,* ed. by Laslett (1949).

the evidence. Some of it can certainly be used against the view taken up here. The claim that as late as 1689 it was still necessary for a Whig writer to go to some trouble to refute Filmer is, of course, correct. Filmer was still being reprinted in 1696, and any acquaintance at all with English political literature up to 1714 will show that Locke was not wasting his publisher's money by including the *First Treatise* in his book. James Tyrell, who knew Locke best as a political writer, had published his *Patriarcha Non Monarcha* against Filmer in 1681, but he found it necessary to return to the attack in 1692. Locke's book reached Oxford early in December, 1689, and when Tyrell saw it he thought of it as an attack on patriarchalism, "a very solid and rational treatise cal'd of Government in which Sr. R. Filmers Principles are very well confuted." In the previous June the English Quaker Furly who had been his host in Rotterdam and was now in England wrote thus to Locke:

> *I met with a scrupulous Cambridge scholar that thought nothing could discharge him of the Oath of Allegiance that he had taken of James II and his successors. I had pleasant sport with him upon Sir R. Filmers maggot.*

But all this goes to show why it was that Locke published what he had written against Filmer in 1689, rather than to demonstrate that he actually wrote his refutation then. It is just possible that a man could find time to do all that Locke is known to have done between February and August of that year, and also to compose a work at such length against the patriarchal extremists. The study of the tracts he acquired makes it quite plain that he interested himself in everything that was written for and against the new regime at that critical time. But it seems extremely unlikely that he allowed himself to be rushed into print in this way, even by circumstances of such supreme importance to him, and even more unlikely that he lost over half his manuscript. Locke was not a man to mislay great bundles of papers, or to permit a printer or publisher to do such a thing. Nor was he a man to do things in a hurry. He never printed his first thoughts on any subject; certainly not on one as important as the foundations of society and the grounds of obedience. It took him nearly thirty years, from his late twenties to his late fifties, to produce in print a single one of the works which made him famous. For nearly all of them we have his drafts, notes and letters which cover the whole of this period. The book on education was composed as a series of letters spread over the years of his exile. Although we do not possess such a series for his major work on government, it seems impossible to believe that they did not once exist. To think of Locke as a man who could write a rationalization of events which had just taken place is to misunderstand his personality. It would have been a psychological impossibility for him to do so.

The view that the work was composed at leisure in the Lockeian manner in the later years of his Dutch exile, say in 1687–1688, the last successive draft of it being ready for the printer by 1689, is no more than guesswork. It accounts for the tone of its political comment, which, as Fox Bourne said, reads as if it was made before William's accession. It allows for an even earlier date of germination. In its favor is Locke's connection with the men who made the Revolution, who, as we have seen, might have expected him to write about it. There is some correspondence of his of 1688 about printing a work which could just conceivably have been this one, but was more probably the philosophical *Essay*. Locke was being pressed from England as early as 1687 to publish his work on toleration, and this might be made into an argument by analogy for the *Treatises*, since Locke on *Toleration* did appear in England in 1689, though he disclaimed responsibility. There is even a scrap of [manuscript] evidence which might be used to show that Locke was working at the text of the *Second Treatise* in February 1687, for he noted in his diary on the 2nd of that month an extract which is found in §14. But it is quite certain that it only found its way into the printed text in the course of publication, for it appears in the later state of the first edition and not in the earlier. This detail, then, may indicate only that the text was in existence in this area at this date, and suggests that Locke did not have it in his possession at the time, but copied his note into it two years later, in 1689 when it is known that he modified what he had written in many places.

It is to the very considerable body of evidence which we have about Locke's reading, his lists of books and his books themselves, their whereabouts and the notes he made on them, that we must turn for positive evidence to prove that *Two Treatises* was complete in some form by 1683. But before we do this we may refer to some obvious and very superficial features of the text of the work itself. In 1689 the words "King James" with no number following could mean one thing only—King James the Second. Yet in the text he had printed in that year Locke refers twice to "King James" when he meant James I, surely a very significant anachronism which he corrected in later printings. It seems strange that this has not been pointed out before, but even stranger that the parliamentary issues and events of the years of the Exclusion Controversy have not been noticed in the constitutional discussion of the *Second Treatise.*

Except, perhaps, in his last chapter, Locke's first concern there is with the summoning and dissolution of Parliament. This was for him the critical relation between Legislative and Executive. It was this which could lead to "a state of War with the People" when the "Executive Power shall use force to hinder the *meeting* and *acting* of the Legislative." Now this was an issue in 1689, but it was between 1678 (or even 1675) and 1681 that it was really crucial. It was then that Shaftesbury, with Locke at his side, had made attempt after attempt to force Charles II either to dissolve a parliament long out of date, or to summon it after an intolerable series of prorogations. The "*long Train of Actings*" of §210, which became the "long train of abuses" of the American Declaration of Independence, includes the underhand favoring of Catholicism ("though publickly proclaimed against"). Now this "acting" was that of Charles II, not James II. James did not find it necessary either to be underhand in favoring Catholicism, or to proclaim against it. . . .

. . . As early as 1679 Locke had begun a work on government, which was to have as one of its objects the criticism of Filmer. But the work he had begun, and which he had written at least as far as §22, was not the *First Treatise,* but the *Second Treatise.* The *First Treatise* seems to have been begun later, perhaps six months later or more, when the influence of Filmer had grown so dangerous that a full-length examination became necessary to Locke, and had indeed already been undertaken by Tyrell and Sidney. The change of plan as well as the writing of the whole work can be attributed to very particular political and personal circumstances. They come from the events of the Exclusion Campaign of 1678–1681, and from Locke's association with the protagonist of that political drama, the first Earl of Shaftesbury.

It is this detailed evidence, refined but exact, which suggests the view of the literary structure of *Two Treatises* here put forward. It does not require minute analysis of Locke's text to feel the force of the suggestion that the *Second Treatise* is the earlier work. As it stands, the printed book is cumbersome and forbidding, two hundred unreadable pages introducing an essay which is lively and convincing, if a little labored and repetitive. We can see why Locke arranged his material thus, though we may feel aggrieved at his insensibility. But there is no good reason for supposing that he thought his thoughts in such an improbable order, or wrote them down like this. Every one of his positions is assumed in the *First Treatise,* but, as we have seen, when he refers to them there he has to send us forward to the *Second.* There is never an occasion to do the opposite. Who would deliberately choose to begin the exposition of a complicated theme by the refutation of another man's system without laying down his own premises? And who would choose to do it not logically, step by step, as Filmer's other critics do, but seriatim, by the pages and paragraphs of a motley assemblage of his occasional writings?

We cannot now do more than suggest this new approach to the book. The question of how complete the *Second Treatise* was when the *First* was begun must be left open. So must the complicated problem of the re-writing and re-arrangement caused by this change of plan. But I believe that the *Second,* the positive statement, was substantially written down when the *First,* the negative commentary, was begun. I believe also that this is the only satisfactory account of the manner of composing the complete book. It can only be valid if it is granted that the whole was written up to ten years earlier than is usually supposed. John Locke's *Two Treatises of Government* is an Exclusion Tract, not a Revolution Pamphlet.

This is as much as is now certainly known and can safely be inferred about the historical occasion for the writing of *Two Treatises.* It leaves a great deal of room for conjecture. Here only one guess will be made, but if it is a lucky guess it explains a very great deal.

There is a document referred to in Locke's papers and in Shaftesbury's papers which had a history corresponding quite exactly with the history of the manuscript draft or drafts of *Two Treatises* as it has been worked out here. The great obstacle to its being accepted as identical is its title. It was called *De Morbo Gallico*—"Of the French disease" (or, the French pox), a euphemism for syphilis. Conspicuous and vulgar, it may be thought, but it must be remembered that cover names are common in these papers, especially for secret, dangerous or embarrassing documents, and, if we are right, *Two Treatises* may well have been thought of as all three. Moreover, Locke and Shaftesbury undoubtedly did think of despotism as the French disease, and when he began his work on the subject Locke had just returned from a four-year examination of the French disease as a system of politics.

When Shaftesbury's papers were seized in July 1681 Locke was in Oxford, but draft A (i) of the *Essay on Human Understanding* was not the only document connected with Locke which was listed. There was "Mr. Locke's book of fruit trees," and his letter on the Oxford Parliament. There was also "Notes out of Mors Gallicus writ in my lords hand." It has never been suggested that Shaftesbury was a syphilitic, though there can be no certainty. But whatever his lordship had noted, it seems unlikely to have been Locke's printed book with the title *Morbus Gallicus. Omnia quae extant de eo,* for it had been printed in Venice as long ago as 1566. In the census of his library at Oxford made a little later in the same month, Locke entered *Tractatus de Morbo Gallico* amongst the folios. His old medical book was a folio, but it is not likely that it would have found a place so close to his Hooker and to two folio notebooks, one of them containing the original draft of his unfinished work on the Understanding. On 19 July he left for London, not from Oxford direct, but from Tyrell's house at Oakley. He often left things with Tyrell, and in his diary on the 18th he wrote—in shorthand—"Left with him De Morbo Gallico." This object then begins to look like something more important to him than a medical treatise, and a year later his medical and political friend Thomas wrote in such a way as makes it clear that it was something which Locke himself had written. "You may send your Observations de Morbo Gallico," send it to Thomas, that is, at Salisbury, and he gives the name of the messenger.

This was in July, 1682. The next reference is in the first letter he wrote from Holland after his flight there in 1683, full of cryptic allusions to his possessions left behind. It is addressed to Edward Clarke, of Somerset, his confidential friend, agent and relative.

Honest Adrian [Thomas] writes me word that the chest is now in Mrs [Smithsby's] custody was not opened, though he had the key and directions to do it. Neither do I ask whether any thing else in her custody was opened, only give me leave to tell you that I either think or dreamt you enquired of me concerning the title of a treatise, part whereof is in Mr Smiths [?Mrs Smithsby's] hands, and it is Tractatus de Morbo Gallico. *If there were another copy of it I should be very glad to have that at any reasonable rate, for I have heard it commended and shall apply myself close to the study of physic by the fireside this winter. But of this I shall tell you more hereafter, when I hear that there are more copies than one, for else it will not be reasonable to desire it. I desire also to know whether Dr Sydenham hath published anything this year.*

It is a treatise and it is in two halves: Locke wants another copy of one half. But no detailed sense can be made of this letter without the missing key agreed upon between Locke and Clarke. The medical references look very like a blind.

The last context is mutilated but clearer. It occurs in another but much later letter to Clarke, written in 1687:

I beg also that the half . . . [hole in original] . . . de Morbo Gallico, which I left with R Smith [Smithsby] sealed up in a little [?box—Rand's guess] about the length of a hand and half a hand in breadth, may be sent into . . . [gap in original].

The letter ends:

You may easily perceive why I would have that tract De Morbo Gallico.

To make it into a package of this size, Locke may have torn out the pages of the folio writing book which stood in his rooms in 1681, and tied up those he thought it safe to preserve. It is tempting to suppose that he wanted them in 1687 in view of the changing political situation.

If our guess is right, and *De Morbo Gallico* was in fact the cover name for the manuscript of *Two Treatises,* all this follows. Shaftesbury read and noted it before July, 1681. At that time it was in Locke's room at Christ Church, written in a large folio notebook, just as was his *Essay on Human Understanding.* Tyrell had it in his keeping for a little while after this, not knowing what it was. Thomas read it in 1682. By the time of Locke's hurried departure in late 1683, it had been split into two parts, and after this we hear only of one of those parts, though we have a confused hint that there may have been another copy somewhere. The fragmentary manuscript was in the keeping of the London landlady, Mrs. Smithsby, at whose house Locke lived in 1689, and who returned other things of his then. She may have kept it until that year, so that Locke never saw it between 1683 and 1689, in spite of his requests to have it sent to Holland. This fits in with the evidence that he did not modify the work before that time.

We must identify this part manuscript with the whole work we now have. The other, longer, piece had presumably been destroyed before he left for exile. It was, of course, the continuation of the *First Treatise,* written, we must remember, not in the middle, but in the later pages of his original folio notebook. His motives for destroying it between 1682 and 1683 can easily be inferred. It was in this continuation that Locke, like Sidney, must have proceeded from the principles of patriarchalism to the practice of monarchs. One of the charges on which Sidney was to lose his head was exactly this, that he had identified Filmer's patriarchal monarch with the king of England and justified forcible resistance to him. Such, it is suggested, was the "Fate which" as Locke tells us in his Preface, "otherwise disposed of the papers which should have filled up the middle, and were more than all the rest."

The history of the composition of *Two Treatises* cannot be said to be very important to the study of Locke. It merely brings that book into line with the others he wrote. It shows that his character was consistent and that he left too much written on paper to conceal the story of the work, however much he may have wished to do so.

Nor will it make much difference to the general historian. The account of the relation of Locke's political system to the English Revolution may have to be modified a little. A few "befores" instead of "afters," some word like "predisposition" where "reflection" or "rationalization" now appears, this will cover the case. Exactly the same chronological revision has had to be made in the case of the absolutists, Hobbes and Filmer. Their systems of authoritarian reaction can no longer be regarded as the result of the attack upon established authority in the English Civil War. It will be as easy to accept, or to ignore, the fact that Lockeian liberalism was worked out before and not after 1688.

But the political scientist may find in this revision further grounds for being critical of one of his accepted concepts, so useful and so inclusive as to be a general category, the concept of Revolution. The name Revolution, in the sense in which we use it, was born in England in 1688–1689, and it is fascinating to watch the old word for sudden dynastic change acquiring its new meaning in the political literature of those months. Because of what happened in England then, and because of the view which contemporaries so soon took of it and which historians immediately elaborated, we talk of the English Revolution, the French Revolution, the American Revolution, the Russian Revolution. We do so because we associate sudden political change with total transformation, political and social, intellectual and even aesthetic. Locke and his political theory, with his epistemology and the rest of his thinking added to it, afford the most useful of all examples of this. But as we have said, the chronology of the English Revolution has to be made so elastic if this association is to be justified, that the phrase itself has become meaningless. Locke was no revolutionary in any case, in the conventional sense. How can we go on associating him with "The English Revolution," whatever that may mean, now that we know that he wrote in anticipation of events? Perhaps it is time we abandoned the phrase itself and the system of muddled and superficial generalization which goes with it.

David Ogg
THE REVOLUTION AS A REINFORCEMENT OF ENGLISH INSTITUTIONS

David Ogg (1887–1965) was a frequent visitor to America. His first major work was Europe in the Seventeenth Century *(1925), followed nine years later by his two-volume* England in the Reign of Charles II. *In 1959 he was appointed Honorary Fellow of New College, Oxford. The following selection is taken from the work that completes his great study of the later seventeenth century.*

One of the best sources for the study of the English Revolution is to be found in the proclamations and declarations put forth by the contestants; never before had the printed word played such a part in political events. On 17 October 1688 James issued a proclamation for the restoration of the corporations, and the removal therefrom of those who had been intruded; three days later came his proclamation ordering a strict watch to be kept on the coasts, and forbidding the spread of false news. On 1 November, the eve of his embarkation, there was an announcement from the prince of Orange, giving his reasons for invading England; next day, James imposed a ban on all public announcements made by the prince. On 6 November the king, after referring to the invasion, promised redress of all grievances; on the 17th a third party—the Lords—intervened with a declaration announcing that war could be avoided only by the speedy summoning of parliament. Then, on 22 November, there were published announcements, from the nobility, gentry, and commonalty of York and Nottingham, declaring adhesion to the prince of Orange; and, at last, on 30 November, a royal proclamation intimated a meeting of parliament for the 15th of January. The conditions laid down by William at Hungerford were published on 9 December; two days later, James, announcing that he had been forced to send his queen and son to safety, confessed that, as he could not trust the army, he would offer no opposition to the prince. On the same day the lords spiritual and temporal, in and about the cities of London and Westminster, intimated that, as the king had with-

From David Ogg, *England in the Reigns of James II and William III* (Oxford, 1955). Reprinted by permission of the Clarendon Press, Oxford.

drawn himself, they had applied to the prince to summon a free parliament, with liberty of conscience to Protestant Dissenters. This date, 11 December, marked the end of the reign of James II and the beginning of the interregnum.

The literary duel continued throughout the interregnum. During his short stay at Rochester, James, on 22 December, put forth a proclamation intimating that he had left Whitehall because of the discourteous conduct of the prince, but he would return at the call of the nation, whenever it agreed to have liberty of conscience. This coincided with an order from the Lords, assembled in their House, requiring all papists to leave London. Next day, 23 December, the prince of Orange summoned all persons who had served in any of Charles II's parliaments to meet at St. James's on the 26th, together with the lord mayor, aldermen, and fifty of the common council of the city of London. These informal assemblies of Lords, ex-Commons, and city magistrates asked William to summon a convention. On Christmas Day the lords spiritual and temporal requested the prince of Orange to take upon himself the direction of affairs until the meeting of the intended convention on 22 January, for which His Highness was asked to direct the issue of writs. His compliance with this request was announced on 29 December. Finally, on 4 January 1689, came a proclamation from James, in the form of a letter to the privy council, intimating the concessions which he had made, and announcing to the world that he had been obliged to leave his country because of his fear of death. The history of the Revolution can be little more than comment on these official pronouncements.

If it be granted that the model revolution is one that avoids bloodshed and maintains a fundamental continuity with the past, then the English Revolution was a model of its kind. Parliament was not in session, but a body of lords and bishops sat in their House, while old parliamentarians met at St. James's, each of which conclaves invited William to assume the administration. The ex-Commons sitting at St. James's had, of course, no official status, but the lords spiritual and temporal, though consisting only of "those about London and Westminster," and though not summoned by a king, had a somewhat stronger position, because they were independent of election. Indeed, they acted in an executive capacity; that they should have done so is one of the many illustrations of the aristocratic character both of the English constitution and of the English Revolution. . . .

The Commons were the first to address themselves to the great constitutional questions raised by recent events; and, as there was a certain hesitancy on the part of new members, the lead was taken by such veterans as Colonel Birch, Sir T. Clarges, and Sergeant Maynard, with the help of those experienced parliamentarians Sir T. Lee, Sir T. Littleton, and Sir Edward Seymour. Birch, who had started life as a carter, had a habit of driving straight through the subtleties and fine distinctions of debate. "These forty years," he declared, "we have been striving against anti-Christ, popery and tyranny." Here was an echo of a far-off past; this link with the Puritan Revolution was evidenced by the passing, on 29 January, of a resolution that a Popish prince was inconsistent with a Protestant state. There was another reminiscence, this time of the Restoration, in Lord Falkland's proposal that, before they filled the throne, they should resolve what powers were to be conferred on the ruler, a proposal which started a hubbub of suggestions—frequent parliaments, independent judges, inviolability of corporations, and many more. That these demands were placed in the forefront may be attributed in part to the influence of Halifax, who was the reputed author of a broadsheet, distributed among the Commons, which counseled them to agree on their constitution before they decided on their governor. So the House resolved that, before proceeding to fill the throne, it would secure the religion, laws, and liberties of the nation. The mistake of 1660 would not be made a second time. . . .

As the Restoration had been followed by an attempt to grant toleration to Protestant Dissenters, so the Revolution raised again the great question of unity within the Protestant fold. Ever since 1679, and even more in the reign of James II, it had been realized that the Protestant Dissenters had been thrown, by the menace of popery, into the same camp as the Anglicans; and to many it seemed that, politically at least, the two had much in common; there was also the example of Scotland, where the Presbyterians had maintained the most consistent opposition to the later Stuarts. Not unnaturally, therefore, it was from the period of the Popish Plot that two abortive measures, a Toleration Bill and a Comprehension Bill were revived. Nottingham tried to secure the passage of both bills. He had little difficulty with the first, but he failed with the second, the more ambitious of the two. This, the Comprehension Bill, would have relaxed the ritual and discipline of the Church of England in such a manner that Nonconformists might attend the parish church without violation of their scruples against such practices as kneeling, and wearing the surplice. It would also have qualified for the cure of souls all Dissenters who took the oath against transubstantiation, and expressed approval of the doctrine, worship, and government of the Church of England. But the strong church party in the Commons successfully opposed the bill, which was dropped on 8 April. The argument had prevailed that, as Convocation was about to be summoned, to that body should be referred the great questions raised by the problem of establishing unity in non-Catholic England.

Another abortive proposal at this time showed how a section, at least of the Convention, was anxious to mitigate the rigidity of the old religious distinctions, and to end the monopoly whereby office-holding was limited to Anglicans. At the third reading in the Lords of the bill for substituting new oaths for the old oaths of allegiance and supremacy (23 March), one of the peers offered as a rider a clause which would have qualified for office anyone who had taken the sacrament either according to the practice of the Church of England, or according to that of any recognized Protestant communion. The rider was lost. Those who protested against this rejection gave reasons which show a remarkable advance on contemporary opinion. By the rejection of the proposal, maintained the protesting minority, a great part of the Protestant freemen of England were excluded from public employment "from a mere scruple of conscience"; moreover, these men professed doctrines which were about to be publicly tolerated in a bill then before the House (the Toleration Bill). This exclusion, contended the protesting peers, might have bad effects on Protestant and Reformed churches abroad, because it turned the edge of a law, intended to penalize Papists, against Protestants and friends of the government as settled by the Revolution. Lastly, in the words of this protest, "mysteries of religion and divine worship are of divine original, and of a nature so wholly distinct from the secular affairs of politic society that they cannot be applied to these ends." In these words, the spirit of 1689 anticipated that of 1829.

It was very different with the Toleration Bill. This did not abolish any of the penal statutes against Protestant Dissenters, but merely declared that they should not be enforced against those who fulfilled certain conditions. These conditions included, for laymen, the new oaths of fidelity to William and Mary, and the standard oath against transubstantiation; for preachers there was added the requirement of subscription to the Thirty-nine Articles, except those relating to homilies, traditions of the church, and consecration of bishops. Some recognition of the status of dissenting ministers (qualified as above) was conceded by their exemption from parish offices and from serving on juries; but no exemption from tithe was given, and it was expressly declared that nothing in the act was intended to give relief to Roman Catholics. No longer were dissenting meetings to be held behind closed doors; indeed, their places of worship were to be certified to the bishop or archdeacon of the diocese. . . .

The coronation of William and Mary took place on 11 April with the customary pageantry. In the absence of Sancroft, Compton officiated, and Mary was crowned as queen regnant. In accordance with the act for establishing the coronation oath, the two sovereigns were obliged to swear that they would govern the people of England and the dominions thereto belonging according to "the statutes in parliament agreed upon, and the laws and customs of the same"; that they would maintain the true profession of the Gospel, and "the Protestant Reformed Religion established by law." Two new things had thus been introduced into the coronation oath, namely, the statutes of parliament, and the "Protestant Reformed Religion." In regard to the first, kings had formerly been obliged to swear observance of the laws and customs emanating from their royal predecessors, especially those granted to the clergy by St. Edward. These are now replaced by the laws and statutes of the realm.

Coronation oaths, though so few in number, are the most precious of all the materials on which the constitutional historian has to work, because they embody fundamental conceptions of the state; they are sensitive to deep-seated changes in these conceptions, and they are sworn in circumstances of the utmost solemnity. Conversely, their misinterpretation, as by George III, may prove of momentous consequence; indeed, if that monarch or his advisers had read the debates in the Commons on the new oath, they would have seen that it was not intended to bind the king in his legislative capacity, for the legislature had in view the fact that important concessions in religious matters were being embodied in bills, to which it was hoped that the crown would assent. Some of the essential principles of both the Revolution and the modern constitution were incorporated in the coronation oath, almost as much as in the Bill of Rights; but the former is much more difficult of interpretation, because so much shorter, and because, even within its brevity, there appears on modern standards to be redundance. About one newcomer we can be certain—the king is no longer the sole law-giver, for thenceforward he is only a part of the legislative body; here is an obvious and noncontroversial change. But it is otherwise with the second newcomer—"the Protestant Reformed Religion established by law." Here the main difficulty arises from its context, since it immediately precedes the obligation to defend the settlement of the Church of England and Ireland, "as by law established." Does this imply that "the Protestant Reformed Religion established by law" was something different from the doctrine and discipline of the Church of England, also established by law? This question was in the mind of one parliamentarian when he objected that the new phrase created another church in addition to the Church of England; moreover, the amended formula "Protestant Church of England" was rejected by the House. So the two apparently similar things were kept apart. Nor is this the end of the supposed redundance, for nowadays "Protestant" and "Reformed" are regarded as meaning exactly the same thing, and it has even been held that to distinguish between the two is mere pedantry.

But before we dismiss the new coronation oath as a piece of pedantry or redundance, we should bear in mind that tautology is often the resort of those who are striving desperately to be clear and emphatic; also, that words which mean the same thing today have not always meant the same thing. Nor was the coronation oath enunciated, as it were, *in vacuo;* on the contrary, it was closely related to historical events, and can be understood only in the light of these events. Unlike previous coronation oaths, this one was drafted by laymen, to be understood by laymen. The legislators provided a guarantee for the Church of England, but, on the other hand, they kept in view the part played by that church in recent history, and how, by its insistence on divine right and nonresistance, it had, in their opinion, done much to encourage the excesses of the Stuarts. So long as the Stuarts had supported the established church, they were free to engage in a policy of crypto- or public Catholicism; and so it seemed to many intelligent laymen that the Church of England had degenerated from the position of a national church into that of a political party. The Seven Bishops had for a time restored this lost prestige, but only for a time, because five of them refused to recognize William; it was also clear that the church was divided, or at best only lukewarm in the cause of the Revolution. Accordingly, guarantee of the Church of England was preceded by guarantee of something else—the Protestant Reformed Religion. The legislators of 1689 were taking no risks.

This dual phrase also derived from the past. By 1689 the term "Protestant" was coming to be used in its modern sense as an inclusive term for all the Western churches opposed to Rome; but it was still distinguished from "Reformed," that is, the more extreme Calvinist and Zwinglian movements of the later sixteenth century which had exercised such influence on the England of Elizabeth. Already the Whigs had emphasized the glories of Elizabeth's reign in contrast with the shame of the Stuarts; and, as that shame deepened, many Englishmen—not necessarily Whigs, for this was well above party distinction—reverted to those great changes of the sixteenth century which, in their view, had created a "Protestant" and "Reformed" England. By "Reformed" they meant the Elizabethan settlement, when some of the most characteristic doctrines of Calvinism had been embodied in the Thirty-nine Articles, where they still remain. Here was a "Reformed" religion, "established by law"; or, in other words, a reminder that if the Church of England had thoughts of taking the path to Rome, it had not yet (so far as the law was concerned) retraced the steps already taken on the way to Geneva. To most churchmen this reminder was obnoxious in the extreme.

"Reformed" was preceded by "Protestant." Here there is great latitude of interpretation. The term may possibly have been used in order to exclude the casuist who could argue that, after the Council of Trent, the church of Rome was a "Reformed" church; or it may have been adopted simply as the widest possible expression to denote those churches of Western Europe which were uncompromisingly opposed to Rome. The term, described in the debates as an "honorable" one, may have included both these things; but it may also have had some reference to Henry VIII's Reformation, with its transference of enormous areas of church lands to secular proprietors, many of them among the ancestors of those who adopted the phrase; indeed, Henry's Reformation was distinctively "Protestant" in the sense that the German or Lutheran reformers had used the word, since their original "protest" was not merely against certain Roman Catholic practices, but against the threat of imperial interference with large-scale confiscations of land. Now Henry's confiscations had also been authorized by law; here was the security by which many members of parliament held their estates. So there was no redundance or pedantry in adding "Protestant" to "Reformed," for these words meant quite different things. Taking the Henrician with the Elizabethan settlement, the view of parliament was that the official religion of England, *as recognized by law,* was both Protestant and Reformed.

These technical matters should not conceal the national importance of what the Revolution government was trying, almost desperately, to do. It was emulating the example set in Elizabeth's reign, when the menace from Spain was countered by association with those Protestant and Reformed communities on the continent which shared our peril; now that we were confronted by a similar menace from France, parliament clearly implied a renewal of this alignment with foreign churches again threatened by militant Catholicism, churches with which Anglicans indignantly repudiated any connection. Nor was this all; for, so long as there remained any doubt whether or not England was Protestant, there was always a loophole for the intervention of the clergy in secular matters; whereas Protestantism (as distinct from the old "Reformed" doctrines) means erastianism, or the complete subordination of church to state. Archbishops and bishops would continue to sit in the Lords, as some of them sat for a time in the cabinet; but in both capacities their position was public and responsible, not secret and irresponsible. Here indeed we have the central achievement of the Revolution; "this coronation oath," declared a member of the House, "is the very touchstone and symbol of your government"; because its dual phrase, so often misunderstood, or resented, or repudiated, has served to enunciate one of the essential characteristics of Anglo-Saxon civilization. The alternative was Bourbon-Stuart civilization, a totalitarian system, having as its agents the priest, the dragoon, and the hangman, a system to which many Englishmen were determined not to submit. It was in accordance with this determination that William III declared war on Louis XIV on 7 May 1689. . . .

The Bill of Rights is our greatest constitutional document since Magna Carta; and, like that document, it emanated from the misdeeds of a king. Both instruments were concerned, not to enunciate abstract principles of government, but to provide safeguards against royal wrongdoings, many of them specified. Some of the omissions from the Bill of Rights are of interest. Reference to the social contract had disappeared in the conferences between the two Houses in February; on the other hand, the whole measure implies some kind of contract between king and nation, based not on law, but on the "complete confidence" which parliament professed in the two sovereigns. There is little about parliament, except that it should be held frequently, and that elections should be free; otherwise, certain executive acts are pronounced legal only if parliament concurs. The suspending power is ruled out altogether; the dispensing power disappeared in a more devious way. At first, it was declared invalid only "as it hath been exercised of late"; but a later clause (II) of the bill enacted that no dispensation to a statute could be allowed unless expressly provided for in the statute itself, or in any statute passed by that session of parliament. As no such statute was passed, the royal exercise of the dispensing power came to an end.

Otherwise, there was no attempt to define the extent of the royal powers. The prerogative of mercy, the king's right to choose his ministers, to declare war and make peace—all these are left untouched. The legislators of 1689 did not even try to make monarchy foolproof; all that they were concerned with was that certain evils within their own experience should not recur. It is mainly for this reason that recent historians have depreciated the value of the Bill of Rights, arguing that it left William, as later George III, with many powers denied to the sovereigns of today. But this is to read the present into the past, and to misunderstand the essentially English character of the document. The Bill of Rights reaffirmed what had been asserted by the great medieval jurists, that the king is subject to law; and that, for many of his most important acts, there must be the consent of those (whether *magnates* or parliament) who could claim to speak on behalf of the nation. True, the king was left with certain important rights; but, meanwhile, parliament had come to stay, and it was only a matter of time before the residual prerogative of the king in person would yield to the rule of king in parliament.

In one more respect modern historiography has done less than justice to the Bill of Rights. With the discredit into which parliamentary institutions have fallen in some quarters, accentuated by assiduous eulogy of the Stuarts, the Revolution has been hailed as a drab or "bourgeois" episode in our history, ending a period of "brilliant" court life, and ushering in an era of dull and not always intelligent kings. But, at least from the point of view of the common man, the advantage does not always lie with the country governed by a fascist ruler, however facetious or devout; indeed, it may be much more enjoyable to read about such kings than to live under them. It was just for these unspectacular, everyday conditions that the Bill of Rights provided. There was not a word about democracy, nor about the economic betterment of the people, nor about the extension of the franchise, but there was a great deal about those elementary legal rights of the subject, rights to which we are now so accustomed that we take them for granted, and therefore assume that they have never been threatened. It is in the guarantee of these rights that the value of the Revolution consists; nor does the fact that we have enjoyed them so long diminish the importance of their origin. "The Bill of Rights is to be as long as we are a nation," declared a member of the House of Commons, and he was not exaggerating.

Lastly, the Bill of Rights evoked from some contemporaries the opinion that it was only the beginning of far-reaching reform. There should, it was argued, be more guarantees for the rights of the subject, particularly in treason trials; the remedy of habeas corpus should be extended, and made more easily available. Most notable was the change in the practice and theory of the prerogative. The clemency of William's rule proved that for all, except the Jacobites, a policy of mercy was perfectly safe, and even the Jacobites were treated with great lenity. Moreover, William's practice was backed by a gradual change in public opinion, whereby the doctrine was repudiated that, for effective government, brutality was necessary. Here are the words of a contemporary, writing in 1692:

> It is a great mistake to imagine that an easie and full power of chopping men in pieces upon a block, or confining them in Newgate or other gaols, can add any strength to the crown, for Englishmen, generally speaking, are fond of a king, not only for his, but for their own sakes. . . . No authority can be so lasting as that which is founded on love and esteem.

Stuart England, like so many continental countries, had found kingship and liberty incompatible; the Revolution of 1688 gave us a constitution in which the two are inseparable. . . .

Sovereignty is one of the most obscure and debated of all political subjects, for hardly any two people can agree in defining either its source or its extent. But in the progress of English civilization one aspect of the problem, namely, legal or parliamentary sovereignty, has steadily acquired clarity of definition and latitude of application, so that today it is almost outside the realm of controversy.

As early as the thirteenth century Bracton had thought in terms of some kind of association for the purposes of government, composed of king and *magnates;* then *Magna Carta* had formulated the principle of no taxation without the consent of the *commune consilium regni.* A more advanced stage was that represented by Coke who, in his Fourth Institute, claimed that the power of parliament was "absolute and transcendent"; but his examples show that he had in mind the High Court of Parliament, concerned with the making of laws, rather than with the direction of policy. Next came Hobbes, whose theory of an unlimited, undivided sovereignty, though postulated of a single, hereditary personality, was easily applicable to a body of men, such as king in parliament, a theory so challenging and absolute as to repel all who thought in terms of balance or compromise, and all who resented the idea that government is ultimately dependent on force. Nevertheless, it was Hobbes's theory, the most logical and the most misunderstood of the century, that ultimately prevailed, though the achievement was indirect and long delayed. In the course of that process the Revolution of 1688 is the dividing line between two periods in the history of sovereignty—an earlier one, in which there was no guarantee for the summoning of parliament; and a later one, in which, though both Houses had an assured and permanent place, the king was still endowed with certain personal prerogatives which limited the scope of parliamentary sovereignty. Hence, in this later stage, it was natural for Locke to popularize at home, and even more abroad, the idea of division of powers, a cordial much more palatable than the distasteful medicine prescribed by Hobbes. But, even then, the formula of Hobbes was in process of application; for there was gradually emerging that omnipotent and indivisible trinity of king, Lords, and Commons in which supreme power and direction are vested today.

Accordingly, in any estimate of the progress made by parliamentary sovereignty in the later seventeenth century, a beginning must be made with those personal rights still exercised by the crown. These rights were legacies from a long and sacred past. The prerogative of the Stuarts had owed much to the sacerdotal element in kingship; and, whatever may be thought of Charles II's virtues, there can be no doubt that, in his exercise of one element in that prerogative—the healing touch—he was (therapeutically) by far the most efficacious of English kings. This literal contact with the body of the subject, never attempted by William, was practiced for the last time by Queen Anne. In spite of the Bill of Rights, there still survived, in English kingship, many powers and exemptions, some of them relics of an older, mystic conception of sovereignty; for the prerogative was thought of as something essentially good, since it did not extend to anything that might injure the subject, or deprive him of his just rights. The king, it was conceived, had an interest in all his subjects, and a claim to their service; he had supreme patronage, appointing bishops by his nomination; as the fountain of honor, he created peers; as the supreme repository of mercy, he granted pardons. He could incorporate a town; and, in the opinion of some, he could revoke a grant of incorporation; he could make an alien free-born; he could put a value on the coin of the realm; he had a right to the lands of convicted felons. His prerogative was an essential part of the common law of England. Such were among the commonplaces of those lawyers who attempted to define this, the most elusive element in the constitution.

As James II had taken the Nonresistance divines too seriously, so he may have been encouraged, in his course of conduct, by the cloudy amplitude of rights and privileges with which the lawyers surrounded the throne. That cloudiness had been clarified in the Revolution Settlement only by dispersal of the fog surrounding the dispensing power; otherwise, most of the old rights remained, including those of summoning, proroguing, and dissolving parliament; dismissing judges (before the Act of Settlement); appointing to high offices of state; vetoing legislation; declaring war and making peace. These were substantial rights. It is one of the paradoxes of English history that the parliamentary constitution dates from an act which diminished the royal power so little, and from the rule of a king whose prerogatives were so great. . . .

It was by means of his moderate and reasonable use of such a vast prerogative that William helped to secure for the crown a permanent place in the British constitution. This is all the more remarkable as he was by nature autocratic and headstrong; but his great self-control kept these instincts within bounds. Almost unfettered by the letter of the constitution, he nevertheless respected its spirit. . . .

The first of these rights, that of summoning, proroguing, and dissolving parliament was limited generally by the clause in the Bill of Rights that, for the redress of grievances and the amending of the laws, "parliaments ought to be held frequently"; and, more specifically by the Triennial Act of 1694. This latter statute was modified by an Act of 1696, the year of the Jacobite Assassination Plot, which enacted that parliament should not determine by the death of the sovereign, but might sit for six months thereafter. These were the legislative measures which ensured for parliament a permanent place in the constitution, and so must be regarded as the most important element in the Revolution Settlement.

It is in these measures, and in the debates to which they gave rise, that we can detect the most striking characteristic of parliament, namely, the gradual adaptation of a medieval institution to more modern needs. . . .

This [article] has attempted, in its references to society and institutions, to connect the development of English civilization with the gradual and peaceful adaptation of medieval survivals; in illustration of this development, the examples of crown and parliament may be cited. In parliament, even as late as the end of the seventeenth century, the Lords, in this little distinguishable from the feudal magnates, still exercised personal privileges which we would consider social abuses; while the Commons were returned by methods, few of which would be commended by the political theorist of today. In both Houses there were thus traces of a perverted medievalism. Nevertheless, parliament had now become permanent and national, directing the state through its first European war, and committing it to another, in which the foundations of world supremacy were to be laid. A similar process of adaptation can be seen in the changed place assigned to the crown in our constitution; and, in the functions now performed by the king, it is possible to detect the sublimated relics of ancient party aspiration. On the one hand, the old Whig, applying his common-law maxim to the prerogative, would acclaim in the sovereign such absolute detachment from party distinction and political initiative as to make public wrongdoing impossible; on the other hand, the old Tory, his religion transmuted into a sentiment, would applaud in the same sovereign a human link, binding together a great commonwealth of free nations, a ruler far more potent than any divine right king. Thus the monarchy is the most remarkable of all these survivals because, while its powers are still regulated by a medieval fiction, it has been adapted to conditions undreamed of in the past. . . .

The art of living together in society is one of the most difficult of all arts, and history is strewn with the wreckage of failures to achieve it. To us, the Revolution of 1688 and the establishment of a Protestant, maritime state may well seem remote, as the thought of Locke may seem trite or commonplace; the first to be taken for granted, the second in danger of depreciation, because anyone can understand it. We may have outgrown these things, but nevertheless they have determined the evolution of Anglo-Saxon civilization in two hemispheres, maintained by communities which are as ready to defend their liberties as they are unwilling to enforce them on others. This voluntary element, this aversion from proselytism and propaganda, this spirit of live and let live is our most precious heritage from the seventeenth century. That its exponents still survive the threats of intolerance and repression is the distinctive achievement which unites the English-speaking world.

Gerald M. Straka

THE REVOLUTION JUSTIFIED BY DIVINE RIGHT

Professor Gerald M. Straka has amplified the theme of the following essay in his Anglican Reaction to the Revolution of 1688 *(1962). He is the author of a forthcoming history of England,* A Certainty in the Succession, 1640–1815.

Since the days of Macaulay and the great reform bill, a number of historians have been at work revising the Whig interpretation of the Glorious Revolution. Just as Magna Carta was placed in its proper medieval setting, clearing it from the misty precedential motives of seventeenth-century parliamentarians, so the Revolution Settlement has been placed more and more in its Stuart setting, freeing it from nineteenth-century positivism. Unlike the case of the former, however, the Revolution era has not as yet been treated in a single volume incorporating all recent revisions of thought. David Ogg's book comes as close as most, but nearly every new survey, when it mentions the Revolution, still repeats the old liberal view, as if the work of the past thirty years had never been accomplished.

Among the vacuous banalities that one finds in revolution rhetoric is the statement that divine right theory died a sudden death in 1689. Of course, those who declare this have in mind—or should have in mind—the divine right of hereditary succession; and, although they might seem to be right, it can be argued that the House of Orange, being in the succession, could claim the divine right of heredity. What is usually meant by the death of divine right, however, is the death of divinely constituted monarchy, and for this there is little evidence. Certainly some minor figures like Charles Blount and John Wildman, as well as a number of court skeptics, derided monarchical divinity, but these were few compared to the majority of Englishmen who did not believe that when James II fled the throne he took God with him. The writings of Bishops Lloyd, Stillingfleet, Tenison, Burnet, scores of pamphlets and books by Anglican laymen indicate that

From Gerald M. Straka, "The Final Phase of Divine Right Theory in England, 1688–1702," *English Historical Review* 77 (October, 1962). Reprinted by permission of Longmans, Green and Company.

divine right continued to exert an influence on men's minds greater than that of a nostalgia for a dead idea. No doubt contractarianism and natural rights gained an ever-growing ascendancy in political thought after 1688, but this is no reason for ignoring the fascinating development within the divine-rightist school. The contractarians have too long given a one-sided view of revolutionary doctrine and we must be made aware that the ardent Anglican who believed in Charles's and James's right could do no less than allow William his divine right to rule. It is my belief that divine right in a new form went just as far as natural right in giving support to the Revolution and that it stood midway between the nonreligious views of Locke and the super-religiosity of the nonjurors.[1]

Jonathan Swift once remarked that every Englishman above the age of forty believed in the sacredness of Queen Anne's person and in her divine right to rule. But in what sort of divinity was it that the post-Revolution Anglican believed? If he read any of the numerous volumes on the subject of divine right or if he, like the pious John Evelyn, attended the parish church at least three times weekly during William and Mary's reign, attended to the sermon or read the sermons in print, he probably believed in some version of what I choose to call the divine right of providence. It is this divine right of providence that replaced the Stuart concept of divine hereditary right and characterized the political theory of the post-Revolution Anglican and his church.

From the summer of 1688 and through the winter of early 1689, the church found itself less and less able to cope with a revolution that it had to a large degree started. Sancroft, the archbishop, had presented a number of "matters . . . judged necessary for his Majesty's Knowledge and Consideration" to James in October, and because it smacked of an ultimatum, James had rejected it. If he had accepted the church's terms, William might have been spared the cost of his expedition, for they were not unlike a first draft of the Bill of Rights, asking among other things for a "fair and free Parliament . . . to sit to redress all Grievances, to settle matters in Church and State upon just and solid Foundations, and to establish

[1] The nonjurors were those who refused to take the new oath of allegiance to William and Mary. Most of them were in the Anglican Church. They maintained that James II was still king and refused to admit that Parliament had a right to change the hereditary succession. Some nonjurors became Jacobites when they actively sought James's restoration.—Ed.

a due liberty of Conscience." But James fled to France in the face of William's army, and Sancroft, to the consternation of future historians, refused to have the same terms put in force by the new government. Sancroft had played much the same part with James as Langton had played with John, but unlike his thirteenth-century counterpart Sancroft had the divine-right homilies of the Jacobean church on his conscience and these clearly forbade rebellion against the Lord's anointed. What Sancroft would not carry through, men like Tillotson, Tenison, Burnet, Lloyd of St. Asaph—all episcopal creations of the revolution—accomplished, and while Sancroft became the leader of the quixotic nonjuring church, the main body of Anglicanism maintained a church, alike in all respects to what Sancroft deeply desired except in its political theory.

Were Anglican leaders under William therefore a pack of trimmers? Did they in fact repudiate divine right in order to save their livings in the national church? Macaulay said they did and Trevelyan hinted as much. So did the nonjurors. Was it so? Let us look at the situation through the eyes of the Revolution Anglican: a national church threatened with disestablishment for want of its leaders' ability to take the oath to the new sovereign, a body of dissenters waiting to fill the offices of all those deprived of their livings because of the oath, the very foundation of the principles of Cranmer, Hooker, and Andrews—good and true principles about the nature of primitive Christianity and the unity under obedience that it enjoyed with the Roman state as the national religion—all in jeopardy. And above all there was the fear that the new church, if disestablished, would abandon the belief of the prophets of old that God was concerned directly for the political management of His earthly vassals. Divine right was far more than a dogma: it was the inarticulate conviction of the peasant and yeoman, the Squire Westerns and Mr. Allworthys who had been raised in Elizabethan piety to believe in the partnership of God, King, and Country.

The new appeals to laws of nature found among the contractarians, associated as they were either with Hobbism or the writings of the regicides of 1649, were anathema to the average Anglican. The church of the Restoration, believing the king was God's viceregent on earth, preached with unlimited vigor that it was mortal sin to rebel against him. It thus became the job of the Revolution church to show how none of these beliefs had been violated by William's accession, that all Anglicans could assent to the new government without losing their souls, and that it was indeed imperative for them to follow divine right, passive obedience, and nonresistance to the throne of William and Mary. James II was to be recognized for what he was, while on the throne, a divine right king of England. But inasmuch as he had misused his holy trust by personally accepting the headship of the antichrist of Rome, by politically accepting the leadership of the tyrant Louis XIV of France, and by subverting the religion and liberties of England, God had judged him unfit, had raised up a new David as a providential deliverer, William of Orange, to avenge Him and save His church. So William, the church declared, held his crown *de facto* after the manner of Henry VII, enjoying his title as conqueror in the trial by battle and as God's chosen instrument of punishment and salvation.

The theme of providential delivery, full of biblical and historical precedent and imagery, became the favorite theme of Revolution church oratory, casuistry, and biblical exegesis, and during William's reign assumed as much importance in church writings as the subject of nonresistance enjoyed after the overthrow of Cromwell's commonwealth in 1660. . . .

. . . National observances in the church calendar perpetuated the habit of thinking in terms of historical providences:

> *Witness an Invincible Armado* [sic], *threatening our Kingdom with perpetual Slavery of Soul and Body, dispers'd and ruin'd by the irresistible Power of God. . . . Witness the dark designs of Hell* [the Gunpowder Plot of 1605], *to destroy our Laws and Law-makers, our Church and State at one blow, betrayed and confounded by a kind of supernatural, and prophetical impression. . . . [These proved] there is not any Church on Earth, that has had more Signal Providences, to approve it the immediate Care and Concern of Heaven, than that we are Members of.*

Gunpowder Day and 29 May, the restoration of Charles II, especially were annual repetitions of the old providential theme. It was even demonstrated how Henry VIII fitted into the grand scheme, for this "high-spirited Prince, a zealous Assertor of the Popish cause, and a Writer against Luther," laid the foundation for a rapid reformation since his personal quarrel with the pope was used by providence to establish the Reformed Church of England.

As the Anglican observed providence at work in history and the perfect balance it seemed to maintain between evil and good, a doctrine emerged that providential miracles always reflected the essential goodness and perfection of God. The consequences of any historical act were the measures of providence's intention, for providence was not mere fortune or caprice. Good would be rewarded and evil punished by some agent—natural, human, or divine. The divine justice was most commonly expressed by the word "judgment," a singular act of punishment by God for a sin that might or might not be known by the sinner. Wars, famines, plagues, any of these could be judgments. Robert Fleming's *A Discourse on Earthquakes, as Supernatural and Premonitory Signs to a Nation* (1693), was a curious mixture of fact and religious interpretation rendered as judgments. The year 1692 had seen an earthquake in London, frightening some into thinking that there would shortly be "heavy judgments from Heaven." Through pulpit oratory people had become familiar with the judgment that was Cromwell's reign, the plague, the great fire, the Dutch war, and the more recent judgment, the reign of James II. Yet however severe the judgment, decisions "were always designed for wholesome and excellent Ends," for providence did not mean the mere permission of God. Even in the grossest evil could be found the "most glorious designs of God's Grace and Providence . . . even the Crucifixion of our Savior himself" or the bloodless victory of William over James.

The churchmen of the revolution, then, considered providence as a hierarchy of divine causes: on the lowest plane it ruled nature and the universe; it considered man and his general history; finally Christianity, Protestantism, and the Church of England. Since the church was under the temporal guidance of the state, then providence's ultimate concern was believed to be tied to affairs of government: "If God demonstrate his Providence in anything here in this World, . . . he exercises it in the Governing, Defending, and Protecting of public Persons and Societies." Atterbury echoed such thoughts when he said, "since the Age of Miracles ceas'd, as it did, when the Testimony of the Gospel was fully Seal'd, the chief way, in which God hath been pleas'd to give Extraordinary Indications of his Power and Providence, hath been by such Signs of the times, such Wonders of Government" as the age's great political upheavals. Such great changes were God's way of achieving "Political Justice." Of course, there was ample biblical justification for these views since Jehovah's direct intervention in the governments of Saul, David, and Solomon provided the church with its fundamental justification for providential political theory. Biblical history, combined with a scholarly knowledge of the providential history of European courts, led churchmen to the conclusion that since the actions of governments affected the well-being of all souls, God's primary point of concentration was on politics, where the battle of good and evil assumed epic proportions. In great public transactions "God has reserved to himself a transcendant Right (as it were a Court of Equity) . . . to mitigate that rigorous procedure, and redress those unequal Judgments [of human politics], which might otherwise reflect upon his Wisdom or his Justice." God's governance of the world was thus taken in its most literal sense, and the theoretical foundation was laid for the assumption that William III had as much divinity in his kingship as the man whom he had dethroned.

The translation of providence from the theological to the political scene was undertaken by every Anglican cleric from Canterbury's Tillotson to St. Paul's new Dean, William Sherlock, who, after a year of soul-searching, took the oath to William and Mary and robbed the nonjurors of one of their ablest theoreticians. Sherlock's *The Case of the Allegiance Due to Soveraign Powers* (1691), now generally forgotten, was the first major work in the new field of providential divine right and was its most controversial exposition. Sherlock was not completely original in his formulation, for the providential conquest and deliverance was a theme that had been in the air throughout the autumn and winter of 1688–1689. He had been hard at work on the idea, however, during the summer of 1690, and by August the major lines of its development were clear to him. He based his entire argument on biblical writ and on the great Jacobean compilation, Bishop Overall's *Convocation Book* of 1606. In brief, his argument ran:

> *God governs the . . . world, removeth Kings, and setteth up Kings, only by his Providence; that is, then God sets up a King, when by his Providence he advances him to the Throne, and puts the Sovereign Authority into his hands; then he removeth a King, when by his Providence he thrusts him from his Throne, and takes the Government out of his hands: for Providence is God's Government of the world by an invisible influence and power, whereby he directs, determines, over-rules all Events to the accomplishment of his own Will and Counsels. . . .*

There were many ways by which a dynasty could be established: by hereditary claim, by election of a people, and by conquest, which Sherlock thought was the most common form of establishment. In matters of succession there were two main categories: "Divine Entail" as in the biblical sense of a direct grant from God, and "Human Entail" made under constitutional procedure; ". . . but all these ways, or any other, that can be thought of, are governed and determined by the Divine Providence, and the Prince thus advanced is . . . truly placed in the Throne. . . ." Thus Sherlock added a new dimension to divine right by maintaining that there was no theological conflict between a legal entail derived by hereditary right and possession derived by conquest:

> It is all but Providence still, and I desire to know why the Providence of an Entail is more Sacred and Obligatory than any other Act of Providence, which gives a Setled [sic] possession of the Throne?

The central idea that Sherlock kept in mind was that all power is from God (Romans 13), and if this divine pronouncement which had been the basis of Stuart divine right were true in the case of one sovereign, it was true in others. Babylon and Egypt had ruled over the chosen people by God's judgment just as Saul, David, and Solomon had ruled over them by His mercy. The distinction between kings *de jure* and *de facto* related only to the laws of the land, but in the light of providence all kings had God's authority if their reigns were sanctioned by God. Regardless of the human legal right of one king over another, the great court of heaven had overruling jurisdiction in its providential acts against which man was powerless. God's primal concern with government for the sake of human society meant that His judgment could not err, neither could it be resisted.

A companion work to *The Case of the Allegiance* was Bishop William Lloyd's *God's Ways of Disposing of Kingdoms* (1691). Not only was this work more consistent with the traditional view of divine right, but it exhibited an erudition beyond anything Sherlock could muster. Lloyd took for his text the verses from Psalm 75, "For Promotion cometh neither from the East, nor from the West, nor from the South. But God is the Judge; He putteth down one, and setteth up another." What gave his book thorough respectability was that the glosses were complete with elaborations from no less an authority than James I, remarkably suited to the English Revolution:

> *"Though no Christian ought to allow any Rebellion of People against their Prince, yet doth God never leave Kings unpunisht when they transgress these Limits."*

Lloyd also linked providence more closely with the responsibility of kings to God:

> *As a Judge, [God] administreth Judgment and Justice both which are said to be the habitation of his Throne. Particularly when he decrees a Conquest of any King or Kingdom; it is either as a Judgment on them for Offenses against himself, or it is by way of Justice to others whom they have injured.*

Just as the temporal power of the sword to enforce justice cannot be denied, "so of God, that when he puts down one, and sets up another, he doth it as a Judge, even [as a] judge among Gods."

The providential theory of the geographer and government licenser, Edmund Bohun, less sophisticated than that of his preceptors of the cloth, was yet the most common Anglican approach to providential theory. Bohun believed quite simply that the providence of God watched over pious princes to preserve them from violence, while those who degraded their office by becoming tyrants were not allowed to end their days in peace. "We are safe," he affirmed, "if we do our Duty, and submit to and pray for those Powers that we find set over us, by Men as the Instruments, by God as the great Disposer of Crowns. . . ." And this was by far the most popular expression of the divine right of providence, appealing to the people's desire to lead quiet, safe lives in timeless resignation to the ways of kings and courts. The right and wrong of an issue mattered little compared to its reality; "sometimes [God] builds us up, and sometimes he pulls us down; but whatever is the success, God is the Author, and Kings are but the Instruments of the Revolution: Which as it is too mysterious for us to understand, so 'tis too sacred for us to oppose."

This application of divine right of providence theory had obviously arisen from the necessities imposed upon the church by the Revolution. When Lloyd or Burnet talked about the irresistibility of providence's disposal of kingdoms, they obviously meant that a providentially ordered revolution must not be opposed. Although their ideas did much to pacify a potentially hostile Anglican element, shrewd critics were not wanting. The nonjurors tended to reject providential divine right; the dissenting contractarians tended to ignore it. It may have been perfectly true that the Old Testament proved regal authority to be founded by divine providence, but some said this method of sacred investiture had such a peculiar relation to the biblical government of Israel that it could not be applied to any modern constitution unless it could be proved beyond doubt that a divine designation had been made. It was vital, then, to prove providential right in the Revolution. Theory and fact had to be linked. The first step taken in completing the linkage was in the definition of what constituted a providential cause:

> First, When it is so surprizing a work, that we can assign no other Cause, from which it does, or can proceed, but God only. Secondly, When, beside the unaccountableness of the Cause, we see the effect is such as we may reasonably believe that God is concern'd for. Thirdly, When we see there was a great and near danger of losing that which God was concern'd for, if this had not happened for its preservation. I think these three that I have named are sure tokens by which we may Judge, without danger of mistake, that any thing that happens in this manner is of God's doing. [From a sermon by Bishop William Lloyd.]

That there had been danger to the Church of England during James's reign, none could dispute. Everyone knew what had been feared—that the destruction of the church and the subversion of English liberties would bring ruin to Protestantism and liberty all over Europe. The popish plan seemed so clever, carried forward with such subtlety, that when the church finally became aware of the danger, it seemed that Catholicism must surely triumph. Then suddenly the plotters broke through the bonds of secrecy and propriety, attempting to carry off liberty and religion at one stroke. "We may remember we were given up for lost by all our Friends in Europe, and did think so to ourselves it being then impossible for us to imagine from whence our Relief should come." And yet, Burnet asked, "Why went [the Jesuits] so fast and so barefac'd? Why grasp'd they so much all at once? Why was the Hook so ill covered when the Bait was thrown out? . . . In a word, all this blasting of Counsels, and defeating of their designs by their own means, was of God, and must be owned to be his doing." This was the first proof of God's ordering of the Revolution: the exposure of the Jesuit plot by its own impatient zeal.

The events of the Revolution supplied the real arguments for a providential right. On 23 December, scarcely a week after the Prince of Orange had entered London, Burnet set the tone of future providential sermons by preaching before William on the text, "It is the Lord's doing, and it is marvellous in our eyes." Flushed with victory, Burnet told his auditors, "We have before us a Work, that seems to ourselves a Dream, and that will appear to Posterity a Fiction: a Work about which Providence has watched in so peculiar a manner, that a Mind must be far gone into Atheism, that can resist so full a Conviction as this offers us in favor of that Truth." He declared that God had deliberately prospered the Catholic powers in order to unite Protestant Europe against them; God had united the usually divided Dutch to a complete support of William's undertaking. Then he asked the worshippers to "consider the steps of Providence . . . the Prodigies and Miracles of Providence, that have attended our Deliverance. . . ." Burnet was not speaking to an unsympathetic audience, for the providential theme had been common from the time when William's plan of invasion was first rumored; even in the autumn of '88 some men regarded it as a deliverance sent from heaven. In the week William entered London many of the clergy offered prayers of thanksgiving that "God in his wonderful mercy has freed us from Slavery both in body and soule by this great and noble Instrument." Many people marveled at the "protestant wind" that not only blew William's sails westward but kept the English fleet in port. Burnet and many others took the wind as a certified sign of divine intervention. Tillotson studied the case of Job, who had submitted to the divine providence, and the question God had posed to him, " 'Hath thou entered into the treasures of the Snow? hath thou seen the treasures of the Haile which I have reserv'd against the time of trouble, against the Day of Battel and War?' " Thus the archbishop was led to the conclusion that one way in which providence worked was through control of the weather, as in the case of William's kindly wind. Bishop Patrick of Ely, struck by the same phenomenon, felt that God "turned the Winds . . . to be so favorable; that if they had been absolutely at [William's] own Disposal, he could not have commanded them to be more obsequious to him, than he found them. For when he was brought to our Coast by a strong Gale, in a very speedy Course; and had over-shot his Port; the Wind changed immediately, and brought him back to his desired Haven." Lloyd, however, made the most of providence by stating that no matter what William's personal motives in seeking the English crown, God had singled him out to be the instrument of James's judgment; though William might not have intended it, Lloyd was sure that God had chosen William to be England's savior. The bishop gave even greater credit to the winds, saying, "They directed him which way to sail. They chose him a landing place, the best perhaps that could have been found in this Kingdom." As if to bear out these assertions, from the little town of Ruan-Minor in Cornwall, came the story of how, on William's coronation day, although the town's church was locked up, the bells rang "for severall hours in great harmony," and when it was observed that no one pulled the bell cords, it was felt that "the noise was rather in the aire than in the Steeple." Another sign of heaven's favor? The month, day, and year of William's landing at Torbay were also auspicious. The day before had been their majesties' wedding anniversary, as well as William's birthday: "Shall I call this our Birth-day? or rather the day of our Resurrection?" Tillotson's impression was

> that God seems in this last deliverance, in some sort to have united and brought together all the great deliverances which he hath been pleased to work for this nation against all the remarkable attempts of popery, from the beginning of the Reformation. Our wonderful deliverance from the Spanish invasion designed against us, happened in the year 1588. And now, just a hundred years after, God was pleased to bring about this last great and most happy deliverance. That horrid gun-power conspiracy, without precedent, and without parallel, was designed to have been executed upon the Fifth day of November; the same day upon which his Highness the Prince of Orange landed the forces here in England, which he brought hither for our rescue. . . .

Finally, the swiftness of William's success seemed so sudden and surprising, that nothing but an almighty hand could have performed it, "none but [God] who fram'd the Machine, and understood the several Movements of it, could so unexpectedly, and with so little noise, have shifted so important a Scene in the World's great Theater; . . . [it] is a thing that cannot be parallel'd in History, and which can only be resolv'd into the over-ruling Providence of God."

With the exception of the few days in London when the usual business of the city was disturbed by popular demonstration against the Catholics after James's flight, there was no period of lawless anarchy or even of sporadic fighting against William's advance guard. So peaceable was his succession, so universal was the acceptance of his actions, that churchmen looked upon the nation's sudden convergence on the issue of the Revolution as a miraculous union of minds. Some obstructions there were, but the wonder was there were not more. Had this comparative unity been providentially achieved? It was known that providence frequently worked through the hearts of men, redirecting human purposes to a concurrence with the divine will. The insufficiency of human planning was an ancient theme, especially in political affairs, "because it depends upon so many contingent causes, any one of which failing the best laid design breaks and falls in pieces. . . . Besides an unaccountable mixture of that which the Heathen call'd Fortune, but we Christians [call] by its true name, the Providence of God . . . does frequently . . . confound the wisdom of the wise, and . . . turn their counsels into foolishness." More than this, God frequently controlled men's thoughts to achieve His purposes. He was commonly supposed to have done so at the restoration, and what God could achieve once, He could do again, for

> *it is Opinion that governs the unthinking sort of Men, which are far the greatest part of the Body of a Nation. And when all these go together, they are like the Atoms of Air, which though taken apart they are too light to be felt, yet being gather'd into a Wind, they are too strong to be withstood. But he that brings the Winds out of his Treasures, he also governs these, and turns them which way he pleases. It is the same great God, that rules the roaring Waves of the Sea, and the Multitude of the People.*

For Burnet, it was "a presage of Moderation in our whole proceedings, that even the less governable Part of the Nation, I mean the unruly Multitude, has been so happily restrained from extravagant acts of fury: for without justifying what they have done, we may well rejoyce for what they have not done, and that Bloody and Outragious Sacrifices have not been made." There was thus good reason to suspect that providence had been at work in bending men's wills to a support of the Revolution.

The lords and commons were not insensible to the value of providential theory, either as divine truth or as propaganda. Upon the framing of the Bill of Rights, a clause was inserted which met with no opposition: "the said lords spiritual and temporal and commons, seriously [consider] how it hath pleased Almighty God, in His marvellous providence and merciful goodness to this nation, to provide and preserve their said majesties' royal persons most happily to reign over us upon the throne of their ancestors. . . ." When the proclamation was read, it was affirmed, "Whereas it has pleas'd Almighty God, in his great mercy to this kingdom, to vouchsafe us a miraculous deliverance from popery and arbitrary power; . . . our preservation is due, next under God, to the resolution and conduct of his highness the prince of Orange, whom God hath chosen to be the glorious instrument of such an inestimable happiness to us and our posterity. . . ."

A revolution that had been providentially directed had to be providentially protected. If there was any danger that the forces of evil would triumph in a counterinvasion, it certainly would be to God's benefit to protect the fruits of His political creation. With William leading the Protestant cause against the French powers of darkness, the war against James II and Louis XIV took on the nature of a crusade. With each success, first in Ireland, then on the continent, the view became general that the crusade was blessed. The victories of the Boyne and at the siege of Limerick first caught the church's attention. William's personal command of the Irish campaign, his many escapes from death, and his victory over the renowned arms of France, indicated to Lloyd that heaven had been with the king. Could anyone imagine how things must have gone had there been no William to assist the salvation of England? At Mary's death, Jurieu, the great French Huguenot leader, published an eloquent *Pastoral Letter* in England in praise of the providential success of the Revolution. When William's life was nearly taken at Turnham Green, the author of *An Impartial History of the Plots and Conspiracies Against the Life of His Sacred Majesty, King William III* showed how "God bared his Arm, [and] shielded his Anointed and our Deliverer" time and again. Bishops Patrick and Moore compared the exposure of the 1696 plot to the providential discovery of the Gunpowder Plot, and other churchmen exhorted the nonjurors to "no longer work to combat the workings of Omnipotence. . . . 'Ye shall not go up to Fight against your Brethren, for this Thing is from [God]. . . .' " The treaty of Ryswick in 1697 gave the final seal of approval to the Revolution, for not only was James II's claim destroyed by Louis XIV's forced recognition of William, but the collapse of mighty France itself was regarded as a providential wonder.

The argument for a providential revolution had its dangers, of course, and Anglicans were warned not to look on the mere seeming favor of providence alone as a sufficient argument of the goodness of any cause. The divine right of providence was a means of continuing in a modified form the more personal divine right of kings, and Robert Jenkin, Master of St. John's College, Cambridge, did a masterful study of Sherlock's providential possession theory with this point in mind. His criticism, although on the whole favorable, was honest enough to admit that the new divine right was actually an able effort to keep a rightful king. James II, from the throne by a subtle modification of the theory that had made him once powerful in his kingship. Divine providence, furthermore, was an argument fit only for revolutions and other extraordinary occurrences. In normal times, Jenkin pointed out, a steady diet of providential theory would be too unsettling for the running of any government which must continue its business under ordinary laws. Yet providence was an attractive argument which even the nonjurors could use when they talked about the fact that Queen Mary had become mortally ill in the very month that "her Father labor'd under an unnatural Rebellion." and that she died in "the Month wherein she was proclaimed." But this was a feeble use of a theological argument that the church employed to better advantage. It must be remembered that providence was not the whole of the Anglican revolution theory, but a necessary supplement to its legal position. The doctrine of right by conquest and the *de facto* monarchy was the legal side of Anglican justification, designed to show William's right under law; the justification by providence was purely a theological position aimed at balancing the legality of William's conquest with a greater moral right. The constitutional precedents established by Henry VII's reign, if used as its sole argument, would have left the church liable to a charge of Machiavellism; but with William's right to the throne granted morally by God's greater designs, no Anglican need have refrained from supporting the new government. This point perhaps explains why the idea of providence enjoyed a brief but intensive period of consideration during the years of William's reign. If a casuist like Burnet admitted "how dangerous and deceitful an Argument this from Providence will ever seem to be," he also would be sure that the groundwork was well laid in theory as well as fact before a providential revolution could be proved. The church was equal to the task, for providence was still the age's leading concept of natural and historical causation into which the Revolution easily fitted:

> . . . there is such a Chain in all things, the most Important matters taking oft their rise of turn from very inconsiderable Circumstances, that it is certain that either there is no Providence at all, or that it has no limits, and takes all things within its care. Yet God having put the whole Frame of Nature under certain Rules and Laws, the greater part of Providence is only the Supporting and Directing of those Beings that do still act according to their own Natures; and in these, tho' Providence is less discernable, yet it is still the Spring of the whole Machine, which, tho' covered and unseen, gives motion to all the parts of it. There are other more solemn Occasions, in which some second causes are raised above their own pitch, and are animated beyond the ordinary rate. . . . This has never appeared with more eminent Characters than in the Revolutions of States and Empires, in which both the course of Natural Agents, the Winds and Seasons, and the tempers of men's minds, seem to have been managed by such a direction, that not only every thing, but every circumstance has cooperated to carry on Great Designs in such a Conjunction, that those who observe them with due attention, are forced on many occasions to cry out 'This is the finger of God! This is the Lord's doing!' And we may the more certainly conclude, that such a Systeme of things is the effect of a special and directing Providence, when the tendency of it is to advance some Design in which the Honor of God is more particularly concerned.

Could any Protestant deny that the Revolution, in destroying papal tyranny and restoring the Reformed Protestant Church of England, had not been to the honor of God?

It is extremely difficult for us to see much merit in what appears to our scientific eyes to be so much theological froth. Nevertheless, the writings of Sherlock, Burnet, Lloyd, and others were responsible, as in the case of the Jacobitical Sir John Bramston, for bringing over large numbers of thoughtful Anglicans to a full support of the Revolution. On the other hand, powerful Jacobite efforts to restore James II were neutralized by the church which continued to remind Anglicans of their duty to maintain the peace, obey the law, and resist the temptation of rebellion against William's government. It was enough, as with John Evelyn, for those who at heart decried the callous disposal by Parliament of their sacred crown, to be obedient Christians if they could not be patriots. The divine right of providence was an Anglican theory aimed primarily at achieving Anglican loyalty for William and Mary by demonstrating that God had given a greater right to rule than the mere hereditary. Thus the Stuart concept of divine right through blood succession was broadened when Sherlock declared that hereditary rights were no holier than providential entails.

The Anglican justification shows that divine right did not cease to be a political force after the Revolution, as so many aver, but marks, if the last, a most vital stage in the history of divine-right thought in England. Divine providential right had its roots deep in medieval and Renaissance political theory and should be interpreted as a justification of the Revolution such as an Elizabethan or Jacobean mentality might formulate. It appealed to an older but still potent piety. Seventeen years after the Revolution providential right appeared in the curious work by Fleming, *The Divine Right of the Revolution*; thirty years after 1688 when the historian Laurence Echard looked back in his *History of the Revolution,* he confessed, "I always thought the Revolution to be a great Deliverance; and I have the more readily asserted it in this History, because it was not only the Opinion and Declaration of the Lords and Commons, Lawyers, and chief Divines of the Nation, but also of several who had the Misfortune not to comply with the Establishment that immediately succeeded it." In the course of the eighteenth century providential right as a justification for the Revolution was to fall before the law of nature in politics as enunciated by Locke. But for this very reason Locke's justification, totally ignored by every Anglican polemicist under William, was to mean far more to the generations of the age of reason than it did to those who had lived through the Great Rebellion and the Glorious Revolution. The generations which had been raised on the Anglican homilies of the Caroline church and works like *The Whole Duty of Man* believed that divine right was part of the rarefied structure of kingship. The question of a king's title to them and to their church was ever above the purview of the subject; the approval of providence working either through normal succession or through conquest was the only means by which a king, be he Henry VII, James I, or William III, could be granted his divine right to an English crown.

Lucile Pinkham
WILLIAM OF ORANGE: CONQUEROR

Lucile Pinkham, born in 1904, received her A.B. from Carleton College, went on to Columbia and Radcliffe for graduate work, and returned to Carleton in 1934 to become the chairman of the history department, which post she occupied until her death in 1960.

William, Prince of Orange, bore a name and a title that were a part of the glorious past of his home, the United Provinces of the Netherlands. By birth and by deeds he could well be identified with that country, where he lived the first thirty-eight years of his life and where, as Stadholder Prince, he achieved a position of note in European politics. Nevertheless, as Stadholder Prince he might have been forgotten or have become, at best, a "minor character" in the *dramatis personae* of the late seventeenth century. It is as William III, King of England, that he is remembered. Names are symbols. Often they tell us not only who individuals are, but also something of what others think of them. The people of that nation where this man once reigned have, throughout the centuries, shown a disinclination to refer to him as William III, a title which would place him firmly in the roster of their accepted monarchs, but have chosen rather to use the patronymic "Orange" or the definitely foreign-sounding designation of "the Dutchman." Why is it that the English have thus refused to take this man to themselves, have considered him an outsider, whose place in their history was almost accidental?

Can it be that he has been rejected because through his mother, Mary, the daughter of Charles I, he was one of the Stuarts, that always-alien family that thought to find in England the goal of their hopes and ambitions but never realized their dreams? Not likely, for the Stuarts were either loved or hated, and to arouse those emotions is in itself a form of acceptance, one that William never achieved. A more plausible answer to our question lies elsewhere. William III came to the throne of England through a revolution that is called "glorious." Cherished in all the nation's annals, from folklore and

ballad to political essay and scholarly monograph, this Revolution
is the proud capstone of a national tradition. Insomuch as William's
contribution is recognized, by just so much must that of the English
themselves be diminished. If the Revolution is to remain "glorious,"
William must remain forever an outsider, an alien prince whose interest in what happened on the island was as incidental to his personal
goals as those goals were to England.

That was not the case. When this man was crowned king he was
realizing an ambition which had influenced him since his boyhood.
No sudden decision nor immediate need had led him across the
North Sea and down the length of the Channel to accept the "invitation" of his English friends to help them submit their troubles to
"a free parliament." On the contrary, his expedition was the result of
plans laid carefully over many years. The setting, both in England
and on the continent, had been judiciously arranged. Public opinion
had been subtly molded in his favor. Even his chosen adherents had
been selected carefully for the weight they would carry for him in
his struggle to win the crown. That hangers-on and potential political
opponents not of his choosing found their way into his camp before
the Revolution was over in no way diminishes the importance of the
above fact.

His significant position in English politics had been recognized
for almost twenty years. The only male heir to the throne who was a
Protestant, in 1677 he had married the one person whose claims
seriously rivaled his own: his cousin Mary, the Protestant daughter
of the Roman Catholic Duke of York. Although he married her, in
part at least, because he did not wish to see her become the wife
of some man who might champion her rights in opposition to his own,
by this deed William accomplished a great deal more than the mere
elimination of possible future disputes. He established himself
throughout Europe as well as in the British Isles as the man who
would one day rule England either in his own right or as consort of
the queen. . . .

. . . Let it be understood here that William wanted the English
crown for its own sake much more than for the advantages it would
give him in diplomatic maneuverings on the continent. These last
play their part, but a close scrutiny of them, especially of the time
element, will reveal, as we shall see later, that they were more a
support for the expedition of 1688 than a cause thereof, and undue

emphasis upon them has obscured the significance of William's personal ambition and its relation to the outcome of the Revolution. We must not lose sight ever of the man with whom we are dealing. We must remember constantly the fact, often overlooked, that William was the grandson of Charles I and that Stuart influence had been stronger in his early life than that of his father's family. Ambitious with the zeal of an able man who *knows* that he can do better than his fellows, he had so far been given free reign in his native country only during a few terrible months in 1672. A youth of twenty-one, untrained and inexperienced alike in warfare, statecraft, and diplomacy, he had taken charge at a time when the United Provinces seemed doomed, and, relying only on himself and the magic appeal of his name to the masses of the Dutch people, he had saved the land. For thanks he won the opposition of the States General. Yet on the three occasions when he visited England he had been cheered. There he had been the darling of the court, the sought-after companion of great politicians. England had no States General made up of proud merchants who felt themselves superior to kings and princes. In England, William could be the king he wanted to be— or so he thought in those days of the reign of James II when so many Englishmen hastened to tell him how thoroughly they were committed to his service.

Two possible courses were open to him. He could maintain the policy he had adopted in the closing years of Charles II: to wait for the natural run of events to bring him his—and his wife's—inheritance. Like almost everyone else he did not expect the interval to be long. As James was not particularly robust there was reason for thinking he would not long survive his brother. The possibility that a rival heir might be born was slight. Even more unlikely was it that James might try to divert the succession either to Anne, if she could be persuaded to apostatize, or to one of his bastard sons. Frequent warnings that this might happen were sent to William, but he was too well aware of his father-in-law's views on indefeasible hereditary right to be particularly disturbed by them. Against this policy of passivity stood William's own impatience and the imperative necessity of taking a stand. James's life expectancy might not be good, but neither was his own, for he was already in his middle thirties and his always-frail constitution did not hold out promise for too long a future. Moreover, he was beginning to receive indications from England that people there, confident that he would oppose James's policies, were expecting him to do so immediately and openly. . . .

If a passive policy was neither tenable nor desirable, the alternative was, of course, direct action. Yet should William choose this course he had to be sure he would win, for the dangers inherent in the failure of an outright assault upon the English throne were too grave to warrant the contemplation of anything but success. In addition to making as sure of victory as was humanly possible, William had to plan a campaign, in both the military and political senses of the term, which would bring him the crown without damaging too severely those very attributes which made it so attractive to him. That is, he did not want a struggle based on purely constitutional issues. Therefore his best means of accomplishing his end in this respect lay in joining forces with the discontented Tories. But like them he would have to compromise with the Whigs, with the Dissenters, and with the malcontents. He must scheme to uphold the Church of England without antagonizing the Dissenters and to protect the prerogative without losing the support of the Whigs. He must pose as the savior of the Protestant religion while he maintained his friendly associations with Catholic Europe: Spain, the Empire, and the papacy itself. . . .

Among most of those in the immediate circle of the prince it was certainly assumed that the crown was the ultimate objective. As early as September 1688, Simon Pettecum, who was one of those most thoroughly acquainted with William's plans, burst out impatiently to the imperial ambassador, "Of what importance is it to the Emperor whether the King of England is named James or William?" Shortly before the expedition sailed, Huygens, William's personal secretary, and brother to the famous scientist, wrote in his diary "Rooseboom discussed what would happen in England *when his Highness should be master there.*" (Italics mine.) The very casual way in which this man, certainly in a position to know, alluded to the future, is highly suggestive. There is nothing surprising to him in the possibility that William might be master of England. The assumption is to be found even beyond the immediate circle. D'Albeville wrote from the Hague on November 23, 1688, that the English in the prince's army "took an oath amongst themselves before their departure that they would never lay down arms till they made the Prince of Orange king, and laughed at a free parliament." If he was not stating proven fact he was at least repeating current gossip. That the idea was not entirely absent even from the minds of those who remained in England is indicated by a letter dated December 2 from Sir Robert Howard to William stating that "they only fix upon hopes of remedy by a total change of persons." . . .

But it is William's own acts which are of greatest interest. In those tense days that followed the flight of James and preceded the meeting of the Convention, he expressed himself to Halifax:

> *Said, hee did not come over to establish a Commonwealth.*
> *Said hee was sure of one thing; hee would not stay in England if King James came again.*
> *Hee said, with the strongest asseverations, that hee would go if they went about to make him regent.*

The implication is clear. William would have the crown or nothing. . . .

After midsummer of 1688 William's relations with England ceased to be those of an outsider. He was now a potential usurper who stood an excellent chance of becoming a *de jure* king. The significance of his position derived from the strength of his military preparations and from his refusal to make any appreciable compromise with his own followers or any compromise whatsoever with James. He was going to invade England and not once did he offer to call off or even delay the invasion in order to give the English people and their king an opportunity to settle their dispute by themselves. Any indication that a solution might be reached without his intervention simply stiffened his determination and gave new speed to his preparations. The impending invasion, therefore, was of paramount importance. Its objective was debatable; its imminence was not. No settlement could be made until it was over. Because of that the England of this autumn became a strange dreamland in which king and people acted with the futility that comes from knowing that the most vigorous activity can be rendered nugatory by decisions as yet unmade. In this interlude, more than at any time after his coronation, William determined what was going to happen in England. The English people were not free agents. They paid the piper, but William called the tune. . . .

. . . The principal line of propaganda in England . . . became that of stress upon maintaining the true laws, liberties, and religion of the country. This would appeal to everyone but the most Jacobite

Catholics and most dyed-in-the-wool Tories and many of the latter were won over by the claim that James was subverting indefeasible hereditary right by a supposititious Prince of Wales. It could also smooth over factional strife, at least for the time being, as both Whigs and Tories could place their own interpretation on "true laws and liberties and religion."

Perhaps the biggest advantage, however, in insisting that his objective was to maintain the established laws was that it enabled William to claim that resistance to him was resistance to legally constituted authority. This was done by casuistry, it is true, but it worked. It formed the basis for that part of his Declaration wherein he called upon the people of England for their support. It appeared in his directions to his fleet when he ordered his admirals to inform any members of the English navy who offered resistance that they would be treated as enemies of the *kingdom* of Great Britain, thus drawing a distinction between loyalty to the king and loyalty to the nation. He used it to form the concluding and the clinching point of his appeal to the soldiers and sailors to desert the ranks of James's army and navy and join his own:

> . . . *I hope God will put it into your hearts at this time to redeem your-selves, your religion, and your country from those miseries which in all human appearance can be done only by giving mee your present assistance who am laboring for your deliverance.*

In addition to appealing to the sentiments as well as to the convictions of the English it constituted a measure of safety against the danger of a charge of treason to those who were engaged with William, a protection, it is true, that was more illusory than real, for the widest interpretation of the statute of treason could scarcely provide foundation for it.

William left little to chance. Weeks before the invasion could be commenced he drew up not only the Declaration but also the appeals to the soldiers and sailors to which reference has just been made. When word from England indicated that the king might succeed in coming to a peaceful settlement with his people a second declaration was prepared, urging that no one be fooled by engagements that could be broken, by promises that could be retracted, and by concessions that could be withdrawn once the danger was over. Thousands of copies of all these proclamations were printed and sent over to various parts of England where they were placed in the hands of secret agents who were ordered to distribute them as soon as they received word of the prince's landing. The equipment of the army included a printing press which was to be used for new broadsheets if the need arose. . . .

The fact that William risked his expedition on such a slender margin is indicative not only of the extent to which he was gambling his whole life on success, but also of his calm confidence of obtaining it. The way he met the problem illustrates the manner in which he arrogated to himself the rights of the head of the government and involved in his cause people who had no idea of making him king. Supplies for his fleet were obtained by the seizure of large stocks of goods kept at Plymouth to provision the English navy. Such a step was not incompatible with the right of conquest, but William did not assert that right. He claimed to represent the true authority of the country. Bolder still was his taking over the tax machinery of Exeter and the surrounding territory whereby he turned that source of James's revenue to his own use. All money in the possession of the receiver of customs was seized and officials who protested were dismissed. William Harbord, a former Exclusionist and perennial malcontent who had joined the expedition shortly before it left the Netherlands, was made paymaster of the forces, and an order was given that all revenues were to be paid to him. Three other Englishmen were set to supervise the collection of the excise. Should William be defeated, these men, together with Harbord, would be hard put to it to explain their actions to their lawful sovereign. It became their interest, therefore, to see to it that William did not lose. Even before the army set out on its march toward London, Bentinck was discussing the possibility of another source of money: that all those who signed the Exeter Association should make contributions in proportion to their wealth. Such a device, if it was proposed, must have met with some opposition or objection, for it was never put into practice. Not until two weeks later was an alternative adopted. This was a voluntary loan, backed by some of the men who had by that time come to join William, notably Sir William Portman, one of the most influential leaders in the Southwest. The sums thus gathered served the double purpose of filling the treasury and of giving their donors additional motive for desiring that the venture they were financing should be successful. With these resources William made his way toward London. . . .

. . . Anyone studying the Revolution of 1688 cannot but be impressed with the way in which previously made plans for insurrection and desertion went into operation throughout the country, but he must reserve his true amazement for the way in which everything that happened, whether in his own immediate vicinity or in distant Yorkshire or Derbyshire was, ultimately, in the control of the Prince of Orange, who used what he wanted to use, discarded what he wanted to discard, and ignored, when it suited his purpose, even such old friends as the Earl of Danby himself. . . .

The insistence of the prince on a minimum of well-defined points, first: no repeal of the Tests, and second: the decision of a free parliament, had a tremendous value, for it concentrated attention on immediate problems and left the nature of their ultimate solution in abeyance. The Whig, the Tory, and the man with no party affiliation could all join a leader with those objectives. At some point, however, there had to be a transfer of authority from the king to his opponent. This had to be done whether or not the intention was to dethrone James. It had been evident since the middle of October that no reforms or promises of reforms were going to satisfy William. He was determined that everything that was done should come as the direct result of his actions, in his presence, and as far as possible, under his direction. He claimed to represent the legally established sovereign power of England which in theory could be interpreted as capable of demanding the obedience not only of the people of the country but even of its king. Whatever James II did, therefore, could be treated with contempt unless it was done under the aegis of the prince. Yet it was hard for most men to separate king and nation in their minds, in spite of, or perhaps because of, the Civil Wars and the Interregnum. King and people must act together. Neither was complete without the other. Only the most fanatic Whigs and those who were touched by the lingering ideas of republicanism felt otherwise. When William claimed to represent the country he was also claiming that the king must act with him. He was not deposing the king unless or until the latter refused to recognize the intangible fusion. He was merely refusing to admit that James had any authority, and opening a way whereby men, even those of rather strong Tory principles, could render obedience to himself without violating their consciences.

William had begun to take steps toward the assumption of authority before he left the United Provinces, although he did not put any of his plans into active operation before the expedition set out. First of all, there was the Declaration with its demand for a "free parliament" elected on his terms. Added to this was the postscript or "additional declaration" with its reiteration of references to a free parliament and admonition to the people of England to place no faith in the reforms that James had granted. William's order to Herbert to treat any English seamen who tried to stop the Dutch fleet as enemies of Great Britain should also be placed in this category, although it was never necessary to put them into effect. Another action of major importance was the making of a great and a small seal bearing the English arms which were given to William's secretary, Constantijn Huygens, to use for the validation of all documents concerning English affairs. Huygens received these seals a few days before the first, unsuccessful, departure of the fleet, and retained custody of them until after the new year when he was forced to yield them to the English William Jephson.

Immediately upon his landing William began to use the authority he was claiming to possess. Although his actions could be construed as those of a successful leader either of a belligerent foreign power or of a group in rebellion against legitimate government, it should be noted that he never for one moment referred to them as such, but persisted throughout in his assertion that he represented the lawful sovereign power in the nation. Upon that assumption he took actions that were normally reserved to the king. One of these was his order, conveyed through Burnet, to the clergy of the Cathedral of Exeter to omit prayers for the Prince of Wales. This, of course, was tantamount to ordering them to proclaim that they did not recognize the child's rights as heir to the throne. The clergy objected, but were forced to yield. The seizure of the tax machinery followed. One of the king's officers who demurred was placed under arrest. Commissions for new regiments were given out, not for a foreign army or for a rebel force, but as lawful acts validated by Huygens with the English seal. Orders were given that anyone who attempted to stop the raising of regiments by arresting men who were on their way to join the prince should themselves be arrested and brought before

Sir Robert Atkins who was commissioned by William as a justice of the peace. . . .

With . . . much irrefutable evidence that William was fast losing whatever popularity he may have had among the English at the time of his arrival, the question very naturally arises how he could have been made king even as a co-ruler with his wife. A statement attributed to Halifax, who is said to have told William on his arrival in London that "he might be what he pleased himself . . . for as nobody knew what to do with him, so nobody knew what to do without him" sums up the situation about as well as anything. James was gone. William was present. Something had to be done, for the country could not continue in a state of uncertainty. We see here also what can happen when a disorganized majority, united only on the common ground of disapproval of what is taking place, is faced by a well-organized minority which, however much it may be concealing dissension within itself, is united in its determination to reach an immediate objective. This minority had been able to gain control of the mechanism whereby that objective could be gained—the Convention. Observers and members of that Convention might note their uneasiness and apprehensive dislike of decisions being made, pamphleteers might criticize, or clergymen denounce, but none of them was in a position to do anything constructive, or even obstructive. Another factor of importance was the presence in the country of a group which wanted to overthrow the monarchy entirely, the existence of which brought about a somewhat paradoxical situation which eventually worked toward William's benefit. The republicans had assisted in the Revolution hoping that the outcome might be victory for their point of view. Once it was over, so far as the actual fighting was concerned, they very naturally turned against William. Never a serious menace, they were still of enough significance to provide a telling argument for the Orangists to convince their opponents that if William was rejected, or if, angered by continual controversy he carried out his threat to return to the Netherlands, a republic might be created to fill the political vacuum. Finally the importance of the time element cannot be too often repeated and emphasized. Not only was settlement imperative. The opposition, caught unprepared, did not have the time to organize, to sort out its own differences, and to reach an agreement upon any other solution than that which the Orangists offered.

Because the latter group controlled the Commons and were the most powerful single element among the Lords, the real debates in both Houses were upon procedure rather than upon objective, and were based on obscure legal points rather than upon fundamentals. The question of "abdicate" vs. "desert" involved the issue of whether or not James had acted voluntarily, for in principle abdication had to be voluntary. It was the fact that if "deserted this kingdom" were the chosen phrase a temporary aspect was given that finally turned the scale, for if James returned, or even tried to do so, he could no longer be said to have deserted. The word "vacancy" suggested a breach in the succession, a denial of the doctrine of indefeasible hereditary right. The issue involved here was much more serious than the other because it gave rise to the suggestion that the office of king was being made elective. When this point was forcibly advanced by the Lords we find 151 members of the Commons voting to drop the phrase. Most interesting is the fact that the doctrine of indefeasible hereditary right was far from being denied at this Convention in spite of later interpretations put upon its actions. Almost no one would admit even that what they were doing might create a precedent, and those who were willing to do so insisted that anything of an elective nature was for this time only. The contention was made that unless the throne was vacant with respect to James it could not be filled by anyone else; to the argument that it would be filled by his heir the old maxim of English law that a living man had no heir was advanced. The real significance of the question lay in whether Mary alone, or William and Mary, should be raised to the throne. On the principle of immediate succession of the heir Mary would have had to be proclaimed and it was only by going through the fiction of a vacant throne that William could be considered unless the members of the Convention had been willing to pass over both daughters of James to adopt a modified Salic law of inheritance. In making their decision, however, the Convention was acting not so much as an elective or legislative body as in their old historic judicial capacity as a "High Court of Parliament." Their job was not to make an heir, since only God could do that, but to find out who was the heir. . . .

As for William himself, he played a more direct part, once the Convention was assembled, than he had been doing for the past two or three weeks. His aims underwent a certain amount of modifica-

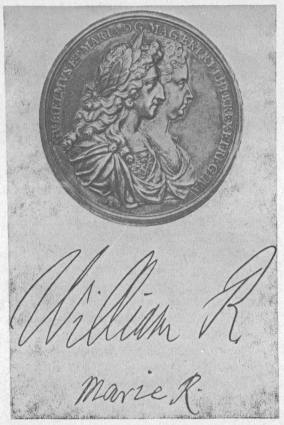

FIGURE 3. Contemporary English medal commemorating the coronation of King William III and Queen Mary II in 1689. (*The Granger Collection*)

tion for it soon became obvious that he could not have his way in his desire to rule alone when even such staunch supporters as Herbert were aghast at the idea. It was probably Dijkveld who influenced him here, by pointing out that insistence on the sole right to the crown would make him unpopular not only in England but also in the United Provinces and with Spain and the Emperor. William, however, was adamant in his refusal to consider Mary as sole ruler or to accept any kind of arrangement whereby his official position was contingent upon hers. That was not selfishness on his part, but merely common sense. No matter how sure he might be that she would survive him, he could not afford to run the risk involved. He knew that as Prince consort he would be expected to undertake and carry out foreign policies and he could not take the chance of being left in mid-air on any of them by his wife's death. His diplomatic position would be intolerable. This, of course, involved coming to some agreement with Anne. The final arrangement—that he should have the crown jointly with Mary during his lifetime, but that any children of his by any other wife than Mary should be superceded by Anne and her heirs, seems to have been worked out in private some days before the public vote in the Convention. . . .

There remains only one further point: the Declaration of Rights, the conditional nature of which has been greatly overstressed. The origin and substance of this document are worthy on their own merits of an intensive study which cannot be accorded to them here. The demand for the declaration reflects the deep need of seventeenth-century England for clarification of many points of its laws. This was the logical time for such a clarification to be made. The Commons' resolution to draw up the declaration came the day after the one on which the resolution declaring the throne vacant was made. A committee appointed to draw up a first draft reported back to the whole House a few days later. During this period, at least up to February 7, the main issue confronting both Houses was the other resolution. Discussion on the two subjects, the declaration and the problem of the succession, went on concurrently in the Lower House, but the discussions were curiously unrelated to each other. Certainly at no time was the offer of the crown made directly or explicitly contingent upon acceptance of the declaration by William and Mary, and it is hard to find much indication of any implicit or indirect condition. In fact, the Declaration of Rights did not receive its final form nor was it adopted by Parliament and given the validity of royal approval until much later in the year, after William and Mary had been safely crowned for some months. A purely accidental circumstance seems to have given rise to the theory of the conditional nature of the declaration. Although the resolution to offer the crown to William and Mary had passed both houses by February 7, not until six days later was the offer formally made to them. In that interval certain differences in the tentative draft of the declaration were ironed out so that, by February 13, the document had been drawn up into what was to be substantially its final form. As far as can be discovered, however, the delay in making the formal offer was caused not by any problems concerned with the Declaration of Rights but simply by Mary's absence. She reached Westminster on Tuesday, February 12. The next day she and her husband accepted the crown.

William was, it is true, somewhat upset at first by the suggestion of a declaration and is reputed to have said that he would not accept a crown with any strings attached to it. Here again Dijkveld is reported to have worked for moderation. Yet a certain amount of moderating was done by the other side as well. All new points were carefully excluded so that the Declaration of Rights which William and Mary ultimately approved contained no limitations not already in existence. Nor was William accepting any theoretical principle that Parliament had an unlimited right of limitation. He agreed to rule according to the laws of England as every king had done who had ever worn the crown.

There remains the task of stating some evaluation of the significance of William's connection with the Revolution. That significance lies in the fact that the original combination of William with the Tories resulted in the end in what was actually nothing more than a palace revolution. William wanted the crown; the Tories the control of the chief offices of the realm. Next to the control of these offices the principal concern of the Tories was the Anglican Church, and the meager concessions of the Toleration Act attest to the hollowness of their glib promises to the Dissenters. To this combination of the Tories with William the Whigs brought some concern for the rights of Parliament, but they too were more interested in the Staff of the Treasury or in the Great Seal than in popular rights. . . .

The only limitations which the Revolution, as embodied in the legislation of the next few years, placed upon the king were to deprive him of the already highly questionable right to suspend the operation of laws, and to make it necessary for him, through financial and other strictures, to call Parliament every year. But, because Parliament must meet and because it could control the purse, what happened was that the royal powers which the king had hitherto been able to use in the interests of whatever group he pleased, sometimes even—God save the mark—the common people, those powers now passed into the control of the landed aristocracy which could control Parliament. In that sense the long struggle that began at Runnymede turned once more in favor of the heirs of the baronial class and for a century and a half the country was more completely in their grip than ever before: the historic counterweight to them, the royal power, was ineffective. The view that the Revolution was essentially aristocratic has been attacked on the ground that the common people supported it. That this assertion cannot be accepted without rather strong qualifications has already been indicated in those parts of this study which deal not only with William's unpopularity but also with devices that were used in such places as York to trick an otherwise loyal populace into taking part in an uprising. Yet even if the assertion could stand unqualified, judgment should be based on results, not immediate participation. Of course many of the "mobile" as they are called in the letters and diaries of the leaders, were enthusiastic. Even if they had not been overmastered by anti-Catholic hysteria they still would have welcomed the prospect of improvement in their daily lives. But the benefits of the Revolution did not go to them. . . .

Stephen B. Baxter
WILLIAM OF ORANGE: PRIME MOVER OF THE REVOLUTION

Stephen B. Baxter, now professor of history at the University of North Carolina, was born in Boston in 1929. Educated at Harvard and Cambridge, he has taught at Dartmouth and the University of Missouri. His wide range of seventeenth-century studies embraces administrative and economic history as well as biography.

It is worth examining the expectations of William III in regard to England in some detail. He expected, as he had since childhood, to inherit the throne. At first he had discounted the rights of the Princesses of York, on the ground that their mother's base origins disqualified them. Later he had been forced to realize that their claims were stronger, in English if not in continental eyes, than his own. What would have been considered a morganatic marriage at a

From Stephen B. Baxter, *William III* (London, 1966). Reprinted by permission of Longman Group Ltd.

German court was sufficient in English law for the transmission of any kind of property right, including a right to the crown. Therefore, to consolidate his claim, William had been forced to marry Princess Mary. He had also had a second motive for the marriage. It would, he hoped, give him control over English foreign policy. In this the prince had been bitterly disappointed. Mary had brought with her a contemptible portion, in influence as well as in cash. Nct until 1685 did her husband receive any tangible political benefits from his marriage. Then and only then did the beam of King James's favor, weak as a February sun though it might be, come to William's aid. The feeble signs that James might follow a Williamite policy were enough to bring Brandenburg and later Sweden to his side, and to reduce if not to eliminate domestic opposition inside the Republic. Then towards the end of 1685 it became clear that James II had changed his mind. The victory of Sunderland over Rochester, the dismissal of Halifax, and finally the dismissal of the Bishop of London from the Council early in 1686 were all indications that the king would not carry out an active Williamite policy. He might well remain neutral, favoring neither Holland nor France; but this was not enough. To redress the balance of power England must do more than remain neutral. She must become active on the side of the allies.

Ever since James's change of policy there have been attempts on the part of French propagandists and of historians of every political hue to demonstrate the existence of a conspiracy headed by William III for the dethronement of his father-in-law, dating from—when? D'Avaux, the most malicious of all, puts the date at 1679. He claims that William was a participant in the movement for the exclusion of the Duke of York. James himself sometimes thought of 1679, at others of the early months of 1685. No serious student agrees with them. A recent American professor [Lucile Pinkham] preferred to date the conspiracy from the famous conversation between the prince and Gilbert Burnet in the summer of 1686. Other scholars, such as Ranke and Klopp, have often considered William's meeting with the Great Elector at Minden later in 1686 as the decisive moment. There are a number of arguments to be made against each of these views, although it is important to point out that not enough evidence survives for certainty. We know that a great many papers of these years were destroyed at the time; we cannot know what they contained. All that can be said with confidence is that every shred of surviving evidence corroborates the latest of all possible dates, which is that given by Gilbert Burnet: the spring of 1688. It is true that the good bishop got the story a little wrong, as he did most stories: he wrote that "Russel coming over in May, brought the matter nearer a point. . . ." Both Russells came in April, with Arthur Herbert, and waited upon the prince at het Loo where he was about to entertain the Elector of Saxony. William refers to the departure of the Englishmen in a letter of 29 April. Obviously they had brought letters, among them two from Danby to which the prince replied on the 30th. Thus we must apparently ascribe to the last days of April the conversation described by Burnet:

> So Russel put the Prince to explain himself what he intended to do. The Prince answered, that, if he was invited by some men of the best interest, and the most valued in the nation, who should both in their own name, and in the name of others who trusted them, invite him to come and rescue the nation and the religion, he believed he could be ready by the end of September to come over. . . .

No sane man prefers a risk to a certainty. In human terms, William III was certain to inherit the throne of England if only he lived long enough. James II was generally known to be diseased and therefore incapable of having any further healthy children. Another child might be born, perhaps even another boy; but not one strong enough to grow up. No sane man would have taken seriously, until well into the spring of 1688, the possibility of the birth of a healthy Prince of Wales. If, on the other hand, William decided to play the role of a Monmouth, he might well share Monmouth's fate. The risk simply was not worth taking, except under one of two conditions. The first was that James could go about to defraud William and Mary of their right. He could do so by selecting Anne as his heir. This, as we have seen, had been a possibility ever since 1683. The Prince and Princess of Orange took the matter seriously. They had been encouraged to learn from Dijkvelt that Anne had no intention of becoming an apostate. This merely made the matter a little more complicated. James might not be able to pass over both his daughters and give the succession at once to the Queen of Spain or the Duchess of Savoy, who were next in line after Anne. But he could obtain the same effect a different way by foisting a supposititious child off on his people as a Prince of Wales. The idea, true or false as it may be, that the king was diseased was an article of faith. Therefore he could not have any more children. Therefore any child he did have must be supposititious. Mary at least was firmly and sincerely convinced that the pregnancy of her stepmother was a fake. . . .

The Princess of Orange did not need the warnings of her sister, contained in a letter of 14 March, to become suspicious of the queen's great belly. She had become suspicious of the whole business before the end of 1687. Then while she was at het Loo with the Prince in April her suspicions were confirmed. . . .

It is obvious that Herbert and the two Russells had to persuade the princess as well as the prince. The invasion could not take place without her knowledge and consent. She, not her husband, was the heir to the throne. She, not her husband, would have to authorize the conspiracy. She, not her husband, would depose her father. For it was obvious from the very beginning that this was what was involved. It was a very great responsibility to undertake, and it seems highly unlikely that Mary would have had the strength to act as she did unless she had been sure that her father was trying to rob her and thus to destroy the true Church. Luckily her firm belief never wavered. . . .

The prince had his own deep religious faith; but he was educated, as his wife was not, and he approached the problem from a broader point of view. Mary could appreciate the idea of her inheritance being stolen from her and could respond to the cry of "The Church in Danger!" Her husband could see another reason for intervention. This was that James had already destroyed the English monarchy, and that the only way of saving anything out of the wreckage was to take direct action. For two generations the Stuarts had indulged in the most fatuous misgovernment, and had done so largely at the expense of the House of Orange. Once before, Charles I had dragged the House of Orange down with him into ruin; what might not be the consequences of the fall of James II? William had every reason to intervene for the protection of his own position as prince; and it is clear that he more than half thought of himself as the head of the Stuarts as well. One might argue that James's first marriage had been morganatic. Or one might argue that James, as a Catholic, was disqualified from being king of England. This did not become the law until 1689, but it had been the deep-felt belief of the Whig party for a decade. And whichever theory William used to justify himself, there was always the demonstrable fact that James had misgoverned and that he had destroyed the monarchy. The favorite remark of Charles II had been that his brother would not be able to govern England for four years. He repeated it again and again. Sometimes he gave James four days, sometimes four years: never longer.

In fact, James II had reigned with success for almost exactly eight months before going off the track. Even then his conduct had not become really outrageous until July 1686. The most likely consequence of his actions since that time would. be that the English people would rise not only against their king but against monarchy as such. The resulting republic would in all likelihood have a Great Person at its head. Poland, the United Provinces, Venice, and Genoa, the four chief republics of the day, all had their great persons. England herself had had one in Oliver. But William III could not expect to be chosen to head an English republic unless he could manage to control the revolution that brought it into being. And he did not want to be the great person in an English republic. In William's eyes, such a place would not be worth having. His task, therefore, was and had been for years to keep himself informed. He would have to listen to the opposition so as to know what was going on. He would have to keep friends on all sides so as to prevent the leadership from slipping into other hands. This was why he entertained Monmouth in 1684, this was why (if he did) he went to the theater rather than fasting on the anniversary of his grandfather's murder in 1685. D'Avaux is our only evidence that William and Mary actually did go to a comedy on 30 January of that year. If they did so, it was to preserve their few remaining friends in England. There were not many of them at that time, and it was only after Monmouth's execution that the Whigs were forced, *faute de mieux,* to turn their eyes towards The Hague.

In the November session of the Parliament of 1685, when the king's plans were thwarted, it was pointed out to him that the opposition consisted of partisans of the Prince of Orange. The situation was not as simple as that. There is no evidence, none at all, that William was directing the opposition. Nor could he have bribed the parliamentary leaders, as has been charged, for the simple reason that he did not have the money. What little he had was to be spent in 1686 on the purchase of het Loo and of the Huis ten Bosch. And since his total income was of the order of that of the Princess Anne or of the

Duke of Buckingham, and his expenditure higher than theirs, there was none to spare for English politicians. What William actually did do in 1685 and 1686 was merely to keep in touch with the leaders of all parties in the British Isles. And we have evidence that he actually disapproved of the conduct of the English parliamentary leaders.

The great bulk of it indicates that in his relations with the English parties William III was on the defensive. Support our plans, said the Catholic extremists, or we will divert the succession from you. In 1686 and the early months of 1687 they hoped for the conversion of the Princess Anne, to be followed by her nomination as heiress-pre-sumptive. Later in 1687, when the illness of Prince George with pneumonia took a severe turn, they were for marrying her to a Catholic prince after a very short widowhood. Still later, after George's recovery, they threatened William III with the establishment of a republic. Antiphonally, the chant was taken up on the other side of the choir. Support *our* plans, said the English and Scottish refugees in Holland, or *we* will set up a republic in England. The prince, like Tarbaby in the Uncle Remus stories, lay low and said nothing. Why should he do anything? Again and again for the last fifteen years he had been threatened with disaster by one English politician after another if he did not act as a puppet in that politician's hands. . . . During the Exclusion Crisis one Englishman after another had told him that all was lost if he did not make a visit to England. William had not come until all was over. And nothing had been lost, except Sunderland's office.

But by the end of 1687 the problem was far more serious than it had been in 1672 or in 1680. The English political situation was completely out of hand. In Dublin Tyrconnel was obviously building a Festung Ireland, which would be a Catholic refuge in case of disaster and which might well be turned over to France in case of need. To such an extent James was clearly dismembering the in-heritance to which the prince felt himself entitled. William also felt, and to all appearances he felt sincerely, that James would join with Louis XIV for a war on Holland as soon as he felt strong enough. Undoubtedly, the prince and Fagel were hysterical. Undoubtedly they read more into the situation than was actually there. In such hysteri-cal circumstances, the pregnancy of the queen took on a most sinister aspect. Mary Beatrice's medical history, to say nothing of her husband's diseases, made a pregnancy most unlikely. What, then, was happening? Was it a fraud? Both Mary and Anne convinced themselves that it was, that their father was trying to rob them and that they must intervene for the protection of their property. Whether or not William thought that the pregnancy was fraudulent we do not know. Even if the queen were truly pregnant, however, it seemed clear that the Jesuits would not allow her to have anything other than a healthy son. If a Prince of Wales were not forthcoming it would be necessary to create one; and here was one miracle that the most skeptical Protestant knew that the Catholics could bring to pass.

There has been a rather general reluctance to think of the English expedition of 1688 as a conspiracy with a short life. The prince must, according to some authorities, have been scheming ever since 1679; according to others, ever since 1685. He may well have considered the possibility of an invasion, at any time after 1684, as one among a number of alternative plans. How else could the prince save his inheritance from the stupidity or malice of his uncles? What else could he do if for example James were to die suddenly and the English chose Anne ahead of Mary? In some circumstances William would have to invade England at short notice, and there is no reason to think that he did not include invasion among his list of *possible* courses of action. But invasion for what? Not to usurp the right of another, but to protect his own right from theft. And there is a wide difference between considering a possible course of action, among many other possible courses, and the adoption of a definite plan of campaign. According to every scrap of surviving evidence, Englishmen and Scots of all parties were pressing William to intervene in England in 1686 and 1687. They wished to force his hand. And again, according to all the evidence we have, the prince listened to each group politely enough but refused to take the advice. In December the situation was altered by the official announcement of the queen's condition. Now a revolution became a distinct possibility. The people of England had been remarkably patient, at least in part because their king was in visibly poor health. Once he died Mary would step in and repair any damage which James might have been able to do. Now the very ill health of the king became the strongest threat to his dynasty. Suppose the birth of a Prince of Wales. Could anyone hope that James II would live long enough to see his son come of age? The idea was preposterous. But the alternative, a regency in the hands of Mary Beatrice, was unthinkable. Barillon reported a very curious story at third-hand about a month before the actual birth of the Prince of Wales, of a plan to seize the boy and bring him up forcibly as a Protestant in the event of the king's death. . . .

Who these conspirators were is not made clear by the French ambassador. There can, however, be no doubt of their identity. At the time of Dijkvelt's visit he had had interviews with the leaders of the opposition at the house of Lord Shrewsbury. The English lords included, in addition to the host, Halifax, Danby, Devonshire, Mordaunt, Lumley, the Bishop of London and Admirals Herbert and Russell. Burnet, who gives their names, informs us that they met often at Shrewsbury's house. Presumably they formed something of a standing committee and continued to meet, as opportunity offered, for a year-and-a-half after the visit of Dijkvelt had first brought them together. In the spring of 1687 there was no thought of rebellion or, at least on the part of William III, of armed intervention in the affairs of England. Such intervention became a possibility in December. . . .

Burnet, who was on the spot and in a part of the secret, has the outlines of the true story. Every writer uses his work, but not every writer bothers to read it through. He says, perfectly clearly, that the prince was being pressed to invade from 1686 on; first by Mordaunt, then by others; that he refused, again and again; that, finally, on the visit of Admiral Russell to The Hague in May 1688, he was forced to agree to participate. Why? Because Russell told him that the English would wait no longer, that if William did not support them they would rise anyway. The threats came from responsible quarters. In May 1688 William had to capture control of a conspiracy. Otherwise, as he himself put it, the English would set up a republic. This would, obviously, deprive both the prince and the princess of their right. Also, and more important, it would be fatal to the Dutch. Of all conceivable forms of English political structure, that of a republic would be worst for Dutch interests. A republic would concentrate on colonial expansion and commercial enterprise. The Dutch knew this from bitter experience. They remembered Cromwell. Their trade had never recovered from the Navigation Acts of 1650 and 1651. Charles II had re-enacted the Navigation Laws, but he had not been able to enforce them. Indeed, he had been obliged by the Treaty of Breda in 1667 to modify them in important respects. But a second English republic could be expected to enforce and even to extend the policy of the Navigation Acts. When, therefore, Russell threatened that if William did not join the conspirators they would go on without him, the prince was obliged to acquiesce. By doing so he could direct the course of a revolution which was going to take place anyway. He could see to it that as much as possible of the English inheritance was salvaged. He could see to it that the revolution did not turn out to the disadvantage of his own fellow Dutchmen. In 1688 he was obliged to sell his inheritance for a mess of pottage; but he chose to sell it dearly, he was clever enough to make sure that the pottage contained as many raisins as possible.

There are usually two arguments raised against this thesis that the prince did not make up his mind until 1688. For one, how could the prince mount an invasion in November if he did not begin his plans until May? How could he raise the necessary forces so quickly? Would it not have been necessary to have formed plans much longer ahead of time? Obviously it would be difficult for a nobody to raise and equip 15,000 men and to provide transport for them in so short a time. But the prince was already at the head of an excellent army and navy. It is much less difficult to expand than to create an armed force. And in fact the records show that the prince did not enter into specific negotiations to raise his forces until 20 July. His plans were delayed by the failure of the English to invite him until 30 June O. S., and also by the illness of Bentinck's wife. This put off the invasion from September to the beginning of November; but it did not do more than cause a delay. The prince, with an army and navy in being, and more significantly with a staff and commissariat in being, could and did mount the invasion of England in less than three months' time. Had he taken longer to do it, the secret would have leaked out and the execution of the plan become impossible. And also, had he taken longer, the expenses would have become insupportable. As it was, William had no money to spare; but if, as his critics argue, he had been making preparations for two or three years, the costs would have been wholly prohibitive.

The second argument against such a late decision to intervene in England is not often expressed in precise terms. It is based on William's character. If he decided to intervene only in the late spring of 1688, he is open to the charge of having intervened for selfish motives, of having intervened because of the Prince of Wales. To avoid charging the prince with having deposed the Stuarts for selfish reasons, it is better to place the decision to intervene as early as possible, and at any rate earlier than the beginning of the queen's pregnancy. William does not need such a defense. Undoubtedly his actions were not dictated by base motives; undoubtedly he was not merely taking candy from a babe. He intervened, not for himself or for his wife but for his faith and for the protection of his native land, the United Provinces. In that cause he had lost his Principality of Orange, his estates in Franche-Comté and Luxembourg—roughly half his income. In that cause he was prepared to risk the English inheritance which was by far the largest asset he had left. It was a real risk, a real sacrifice. He might well have decided not to make it had he had a son. Since he did not have one he was free to act in the public interest. The fact that the prince's gamble succeeded is irrelevant. It was a great gamble, and only a man of the highest devotion to duty would ever have consented to make it.

There are other arguments against the idea that the prince's plans should be dated 1686 or earlier. Until 1686 he did not have control over the Dutch navy, and until then that force was too weak to be of any use. It was only when the Customs duties were put to farm and the revenues placed under the prince's control that the rebuilding of the navy could proceed, and even when those revenues became available the process of strengthening the fleet took years. . . .

When the prince did decide to intervene, he insisted on directing the conspiracy in his own way. The English wanted him to bring a small number of men, but a large fleet. William insisted on bringing enough soldiers so that he would be able to act independently. There was enough unrest in the army of James II so that it might well not fight. And, of course, its quality was such that even if it did try to fight it could not put up much resistance. Yet the prince would leave nothing to chance. He would take over more than enough men to destroy the royal army in the field if that became necessary. It is also very likely that the prince foresaw the actual result of the invasion. His wife, in her *Mémoire,* spoke of William going to dethrone her father. In all probability this is precisely what the prince intended to do. Only Parliament could make him king, and he might have to settle for less. But any compromise solution, such as a regency for James or for the Prince of Wales, simply would not work. He had no desire for the external glories of monarchy. The pompous ceremonies of the English court bored and disgusted him, and even if he had been able to perform them, as he never was, he would have slighted the public functions of kingship as much as he could. What the prince wanted was power, power enough to bring England into an alliance against Louis XIV and to keep her there. He could do this only as King Regnant. . . . Any lesser position would have been much too weak. In 1686 Burnet discovered that Mary hoped that her husband would become King Regnant. The task now was to lead the English into agreeing with her wishes. . . .

William carefully fostered the illusion that he would attack on the Rhine by mustering his army near Nijmegen. Solemnly the ammunition boats went up the river to the camp; but the stores remained on board, and the boats went downstream more quickly and far more secretly than they had gone up. The news of the French siege of Philippsburg reached The Hague on 27 September, proving that the prince's cover-plans had successfuly bemused the French. At the report, which meant that the Republic was safe for the moment, the stock market rose by 10 percent.

On 8 October the prince told the Deputies for Foreign Affairs of his plans. . . .

. . . The States General approved the report, and thanked both the Deputies and his Highness. The die was now cast.

There is, of course, one element of truth in the prince's statement [made to the Dutch] that he did not mean to make himself master of England. Obviously he went, as he had told his wife months before, to dethrone the king: so much of his statement to the Deputies was misleading. But he did not mean to follow the example of Henry VII, to proclaim himself king first and only then to summon a Parliament. Such a Parliament would not be free. Now and later William was to insist that Parliament should invite him to assume the crown. William the Deliverer would be in a much stronger position in the long run than William the Conqueror. And William the Deliverer would be justified, not only by the Dutch Deputies for Foreign Affairs, but by a far higher authority in the world of philosophy. Did not Bodin hold that it was just for a sovereign prince to intervene for the liberation of an oppressed people, though that people might not lawfully rebel themselves? It might be necessary for those holding the complete doctrine of nonresistance to suffer a second Nero with patience, although their patience was wearing thin now that the second Nero was at hand. But Bodin, referring most probably to the conduct of the prince's great-grandfather William the Silent, had approved the intervention of that prince as a sovereign—of Orange—even though he could say nothing for the conduct of the Dutch rebels against Philip II. Now Bodin's words seemed to have a new relevance. William's conduct in 1688 stretched the legal fiction of his sovereignty over Orange to its full limit. But it was a very useful legal fiction, justifying his own conduct and freeing the Dutch from the charge of aggressive war against England. Certainly the claim to the sovereignty of Orange was far nearer the truth, and far more specifically endorsed by every European treaty since 1544, than some of the claims of Louis XIV as brought forward in the Chambers of Reunion.

*   *   *

One of the great myths of the Revolution of 1688 is that it was made by the nobility rather than by the people of England. It was not. The ultimate cause, of course, was the misgovernment of James II which so alienated the people that two abortive risings occurred as early as 1685. Here we mean all the people, what were known at the time as the *menu peuple* [common people], rather than the tiny group which formed the political nation. Had the *menu peuple,* the countrywomen with their pipes and their offerings of apples, not been bitterly hostile to the Restoration government it would not have fallen at the first sight of 15,000 armed men. The fact that the militia so hated the king that he did not dare use it is a most significant fact. It is undoubtedly true that the upper class went along with the invasion once it had established a beachhead and that a few of the early arrivals at Exeter, such as Lord Colchester and Sir Edward Seymour, deserved perhaps even more from the prince than did the Immortal Seven [the seven lords who formally requested William's invasion]. Colchester and Seymour gave courage to the fainthearted. But the prince could easily have argued that his political debts were limited to those two men and to a very few others. His debts to those Englishmen who accompanied him were of course very large. His debts to the gentlemen and nobles who had stayed in England were not.

This, perhaps, is the ultimate basis of the conquest theory of the Revolution. There was an opportunity for William III to claim that he had done in 1688 what he had done in 1672 [in the Netherlands]:

leading the *menu peuple* in a revolution against the political nation. Such a claim would have meant that the Revolution of 1688 was a class war. It might well have led to a second supersession of the House of Lords, a return to the constitutional position of March 1649. Levellers and Diggers and the like might reappear, with demands for political and perhaps even economic equality. This is presumably what James meant when he told the peers at his *levée* of 16 October that they would all find the Prince of Orange a worse man than Cromwell. William III, however, avoided this trap in 1688 as he had avoided it in 1672. He did not want to be a traitor to his class, to overthrow the political nation. All he wanted on both occasions was what he felt to be his rightful place in the existing polity. He certainly used the *menu peuple,* and in doing so he laid the foundations for the bitter hatred of the magnates against him. They were terrified by the possible consequences of his conduct, and they were to resent as the Stuarts had the threat posed by his popularity. But William III was no Cromwell, no Napoleon, no Lenin. He had no need to be. It is possible to compare him to George Washington. It is not possible to make him into anything resembling a true revolutionary. It is equally impossible to give the English magnates much credit for the conservative nature of the Revolution of 1688. It was indeed a conservative revolution. But that happy result was the effect of an act of will on the part of William III. In December of 1688 he could have had anything he wanted. As Halifax told him, the English did not know what to do with him; but neither did they know what to do without him.

In other respects than finance the conduct of the Convention [Parliament summoned by William after his arrival in London] was also obnoxious. Although a Toleration Act was passed, its provisions were narrow in the extreme and it was only by a consistent refusal to enforce the penal laws that the king [William] was able to give the English the blessings that are so inaccurately associated with the statute. William's hopes for a Comprehension Act and for the repeal of the Tests in so far as they affected Protestant dissenters were blasted. Habeas corpus was suspended, but not long enough to give the king any real personal safety. It was not until 7 May that war was declared on France. Worst of all, William's plans for the succession were only to be carried out in part. He had hoped to have the Duchess Sophia of Hanover, the next Protestant in the line of succession after the Princess Anne, mentioned by name. This would secure the Protestant succession, since Sophia had several sons. It would also secure Hanover, an important piece in the diplomatic jigsaw puzzle and one that happened to have a treaty with France at that moment. But the Convention would not agree, and Sophia's claims were not to be recognized by Parliament for another twelve years. . . .

On 20 August the king was obliged to prorogue the Convention, which had been spending its time in attacking his ministers rather than in providing him with any assistance. By this time, despite the antics of the politicians, the Revolution was visibly prospering. England was much more confident of the stability of the new regime than it had been in the spring. Scotland was well on the way to order. In Ireland things were going better, if they were not yet going well. On the continent an alliance had been formed which was gaining ground from the French. Even the Princess Anne had done her share by giving birth in July to a boy. The life of the little Duke of Gloucester, frail though he was, gave a promise of permanence to the dynasty. The king, however, had little to hope for from his present ministry or from the Convention. Halifax, able as he was, was neither an administrator nor a party leader. William wanted to forget the past; but the Commons had not passed a bill of indemnity, nor had it settled the revenue. During the parliamentary recess the king went to Newmarket and politely lost four or five thousand guineas in an attempt to court popularity with the nobles. His efforts were not very successful. As he remarked gloomily to Dijkvelt, "I see that I am not made for this people, nor they for me." . . .

In February [1689] the king and queen had accepted the crown of England on conditions, those contained in the famous Declaration of Right. William III was annoyed at any reduction of the royal power and hoped that the crown would not be the worse for his wearing of it. At the time, the Declaration was explained to him as being a mere restatement of existing law. Whatever it might be, he hoped to have heard the last of it. Yet at the end of the year the Convention made the Declaration into a statute, known as the Bill of Rights. In one important respect the bill went further than the Declaration. The suspending power had been declared illegal in February, and so too the dispensing power "as it hath been assumed and exercised of late." In December the dispensing power was quite taken away.

At the same time that the royal powers were being whittled away, no progress was made towards a Bill of Indemnity. The Whigs also attempted to ruin their enemies by means of a Corporation Bill, put before a thin House during the Christmas festivals. The Sacheverell Clause of this bill would have disqualified all those who had taken part in the surrender of the old charters to Charles II and his brother from holding municipal office for a period of seven years. Had the clause taken effect, a very large number of the best qualified men in the kingdom would have been proscribed. The king was warned that the Whigs would withdraw their loans if he opposed the measure. Luckily the third reading of the bill did not take place until 10 January, and by that time many Tories had been able to return to their places. After a long debate, the clause was rejected. Some angry men did demand their money from the Exchequer, but other lenders were soon to come forward.

*   *   *

When he had first become king, William had been overheard to say that the crown should not be the worse for his wearing it; on which one sour prerogative man commented that he had made it little better than a nightcap. Perhaps this is not fair comment; but the powers of the crown were certainly far more limited in 1702 than they had been in 1689. For the most part the initiative which the crown had lost passed to the parties in the House of Commons. A situation had now arisen, however, in which the parties, by their equal strength, cancelled each other out. William, as arbiter between them, resumed much of the authority which had been lost since the Revolution. His followers realized how great was the present advantage and hoped that it might endure. . . .

The place of William III in European history depends on two separate developments: his defense of the United Provinces and his creation of a modern government in England. There can be no question as to where his heart lay. He was and remained throughout his life Dutch William. Perhaps, in a superficial view, he was a failure on the continent. . . .

In England the task of William III was different. Here he was creating something new rather than defending the old. It was not to be expected that his work should be appreciated at its true value.

He had their Rights and Liberties restor'd
In Battle purchas'd, and by Peace secur'd:
And they with English Gratitude began,
To feel the Favor and despise the Man.

Or, as it was put in another pamphlet a year later:

He that's fallen into a Pit, may chuse whether he will be help'd out, or no;
and if he stretches out his Hands, and strains his Lungs in begging for
Help, 'tis hard that all this Fatigue must pass for nothing, but that he
who only lends his Hand, should set up for his sole Rescuer. Yet thus
stupid were all the Parliaments in K. W.'s Reign, and gave him the only
Honor of a Redeemer, when 'tis notorious, that the whole Kingdom was
as fond of being redeem'd, as he was of coming to their Rescue.

Most Englishmen, once the king was safely dead, were able to take
a more balanced view of his work, even if they refused to go so far
as Bishop Burnet and apply to him the words of the Psalmist, "The
man of God's right hand, whom He made strong for Himself." Obviously enough, William III was the Deliverer of England from the
tyranny and arbitrary government of the Stuarts, as he was the Deliverer of Europe from the tyranny of Louis XIV. But in England he
was more than this. He repaired and improved an obsolete system
of government, and left it strong enough to withstand the stresses of
the next century virtually unchanged. The army of Marlborough, and
that of Wellington, and to large extent that of Raglan, was the creation of William III. So too was the independence of the judiciary.
In law he might, like the Stuarts, have displaced judges for decisions
he did not care for. Voluntarily he refused to do what his successors
were prevented from doing by the Act of Settlement. How great a
portion of the success of the Revolution Settlement do we not owe
to him for his refusal to accept the crown of England by the title of
conquest! In 1688 almost all the lawyers would have preferred that
he usurp the throne by such a claim, but William refused to make it.
He may not have foreseen all the consequences of his decision, and
he certainly did not enjoy all the difficulties in which that decision
later placed him, but the credit for it is William's and William's alone.
So too is the new moderation of political warfare after the Revolution. We should not blame him for the fact that he was the last
English king to execute a man by Act of Attainder. It is, rather, to his
credit that Fenwick was the single victim of such a barbarous procedure in his own reign, and that Fenwick has had no successors. . . .

III THE REVOLUTION AND THE EMERGENCE OF PARTY POLITICS

The Jacobites
THE REVOLUTION AS IMMORAL, ILLEGAL, AND ANTI-MONARCHICAL

This pamphlet, like most Jacobite works, is anonymous. Anonymity was a device resorted to frequently to forestall charges of sedition or libel. The pamphlet is representative of many, expressing the ultra-legalism of the Jacobite movement and the bitterness caused by the events of 1688–1689. The author insists that only a firm adherence to the laws of succession and nonresistance can restore the rule of law in England. Note that "K. J." and "K. W." refer to King James and King William; and that "P. of O." means the Prince of Orange (William).

If it be true that interest is often mistaken, though it never lie, and that standers-by sometimes see more than gamesters, though they do not understand the game so well, it may not be false that the politic drivers of our late revolution in England (who, 'tis to be feared, have too many of them designed their private interest at least as much as that of the public), have mistaken their way to both, and that one who has been no more than an indifferent looker-on, and who pretends not to be clearer sighted than others, has observed some things which the abler gamesters have not been aware of. Whether it be so or not, who pleases to read the following observations may judge. I will preface no more to him, whoever he be, than that if he examine them, as they have done the matter of fact on both sides, without prejudice to any, he will judge the better; and that since my kindness for my friends and country is the only motive I can have to expose my thoughts of this nature, he will be very unkind if he does not forgive what he does not approve.

First Observation. That though religion in the contrivance of this turn was called upon at first to serve the turn of interest, as it has ever been put to do in changes of this kind, and did sanctify a little while the pride and ambition of private men, with the name of Blessed Reformation, and made saints among the ignorant people of the worthy gentlemen so qualified, it has nevertheless been treated by them with less ceremony, than has been shown it before on such

From "Observations upon the Late Revolution in England," in *A Collection of Scarce and Valuable Tracts [Somers Tracts]* (London, 1813), vol. 10.

occasions. That mask was immediately thrown off here, and interest appeared bare-faced in everybody's mouth from the very beginning. . . . In short, men of war, men of law, men of gospel, men of all kinds, professed plainly to stand up for their liberty and property against their king; and that not so much by covering them, under the defense of their religion, as by discovering their religion was to defend them. So that though religion was advanced sometimes to lead up the common people, and marched along with liberty and property at the head of parties and pamphlets, when there was occasion to appear in public, it was plain that my lords and gentlemen had no other use of it, than to gull the commonalty; and that the profits and preferments of the government, to which the laws and possession gave them a title, were the things they would never part with, if any other king, or if no king, would preserve them to them.

Second Observation. That their redeemer, the P. of O., had the same occasion, and made just the same use of religion as his religiously aggrieved inviters and assisters into England; his declaration setting forth the deep sense and concern he had for it, as plainly as they could speak and write theirs. . . . [Furthermore,] whoever observes that the shoe pinches chiefly in the point of the Prince of Wales, who put the Prince of Orange by [out of] his hopes of succession, even more if it were true, than if it were fictitious, and that therefore . . . it was absolutely necessary to make him appear fictitious if possible; and whoever considers these other proceedings of the Prince of Orange upon all occasions; the trouble he gave himself of coming over into England about ten years ago, on purpose to help forward the Bill of Exclusion against the Duke of York; his entering into a conspiracy (which is averred from the mouth of one trusted by himself at the very time) for . . . deposing K. Ch. II.; his unwearied diligence in thwarting every thing K. C. or K. J. had a mind to have done by their own subjects; his great goodness in providing well for all those persons, who, for some goodness or other, had incurred their displeasure, and were banished or proclaimed traitors by those two kings; his generosity in sending and making use of the Duke of Monmouth, like foot of whelp, to burn his paws with setting up for king in England, without men, money, or arms; his courage afterwards, so much extolled, in coming himself, when, being rid of Monmouth's pretensions, he had the consent of the greatest part of the people and army of England, and knew he was not to strike any other kind of stroke for it than such . . . as he gave with his whip on a gentleman's shoulders at Newmarket, for riding before him, wittily enough observed then, to be the first he struck for the kingdom; his great care of K. J. when he was betrayed by his own army, in sending him a Dutch guard to Whitehall at eleven o'clock at night, without his knowing anything of it; . . . his constant and firm adherence, after the king's departure, to his declaration (the confidence of which had drawn in all the people to him); first, in his calling a free and legal parliament, than which he declares to have no other design; secondly, in the particular care he took for electing to his parliament, called the Convention, all true churchmen, all such as had been discountenanced, or brow-beaten before, in the way of outlawries, or so, by King Charles the Second, or King James; all such as could possibly be found, who had any hand of their own, or relation to those who had, in bringing his grandfather King Charles the First to condign punishment; and, thirdly, in his not suffering any business of the kingdom to come before or be thought of, by his honorable convention; not so much as his dearly beloved consort the princess, who, though she was graciously mentioned in his declaration, to have so great an interest in this matter, and such a right as all the world knows, to the succession of the crown, was not then permitted to come into England, till they had altered the fundamental constitution of the government, and made him king in his own right; his transubstantiating (as it has been called) when he was king, the same convention into a parliament, without writs or new elections, lest he should not get the people, who had been deceived by their conventionary members doing what they never dreamed of in making him king, to choose such parliament men as would serve the turns he had to come hereafter; . . . his filling all places of trust and profit throughout the kingdom, as far as could be found, with persons of the church of England, and of good life and conversations; his sending out of England even for Mr. Ludlow, one of the regicides of his grandfather, attainted and condemned by act of parliament for hanging up without a trial, to be advised with, if not preferred in the government here; his free disinterested submission of this kingdom's business to this free parliament, without any of those tricks as were played by former kings to influence or bias the members, as appears by its being so well an officered parliament, as it has been observed to be in the House of Commons itself; by the lords' sons he has called up, and the new peers he has created, by his sending his own Bentinck, whom he never parts with, when he has no particular interest driving elsewhere, out of his closet, to vote for Mr. Oats's being a good evidence again; . . . his religious way of taking and keeping coronation oaths in England, to defend episcopacy, and the church of England, as established by law; for the special performance of which, all England sees itself obliged to his weak endeavors; in Scotland to abolish episcopacy, root and branch, and to establish a church more conformable to the word of God, for the godly performance of which, all Scotland see no church at all. To conclude, upon this whole matter, it is observed, that his Dutch highness, as well as his English factors, consulted his private interest and ambition in the redemption he brought to England, at least as much as he did the good of religion, or the interest of the kingdom.

*   *   *

Fourth Observation.   That setting aside the question, whether the proceedings of the people of England have been just or lawful, it is observed that what they have done, is directly against their dearly beloved and espoused interest, and worse for themselves, in the same kind, than any inconveniences King James could have brought them under; that is to say, that those very inconveniences, of what kind soever they were, which they apprehended from him (and everybody knows they were not more than apprehended), are actually insupportable under this change of government already, and that they will grow worse and worse still, without other remedy than restoring him again; which will appear best by comparing what we feared then with what we feel now. . . .

We feared for our laws, not so much I believe for what was done, as for the manner of doing it, for I am persuaded a good part of what King James did might have been done for him in a legal way, and with the consent of the people; but when we saw him assume a dispensing power, not vested in him by law, we were sensible that the same power which overruled one law, might overrule another, and all, and feared the pernicious example: This, I think, was the case and the disease. The antidote now which we have taken against the poison of this bad example, is it not an example as bad, or worse, and our remedy against one illegal power, which we have pulled down, a setting up another altogether as illegal?

For the law acknowledges not for a legal parliament, any number of men, who are strong enough, a legal call; no, though they convene in the parliament-house, and vote themselves a parliament, nor that man for a king, whom the law places not in the throne. Unriddle me now, who can, in what an illegal dispensing power was more dangerous to our laws, than an illegal enactive, or an illegal executive power is; or in what the abdicated example of K. J. to dispense with some laws, was worse than the example set up now, by which any number of men who are strong enough, may assume an absolute power to dispose of all our laws, our religion, our bodies, consciences, and purses as they please, with no more ceremony than the formality of a transubstantiating vote. A liberty- and property-defending army of Englishmen, has done little less within the memory of man, and if our Dutch redeemers should take it for the fashion of the country, and to complete our redemption, set up for the parliament of England, which way can we plead our laws in bar to them, which we have overruled already ourselves? In short, illegality is always illegality, and if that were the intolerable pernicious thing before, it is so much the more intolerable now, by how much a legislative illegality is more pernicious than a dispensative one, and an usurped executive power more dangerous than a legal one; and yet the wisdom of our fears has drank down one, as a destructive disturbing, and the other, as a healing settling draught. I am far enough from kindness to either, but I will say for the destructive one, that it has been, at least, the more modest of the two, for it only made bold with a single superstructure, by dispensing with the test-act, without which our government had stood many a fair age, and that too with a pretense on its side of its being law, in the interval of parliament, and of referring it to a parliament when it met; whereas our settling illegality has fallen confidently upon the very foundations of our constitution, and pulled them quite away. The English government has hitherto stood upon these fundamental maxims, that the king never dies, and that all authority is derived from him. For our wise ancestors were so sensible of the ruinous consequences of interregnums, elections, seditions, and saw so well that nothing could prevent them but a legal king always in being, that they would not allow to death itself, with all its irresistible power over the man, any power over the king, but made the same moment which received the last breath of the man breathe his regal power into the next of blood; and then placing the fountain of all authority in this immortal king, stopped up forever all pretending streams of sedition. By this it was made impossible, for any pretense to cheat or hinder the people from distinguishing the seditious, which they were to avoid, from the just power which they were to obey, there being no more to do, but to ask which flowed from that fountain which they had contrived should always run. Now we have introduced vacant thrones, filling them as pleasure or humor, not as blood directs, and a new power over our fundamentals themselves, not derived from the old only fountain; and now to make the hinges straight, upon which how much soever they swayed before by dispensing, our government still moved, we have knocked them quite off. I will not be the melancholy prophet to foretell what will be the consequence, but leave every one to guess, who will reflect what they have seen and felt in one year's time. . . .

*   *   *

Sixth Observation. That though we thought to make our court to our new king by deserting our old, as we are generally an honest, upright people, our consciences possibly, if they were not ashamed to speak, could tell strange stories of the self-denial this compliment cost us, and the hard shifts and pains many of us made, and took to mortify the struggling rebellion of nature against that which we unnaturally hurried ourselves into against our king. And for getting the better of ourselves, for the fruits of this glorious victory, our ears tell us every day, that cowardice and treachery (reproaches heretofore unusual to Englishmen) fly in our faces from the mouths of our conquerors, from such of them at least as cannot be hindered from saying what they think, which is enough to instruct us what the reserved rest have to say, whose time it is not yet to speak their thoughts. Our eyes tell us, that no Englishman is trusted in anything, no not those who for form-sake sit in places of trust, for as our English estates are often settled in trust, our English trust itself is in trust now; the fine titles worn by our ministers and privy-counselors of England being nothing but gay liveries, to make them show the handsomer tools to finish up the work cut out by Dutchmen in the closet. And our reason will tell us we cannot complain, nor expect it ever should be otherwise. For no wise prince will trust a man whom he has cause to suspect will not be true to him; and our K. W. cannot forget that he was not born in England, that he did not inherit the crown, that he cannot reign without wars and taxes: and that therefore he cannot (though he would never so fain) securely count upon those men, whereof every one who presents himself for employment, must of necessity come with this speech in his mouth: You, sir, are king *de facto,* and may be sure of me; for I am just come from being false to a king *de facto,* and *de jure* both, who was my countryman, besides, twenty to one, my particular benefactor, and whose reign was a reign of peace and plenty. Our compliment therefore has put an inevitable necessity upon our new king, never to trust us to counsel or fight for ourselves, but under a sure guard, and to furnish himself with store of foreign heads and hands, to carry on the interest of England; at which we are neither to wonder nor complain, for necessity has no law.

Seventh Observation.   That all this mischief cannot follow only (as some would have, and do infer) from K. James's going away, called Abdication; for though abdication is a hard word, which I will not pretend to understand, because my dictionary does not, I am sure it means not what his going away plainly was, trying to escape a foreseen restraint, and escaping at last an actual one. But I guess what they would have meant by it is, that K. James when he went away, ceased to be K. some way or other, which yet was neither giving away out of liberality, nor selling for money, nor losing his crown by chance, nor forfeiting, nor surrendering, nor dying. But what unintelligible way soever it were, the moment in which he ceased to be king (according to our constitution) some other was king; in which case we had no more to do but to let our government move upon the old sure wheels, and our happiness would have gone on along with it under the new king, whom God and nature, and the law of England, have always in readiness for us when the old fails. So that let abdicating signify what it will, I see no necessity of shaming ourselves with the imputation of a faithless, simple people, neither to be trusted by any king, nor so much as with our own concerns and interest: No necessity of foreigners, and the calamities they must bring along with them: None of subverting the foundation of our constitution, and crushing ourselves with the falling building.

It had been but keeping the laws, and they would have kept us. But as we have handled the matter, with our anteponing and postponing, we have brought the government of England to the domineering of a [mob], with all their whimsies, and all their violence, with only a more formal outside: for there is no such thing as a government left, to which anybody is obliged to submit for any reason but fear: No such thing as law, which has been, or can be legally made or executed; and let a man have deserved to have been condemned never so much the last year, he needs his pardon who condemned him. In short, we are absolutely in the state of nature before society, where all the power which one man had over another was his greater strength, and all authority violence. 'Tis by violence K. W. calls conventions and parliaments; and violence is all the validity of their acts. They have no other authority than the laws which thieves make among themselves to rob the more methodically and safely; and we submit to both, for the same reason, fear of worse. Violence seizes our money and our liberty, and we yield to it, just as we suffer stronger highwaymen to bind us and take our purses. Were the just scales of the law in use (for the dispensing with which in one particular we were in such frights before), every order now for a tax, every assessment, every collection, and perhaps (if necessity help us not off) every payment would weigh more than felony, downright treason: And what the men of might do to us, every one of us, who happens to be strong enough, may with as much right do to them.

Eighth Observation. To conclude: Here we are, and here we must be eternally, till we learn wit of a carter, and set the overturned cart on the wheels again; in plain terms, till we re-settle King James on his throne. The happiness of England depends upon a rightful king, we see it always went out with him, and 'tis in vain to hope it ever will, or can return without him. . . .

We may have a lawful government and true parliaments again, security of our religion, laws, and rights, and be once more the freemen we were born, re-enfranchized from wars and taxes; for all these things are waiters in ordinary, and return with the king of course. If any remnant of our former fears hangs still uneasy about us, he is not so far off, but a willing mind may have recourse to him, whither he has more than once invited us for that purpose, and be eased. And it is not now to be suspected, he will boggle at condescending to anything that is reasonable in our fears, much less that we shall ever have reason to complain hereafter of non-performance. For as there is no security like interest, and he cannot but be sensible of it, who sees that not to keep his word, is not to keep his kingdom; if we have but wit enough to judge as the wise Romans did, even upon the suggestion of a conquered enemy, that a reasonable easy peace on both sides, is sincere and lasting; an unreasonable grating one on either side, of no longer durance than till the next opportunity for war, and so keep ourselves from grating unreasonably upon him; the wit of a burned child in him will set our hearts at rest for that matter: But have him we must on any terms, or be the most wretched nation under the sun: For the fire of war is kindled, which of necessity must otherwise consume us. . . . We live in an island, where, conversing only among ourselves, we are apt to think the world goes as the cry goes with us, and perceive not how abominably we stink in the nostrils of all mankind besides; not excepting the very Turks, nor our delivering masters themselves, for the glory of wearing whose chains we have made ourselves so wretchedly despicable. Not to flatter ourselves, all Europe loaths a nation which, having murdered one king, is now murdering another, and that not by a ragged [mob] whose unthinking fury starts more excusably into horrid crimes, but by a [mob] of another make, a [mob] of honor dressed up in the wisdom and devotion of the nation; a thinking godly [mob], which kills in cool blood, and fasts and prays to sanctify the murders. To be plain, all Europe hates our hypocrisy, who, pretending zeal for the protestant religion, are all the while worse than the very worst of papists.

Alas! that England should for our sakes bid fair to lose its old name, and be known hereafter by the name of the barbarous, the king-killing country; and our religion the faithless, the hypocritical religion!

But it is time to end, and I will, if I can, end with demonstration. It is demonstration that, unless we recover our old constitution by consent, we must, besides the intermediate miseries, sink at last under arbitrary power. It may be monarchical, and it may be republican. But arbitrary it must be, if we suffer it to come either to a conquest of King William, or King James, or to a commonwealth; which, by the way, would be the worst of all; we can at least complain under an arbitrary prince, and the shame and vexation of just complaints is some check to him, let him be never so absolute. Under a commonwealth there is not so much as that poor ease; as imaginations of law or fancy, I know not whether, makes us do whatever our representatives do; no burthen can pass for oppression, nor complaint for just. For we oppress ourselves all the while, and must complain of ourselves, and whatever we suffer in reality, all is ease and liberty in imagination. But this is no place for the dispute betwixt monarchy and a commonwealth. It is enough that conquest makes a conqueror absolute; that nothing can be more arbitrary than a commonwealth must be, and that a weight weighs its weight however it be laid on. It is demonstration that we cannot recover our old constitution, without our old king. It stands upon right of blood, it fell with that right, and we may as soon build a castle in the air as think to rear and prop it again with our politic fancies. . . .

George L. Cherry
WERE THE JACOBITES RIGHT?

George L. Cherry was born in 1905. He received his graduate training at Northwestern University, where he was awarded his doctorate in 1938. During the war he served with the Air Force, and after his tour of duty, returned to teaching. Currently, he is an associate professor of history at the University of Southern Illinois. He has devoted most of his attention to monographic studies on the reign of William and Mary.

The mosaic of political concepts advanced during the interregnum for the settlement of the English government has remained incompletely constructed. This deficiency has resulted largely from three factors. In the first place, the Whig foundations of the arrangement have received greater emphasis than the alternative proposals. The Whig concepts sounded the death knell to absolutism and provided for the beginnings of a limited monarchy, under which form of government England was to rise to new heights of wealth, power, and

From George L. Cherry, "The Legal and Philosophical Position of the Jacobites, 1688–1689," *Journal of Modern History* 22 (December, 1950): 309–321. Copyright © 1950 by the University of Chicago. Reprinted by permission of the University of Chicago Press.

prestige. To emphasize the principles that seemingly motivated this startling development would therefore be natural. In the second place, writers have considered the discussions of the interregnum, and particularly the debates in the Convention Parliament, less important than the philosophy of John Locke, who wrote after the settlement, or that of Filmer and Harrington, who wrote before the revolution. A typical disparaging analysis of the Convention deliberations is given by the historian James Ralph: "The whole Dispute about the Words *abdicate, desert,* and *vacancy,* was fitter for a School than a House of Parliament, and might have been expected in some Assembly of Pedants." Subsequent authors have but little altered the opinion of Ralph. Some of them have paraphrased the major speeches; others have given almost no attention to the discussions; a few have omitted them entirely. All of them have neglected to reveal the pattern of political concepts. In the third place, Jacobite ideas have received no special attention. This omission resulted from the unpopularity of these concepts and the belief that Jacobitism from the beginning was a lost cause. But Jacobitism did exist.

The importance of Jacobitism as a political force for the half-century after the revolution warrants an investigation of its foundations. At the time of Jame's first flight, the party consisted largely of Catholics. The nucleus grew when the captured king was returned to London. This group was increased by the action of William when he forced the king out of England. During the election in January 1689 the Jacobite faction was one of the groups to compete for Convention seats. The party was much larger than was generally supposed. When the Convention met, 200 of the 513 members had served in the parliament of 1685. The fight in the commons for retaining James in some status was led by Lord Charles Fanshaw, Sir Christopher Musgrave, Sir Edward Seymour, and Mr. Heneage Finch. When the resolution on the vacancy was brought before the house, 151 members voted in the negative. In the upper chamber Jacobite strength was greater. On the question of the regency 49 peers voted for retaining James, while 51 voted against him. Among the leaders supporting the regency were the Earls of Clarendon, Rochester, and Nottingham; Sidney Godolphin, baron of Rialton; the Bishop of Ely; and the Archbishop of York. These lords were vigorous in their opposition to the commons action until the final decision on the "vacancy" resolution was reached. On this question 45 lords voted nay, and 39 of the peers entered their protests. Those figures give evidence of the strength of the group in the Convention. During the remainder of the Stuart period probably no fewer than fifty Jacobites held seats in parliament. These leaders worked actively for the restoration of the old order, while the majority of the party remained aloof from the government and engaged in plots for the return of James or his heirs. "Jacobitism remained a serious and powerful political cause until 1746." In view of the significance of Jacobitism, its concepts will be presented in this article through an analysis of Jacobite ideas on the following topics: the institutional authority to solve the constitutional problem; the divine-right theory; the compact theory; the plan for a regency; the royal hereditary rights; the abdication principle; and the vacancy of the throne.

An important question under discussion during the interregnum was the authority of the English institutions, in the absence of the king, to settle the constitutional crisis created by the flight of James II. The Jacobites maintained that the Convention was without legal authority to make the settlement through a breach of the line of succession. . . .

The flight initiated the second phase of the problem of stabilizing the English government. In this phase the government was operating without a king and there was danger of the governmental balance being upset. During this period a temporary expedient was advanced by the lords and commons who had served in the parliaments of Charles II. The lords, who considered the possible alternatives, had been urged by Lord William Pagett to declare the king's withdrawal a demise and to select Mary as queen. The motion was not carried because of the vigorous opposition of the Earls of Pembroke and Nottingham. Two days later the prince asked the group to suggest ways and means for implementing his declaration to preserve the institutions of England. At this meeting of the delegates the body asked the prince to take charge of the government and to issue a call for a convention. In spite of the majority decision, the opinion was widely held that the convention would have no power to deal with the crisis because a legislature was without authority when the king did not participate. Although some of the leaders favored inviting James to return, provided that he would make certain guarantees, the clergy generally favored a regency through which a parliament could be called within the limits of the constitution. The apprehension of the Jacobite leaders was aroused by these developments. In a discussion of the implications with the Earl of Clarendon, Pembroke argued that in the approaching convention strenuous efforts must be made to guarantee the safety of James's interest while the political settlement was designed.

The third phase of the crisis developed during the meeting of the Convention. During this period the Jacobites were working to prevent what they considered to be an illegal legislature from jeopardizing the traditional balance of the constitution. When the Convention met there was much discussion about the authority of the body to deal with the critical problem. Frst came the question about the seat of authority after the king fled. Some observers agreed with a pamphleteer who analyzed the departure of the king as a dissolution of the government when he wrote, "If the Departure of the King amounts to such a Desertion as dissolves the Government, then the Power must necessarily revert and vest in the People, who may erect a new one, either according to the old *Model,* if they like it so well, or any other that they like and approve better." On the other hand, Nottingham expressed the belief that precedent gave the peers of the realm considerable authority under these circumstances:

> In the absence of the King . . . I would not be understood to say, the government devolved upon the Lords; but I may say they are the government's great council in the interval of Parliaments, and may have greater sway by the privilege of their birth, in the exigencies of state: As appears in several instances, and particularly the first of Henry the sixth, and during his infancy.

Deeper legal implications were seen, however, in the query put by Sir Christopher Musgrave to the legislative body. He said, "I would be clear whether the intent is to depose the King; if he has forfeited his Inheritance to the Crown, I would know from the Long Robe whether you can depose the King or no." This led to doubts as to the authority of the Convention to settle the question. It was emphasized that a convention was not a body that could be compared with a parliament. Because the king's writs had not been used to summon the body, it could have no legislative powers. Further clarifying the status of the Convention, one of the lords said, "As our Laws stand; We have misled a legal and free Parliament, and have got a Convention that cannot make Laws, nor call a Parliament

that can, but what will need a confirmation from a better authority."
Referring to legal precedents in his interpretation of the authority, the
Bishop of Ely recalled that the heir to the throne had been set aside
by parliament on previous occasions. The bishop emphasized, however, that it did not follow "that every breach of the first original contract, gives us power to dispose of the lineal succession." This
position was generally supported by the clergy, who were apprehensive about recognizing deposing powers. The spokesman for the
group, Ely, gave a more complete analysis of the authority of
parliament. Relating the powers of parliament to the original
compact, he asserted that through this agreement the king
and parliament had the authority to make and amend laws. Since
the law of succession was a part of the compact, the powers
of parliament did not include dealing with the crown until all
heirs had abdicated. He doubted whether the precedents on the
interruptions of the throne provided power to set aside the lineal
succession because of the allegiance laws enacted under Elizabeth
and James I. Since these laws were a part of the contract, parliament
could not alter the succession except through the regular legislative
process. Thus the Jacobites concluded that the Convention had no
power to deal with the constitutional crisis. In spite of the solid legal
foundations of their arguments, the Whig majority pushed ahead
to settle the government. The widespread discussions during the
interregnum defined many ideas on the nature of government; among
them were those relating to the divine-right theory.

It was assumed during the eighteenth century that the Jacobites
believed in "dispensing Power in the Crown, with indefeasible Hereditary Right, *Jure Divino.*" This idea has persisted for over two centuries. In his recent article about the revolution J. L. Duncan wrote:

> *On the one hand were ranged all believers in political absolutism, who
> then maintained that the King virtually stood above all law and reigned
> by virtue of divine right. His actions were regarded as sacrosanct and
> unchallengeable by any subject. In particular it was held that no circum-
> stances could ever arise which would justify a subject in resisting by
> armed force any dictate of sovereign power.*

The evidence, however, does not support these positions. The facts
reveal that, while the settlement was being accomplished, the majority
of the Jacobites exchanged the divine-right theory of the Cavaliers

for the more rational compact idea based on the precedents of constitutional growth. Some of the former remained, however, expressing themselves in letters, speeches, and pamphlets. A few of them believed in political absolutism, maintaining that the king was above the law and reigned by divine sanction. The most significant proponent of these ideas was James II, who wrote to the lords from Saint-Germain-en-Laye: "No change of fortune shall ever make Us forget Ourselves so far as to condescend to anything unbecoming that high and royall station on which God Almighty has by right of succession placed us." This position, however, was not widely accepted in official circles. During the Convention, occasional references were made to the absolutist theory of control. This attitude was referred to by Sir Robert Howard, a Whig leader, who in his speech on the state of the nation said, "I have heard 'that the King has his crown by Divine Right.' " Public discussions, however, were different in tone. . . .

At the meeting of the Convention the majority of James's followers supported the compact theory of government through which the lords and commons participated, under the leadership of the king, in the control of the nation according to constitutional precedents. Their position was revealed through the discussions of the Convention and indicated concern about the preservation of their laws, their estates, their religion, their standing in the country, and the consequences of a drastic change in the hereditary rights of the crown. It also revealed a fear of an elective monarchy and a commonwealth. In origin it did not show a dependence upon Filmer and Harrington, but rather a relationship to the philosophy or legal principles of Richard Hooker, Hugo Grotius, the Bible, Sir Edward Coke, Sir John Fortescue, the coronation oath, and Tacitus. The speeches and writings revealed a more significant reliance upon the opinions of the learned counselors of the law than upon any other source. Those serving as counselors included Sir Robert Atkyns, Sir Edward Montague, Sir William Dolben, Sir Cresswell Levinz, Sir Edward Nevill, Sir John Holt, Sir William Whitlocke, George Bradbury, and William Petyt. In order to present clearly the political concepts of the Jacobites on the contract theory, an analysis of their opinions will be necessary.

When the Convention lords received the commons resolution, the peers requested the opinions of the counselors about the legal status of the compact theory. The majority of them asserted that, although the lawbooks did not refer to the original contract, they believed in its existence. Two of the counselors were evasive. Atkyns said he believed the term referred to the first step in government, when the king and the people formed a limited monarchy. He cited Hooker, the preamble of the act concerning Peter's Pence, Grotius, and the Bible to substantiate his opinion. When asked about the term, Dolben asserted that Coke spoke of approximately the same thing. If the principle did not exist, subjects could not demand that the king must live within the law. Whitlocke argued that the limited nature of the monarchy was derived from the king's compact with the people, and he recalled that King Alfred was limited by his coronation oath. After confessing that he had been incorrectly taught at Oxford that no contract existed, Bradbury stated that no government could subsist without an agreement between the king and the people, and he believed the body of common law was the original contract. Analyzing the body politic of England, he saw three parts: king, lords, and commons. This idea was used again and again by the lords when defending the hereditary monarchy through the concept of the original contract. Petyt emphasized the coronation oath as evidence for the existence of the original contract. After referring to the selection of rulers by acclamation in Germany, he said there was always agreement between the king and the people in Saxon times. He affirmed that, since Statute 25 Edward III, the king had been bound by his oath to rule justly. The oath, he pointed out, was administered before any subject did homage.

This uncertainty of the legal status of the original contract was reflected in the debate preceding the settlement. A pamphlet asserted, "Most men believed that the pretended Breach of that they call The Original Contract, was designed for no more than a popular Flourish." The Earl of Clarendon, however, was more profound in his analysis when he remarked at the Convention:

> I may say . . . that this breaking of the original contract is a language that hath not been long used in this place; nor known in any of our law books, or public records. It is sprung up, but as taken from some late authors none of the best received.

Less skeptical was the Earl of Pembroke, who outlined the character of the contract when he said:

The laws are certainly part of the original contract; and by the laws made, which established the oath of allegiance and supremacy, we are tied up to keep the hereditary line, being sworn to be true and faithful to the King, his heirs and successors; whereas the old oath was only to bear true allegiance to the King. There (I take it) lies the reason why we cannot (of ourselves) without breaking that contract, break the succession.

A more penetrating deduction was expressed by Nottingham, who denied the ability to destroy the compact. Granting a breach of the contract, he insisted that the next in line could not inherit the crown because an individual cannot be heir to a person who is alive. Furthermore, he pointed out, by accepting a dissolution of government and selecting a new line, the Convention would commit "the same fault we have laid upon the King." Accepting the analysis of the Oxonian Bradbury, he saw the English government as a body politic consisting of three parts, with the king as the leader of the lords and commons. With the removal of the sovereign, the remainder of the government was endangered. "For they are knit together in their common head; and if one part of the government be dissolved, I see not any reason but that all must be dissolved." A similar point of view was expressed by a pamphlet, which in discussing conditions in England emphasized the distinction between parliament and the Convention. Because the latter was not called by writs (a function of the king), it had no legislative powers.

By accepting the compact idea of government as a means for the preservation of the hereditary monarchy, the Bishop of Ely agreed with Bradbury's analysis of the body politic. The bishop conceived the compact as an agreement made when the state was first instituted. In the agreement were the conditions under which the government (king, lords, and commons assembled) should function. The body politic was obliged to make new laws and to alter old ones. Among these was a law of succession, which was as much a part of the original contract as any other statute. In the case of abdication, the disposition of the crown would not be a prerogative of parliament until all the heirs had abdicated. The bishop recognized the seven interruptions in the succession since the Conquest, but he cited the statutes of Queen Elizabeth and James I on allegiance as part of the contract, which required obedience until altered by a lawful parliament. By observing these principles, he believed England would avoid an elective crown.

In the commons, the Jacobites analyzed the nature of the government, in the case of drastic changes, with a concern equal to that of the lords. Heneage Finch believed the destruction of the contract would be a serious act. The problems created by the breakdown of the constitution would be almost insurmountable. If James were no longer king, he believed, the throne should be filled with the next in line of succession. It was true that the king could forfeit for himself, but he could not resign or dispose of the inheritance. In the case of James, his escape did not seem a complete renunciation. Yet the English people would endanger their security by sending proposals to James. Finch believed a satisfactory solution for the preservation of the contract would be to establish a regency during the life of the king. A more liberal view was taken by Sir Christopher Musgrave. Adhering to the ideal of the hereditary monarchy as an element of the compact, he believed the king could violate the contract and not destroy the constitution. To avoid disturbing the constitution, he would follow the dictum of the Bishop of Ely in distinguishing between the right to, and the exercise of the right to, the crown. The third point of view was expressed by Sir Thomas Clarges. He supported the idea of hereditary right and believed that to declare the crown void would have unusual results. It would disturb the constitution by changing the status of the king. Filling the vacancy would be more serious. Clarges thought the selection of a successor to James would convert the kingdom into a commonwealth. This development would imperil the constitutional principle of hereditary rights.

The commons as well as the peers supported the principle of a hereditary king and expressed apprehension of instable government if the lineal succession were disrupted. Although the number of Jacobites was not great in the commons, this point of view was advanced by Finch, who in a debate on January 28 expressed his belief in the hereditary nature of the crown with descent through an uninterrupted lineal succession. The king, he thought, might give up his position as in case of malfeasance of office, but in that event he would relinquish only the exercise of the crown. His departure would cause transfer of governmental control into the hands of his successor because the king could not lose his title or inheritance.

In the upper chamber the Jacobites, holding ideas much like those held by the Tories, took views similar to those held by Finch. Many of these concepts were formed upon the putting of the question "whether king James having broke that Original Contract between him and his people, and deserted the government whether the throne was thereby 'vacant'?" One group stoutly maintained that the "king never dies." The concept of a hereditary king, however, was amplified in the conference between the lords and commons in an effort to iron out their differences. Clarendon and Nottingham were the principal defenders of the lords' position. Replying to the aged Sir John Maynard, the former said, "I think, no act of ours can alter the lineal succession; for, by all laws we now have in being, our government appears to be hereditary in the right line of descent: And upon any descent, when any one ceaseth to be King, allegiance is by law due to his heir as successor." When asked by Henry Pollexfen, a house conferee, who should succeed James, he queried, "Must it not be supplied by those that should come if he were dead?" Uneasy about the status of the crown because the commons had indicated that they did not want an elective crown, Clarendon stated that a breach in the lineal succession at this time might act as a precedent which would make the throne perpetually elective. Another of the conferees, the Earl of Nottingham, discussed the nature of the crown by citing cases from English precedent. Nottingham was an ardent disciple of hereditary right. In analyzing the position of the king, he contrasted it with the status of the commoner. Because the inheritance of the commoner can be halted by an attainder, it is weaker than the royal line as defined by the lawyers of Henry VII. The status of the crown had been defined by the statute dealing with the king's succession during the reign of Henry VIII. By this law, said Nottingham, succession was limited to the king's children. If the king chose to relinquish his position, his act would not exclude his heirs. Furthermore, Nottingham, relating incidents from history, demonstrated how, in cases of disturbed succession, claimants had not taken the throne unless they had "some specious pretence of an hereditary title to it." In this manner he revealed that the throne might be vacant as to a particular person, but it would not be to the successor because the English laws recognized no interregnum. Upon the death of the ruler the next in line is the sovereign at one and the same instant. The coronation oath, in the mind of the Jacobites, did not greatly alter the hereditary position. Clarendon further amplified this condition by relating the regal position to the oath. He explained that the king must live within the law before as well as after the oath was administered. In this way allegiance is due from subjects as soon as the crown descends upon the next in line by succession. A more complex view of the oath was presented by a pamphleteer who wrote, "Though the King do not perform his Coronation-Oath, yet his Subjects are not therefore absolved from the Oath of Allegiance; and on the contrary, the King is bound by his Coronation-Oath, though his Subjects do not keep that of Allegiance." These concepts provided the foundation for the resolution for the regency in spite of the more conservative ideas expressed in other pamphlets.

The position of the Jacobites in the house of lords as well as in the commons followed with amplification the ideas expressed by the learned counsel of the law on the question of the regency. The discussion of the possibility of a regency was begun in the upper house when the commons resolution on James II was received, although doubts were expressed about the status of the king in relation to the regency. Turning to the Civil War precedent, the incident was cited wherein the commons had enacted a measure to execute the king, and the lords had rejected it on December 29, 1648. This position was sustained from the legislation, Statute 22 Edward III, which resolved that the king has no peer in the realm and cannot be judged by men. The status of the king was further clarified by the statutes of Henry VI's reign, which stated that the king could not dispose of his kingdom. Although John had tried to subvert the crown, he could not do so. In view of these doctrines, and considering the flight of James, it was concluded that the best remedy for the situation would be a regency, since it came nearest to meeting the requirements of the law. The counselors were then asked for an opinion on the legality of the regency. Sir Robert Atkyns replied that in law the regent is a guardian and a protector. If royal power were assumed, the regent would differ little from a king. With these opinions as background, the Jacobites waged the struggle on the question of the regency in both the lower and the upper houses, but the idea was more widely accepted in the latter than in the former. In his debate on the state of the kingdom in the commons, Finch proposed the establishment of a regency during the lifetime of the king. An acceptance of the plan was urged because of the stability it would provide. Although Finch thought James should not be given regal powers, he was certain a sound administration would result. These ideas did not win the approval of the commons, but they were accepted by a near majority in the house of lords. A resolution for a regency during the life of James II was introduced in the upper house by Nottingham, and its introduction was followed by a long and bitter debate. Nottingham, the leader of the discussion, by citing the instance of Don Pedro, who was regent while the king of Portugal yet reigned but did not rule, exercised great influence upon the peers. His ideas did not prevail, however, as the resolution failed to carry by a narrow margin of two votes. The failure of the motion to pass made necessary the consideration of the legal position of the exiled king.

Although the commons accepted the idea that by fleeing James had abdicated, the lords, adhering to the hereditary concept of the monarchy, believed the king could not abdicate. Their position was determined in part by the analysis of the abdication principle by the counselors of law. Four of them agreed that the term was not found in common law. Atkyns pointed out that the term was included in the dictionary, while Dolben asserted that it was used in Roman law. Whitlocke and the more profound Bradbury agreed that the term could not extend beyond the person involved. Furthermore, the circumstances of James's flight were closely related to the opinion of his status. It was widely believed that, because the king was in danger, his action could not be defined as an abdication. There was, indeed, much evidence to support this analysis because a portion of the army had deserted and the remaining forces were of slight value. Furthermore, the subjects expressed a strong resentment against the king, and disorders were widespread as William's army swept inland. Under these circumstances the Jacobites believed James had withdrawn to protect himself and his family. His hasty departure had precluded the appointment of officials to administer the government. "And since his Majesty had sufficient Reasons to withdraw, these can be no Pretense for an Abdication: For we are to observe, That to abdicate an Office, always supposes the Consent of him who quits it. That this is the signification of the word Abdico, appears from Tully, Salust and Livy; to which I shall only add the Learned Grotius, De Jure Belli . . . where he makes Abdicating the Government, and plainly Giving it up, to be Terms of the same importance." Grotius, however, had been more explicit when he added that a

"Neglect or Omission in the administration of Government, is by no means to be interpreted a Renunciation of it." In addition to referring to foreign authors, cases in English history were cited.

We have but two Instances with us, which looks like an Abdication since the Conquest; which are the Reigns of Edward II and Richard II both which were unjustly Deposed by their Subjects. However they did not renounce their Allegiance, and declare the throne Void, till they had a formal Resignation under the Hands of both those unfortunate Princes.

In the commons the proponents of these opinions were Lord Charles Fanshaw and Sir Thomas Clarges. The former in a talk on the state of the nation observed that the king had been forced out of the kingdom because of fear of his own subjects. Clarges could not accept the principle of abdication. Following precedents, he believed the principle referred to voluntary action.

The opposition of the peers to the application of the abdication principle to James revealed opinion similar to that of the counselors, the pamphleteers, and the commoners. Theirs was largely expressed in the conference with the commons by Nottingham, the Bishop of Ely, Rochester, and Clarendon. Upon the receipt of the commons resolution on James II, the lords refused to accept the principle of abdication. Their reasons were given in a resolution returned to the house of commons, which stated that, as the term was unknown in common law, the lords desired to use a word upon which there was general acceptance. It was pointed out that, when the term was used in civil law, it indicated a voluntary renunciation. Obviously, James had not left voluntarily. The free conference between the lords and commons brought greater amplification on the nature of abdication. Although the three major speakers, Ely, Clarendon, and Nottingham, presented conflicting details in analyzing the principle, they agreed that the word was not found in common law; that when the word was used in civil law, it meant voluntary action; and, if the principle were applied to James II, the hereditary succession would be endangered. Their major concern appeared to involve the declaration of a vacant throne.

The lords were apprehensive about the use of the word "vacant" to describe the condition of the throne. This concern probably developed from the reluctance of the counselors to render exact opinions. They were evasive and vague. Atkyns, Levinz, and Montague believed the question could not be answered by reference to common law but was a case for the high court of parliament. Although agreeing with the other counselors that the decision should be made by the high court, Bradbury was willing to speculate on the principle. He believed that a vacancy might exist, and, if the royal family were extinct, he thought there would be no question about it.

Using Bradbury's statement as the foundation, the peers vigorously opposed the commons resolution on the vacancy. While considering the resolution, the lords struck out the clause "and that the throne is thereby vacant." In a statement sent to the lower house, the lords explained their rejection of the word "vacancy" on the following grounds:

> *(1) Because, by the Constitution of the Government, the Monarchy is Hereditary, and not Elective. (2) Because no Act of the King alone can bar or destroy the Right of His Heirs to the Crown; and therefore . . . if the throne be vacant of James the Second, Allegiance is due to such Person as the Right of Succession does belong to.*

Not much was added to these statements by the speakers at the free conference. The Earl of Nottingham refused to accept the idea of vacancy because of its consequences. If the condition applied to James's heirs, the crown would be elective. Clarendon went further in his thinking about the results of declaring the throne vacant. In a debate with Pollexfen he asserted, "If then you say this government is vacant, that would be to put all those by that [i.e., to remove all those who] should take the succession." Furthermore, he believed the nation might become a commonwealth. The Earl of Rochester, commenting on the difference between hereditary and elective governments, observed that in the former, upon the death of the occupant, the "next heir was immediately in the throne." This was not the case in elective kingdoms:

> *Indeed, in Poland when the king dies there is a vacancy, because there the law knows no certain successor: So that the difference is plain, that whenever the monachy is hereditary, upon the ceasing of him in possession, the throne is not vacant: where it is elective, 'tis vacant.*

The Earl of Pembroke, however, was willing to recognize an expediency to solve the problem. Explaining his position, he said, "We should make it a case of demise of our kings, as our law calls it; that is, the king is dead in law by this Abdication or Desertion of the government, and that the next heir is to take by descent."

On the question of the vacancy as well as on previous issues, Clarendon stated that it was the general belief among fair-minded men that the Jacobites had the most logical arguments. Disregarding the legal and philosophical case advanced by the supporters of James II, however, the Whigs and their Tory allies forged ahead to depose James and to elevate William and Mary to the English throne.

Throughout the interregnum the Jacobite political concepts had developed along a pattern that would preserve the continuity of the constitution. The bulk of their ideas that were advanced in the debates, public and official, were based on legal and constitutional precedents and on the opinion of the learned counselors of law rather than on the divine-right theories and practices of the early Stuart period, as has generally been assumed.

Henry Horwitz
THE ROLE PLAYED BY PARTIES IN THE REVOLUTION

Professor Henry Horwitz, born in New York in 1938, studied at Haverford College, served as a Fulbright Scholar, and received his doctorate at Oxford. Now a professor of history at the University of Iowa, he is becoming noted as an expert on the politics of the Revolution era.

For the past four decades, students of early modern English political history—under the spell of the late Sir Lewis Namier's analyses of mid-eighteenth-century politics—have been engaged less with narrating and explicating the political *events* of this period and more with investigating and reconstituting the very *structure* of politics.

From Henry Horwitz, "The Structure of Parliamentary Politics," in *Britain after the Glorious Revolution, 1689–1714,* edited by Geoffrey Holmes (London, 1969). Reprinted by permission of Macmillan, London and Basingstoke; and St. Martin's Press.

Traditional assumptions have been thrust aside, new interpretations asserted, and in turn the work of the "Namierite" revisionists has itself been called into question. And perhaps nowhere, outside the mid-eighteenth century, has there been more controversy or confusion over the character of politics and the nature of political divisions than in the days of King William and Queen Anne, at least since the appearance in 1956 of Robert Walcott's major venture in revision, *English Politics in the Early Eighteenth Century.* The object of this essay, then, is twofold: first, to review the background, course and current state of this debate over the structure of politics in the post-Revolution years; and second, to grapple with the chief issue in dispute—the question of whether politics at Westminster during this period was carried on within a two-party or a multi-party framework.

The view that parliamentary politics between 1689 and 1714 revolved around the conflict of the Whig and Tory parties is deeply rooted in the historiography of this period. And in the years just before and immediately after the publication in 1929 of Namier's *The Structure of Politics at the Accession of George III,* this interpretation was given renewed and most knowledgeable statement in W. T. Morgan's *English Political Parties and Leaders in the Reign of Queen Anne* (1920), K. Feiling's *History of the Tory Party* (1924) and G. M. Trevelyan's *England under Queen Anne* (1930–1934). Yet each of these scholars, while giving pride of place to the Whig-Tory struggle, also drew attention to other elements on the political scene which tended to divert and sometimes even to blunt the thrust of party— the important part played by the monarch (not only Wiliam, but even Anne), the continuing role of the Court and the placemen as a third force within the Houses, and (as Feiling particularly stressed) the persistence after 1689 of the older conflict between Court and Country. Moreover they recognized the existence, at times, of substantial divisions within the two parties, while Feiling—dealing with the entire period—also emphasized the significance of the partisan realignment of the 1690s.

The 1920s and early 1930s, then, saw the formulation of some important modifications to the two-party interpretation as expounded by the "Whig" historians of the nineteenth century, but in the event these proved to be only the preliminaries to Walcott's frontal assault. As early as 1941, Walcott—taking aim particularly against Trevelyan's earlier works and the tradition they epitomized—advanced the argument that "the description of party organization under William and Anne which Trevelyan suggested in his Romanes Lecture [of 1926] on the two-party system is less applicable to our period than the detailed picture of eighteenth-century politics which emerges from Professor Namier's volumes on the age of Newcastle." Walcott's invocation of Namier's studies was, indeed, a notable testimony to the growing influence of the methods of structural analysis and collective biography—with their concentration on the personal background, electoral circumstances and political record of every individual M.P. —that Sir Lewis had so skillfully exploited. And in his full-dress work of reinterpretation of 1956, Walcott once again acknowledged the inspiration of Namier's researches.

However, as one reviews Walcott's contributions to the study of the political history of William's and Anne's reigns, it becomes evident that his indebtedness to Sir Lewis extended beyond the approach he adopted to the substantive conclusions at which he arrived. As W. R. Fryer rightly observed, Walcott's "view might be summed up as the interpretation of Sir Lewis Namier, extended backwards to this earlier period." Above all, just as Sir Lewis had maintained that "the political life" of the mid-eighteenth century "could be fully described without ever using a party denomination," so Walcott denied the validity of a two-party interpretation of post-Revolution politics, whether in its traditional form or in the modified versions of Morgan, Feiling and Trevelyan.

Walcott based this contention on two main grounds: (1) the voting behavior of M.P.s during the period as a whole; and (2) the parliamentary alignments of a single session. On the one hand, in surveying the twelve division lists from these years of which he knew, Walcott asserted that a substantial proportion of members did not vote as consistent Whigs or Tories. As he put it, "on each of these issues there was theoretically a 'Whig' and a 'Tory' position, and Members should have voted consistently on one side or the other time after time. Unfortunately, the lists do not square with this theory. The 'Tory' side in any one division inevitably includes many who at other times voted 'Whig' and vice versa." On the other hand, in a detailed examination of the parliamentary session of 1707–1708 Walcott laid bare this sort of inconsistency in the behavior of the supposedly united Whig and Tory parties. On some questions he found Whigs and Tories outside the ministry combining to oppose the administration, while at the same time he discovered the head of the ministry, Godolphin, mustering a body of "Lord Treasurer's Whigs" in his efforts to push through the government's measures. Moreover, in tracing the outcome of this bitterly fought session and the General Election which followed in the summer of 1708, Walcott suggested that the eventual outcome was not the formation of a strictly Whig ministry, as some of his predecessors had supposed. Rather, the ministerial changes of 1708 were, at least at first, made in favor of the "Lord Treasurer's Whigs." Thus, in Walcott's view, the evidence about group alignments and individual voting in Parliament could hardly be fitted within the confines of a two-party framework; instead, it revealed the need to formulate a new interpretation which would consort better with the facts of political behavior.

When Walcott turned from the work of destruction to the task of reconstruction he again followed closely in Namier's footsteps. For one thing, he suggested that the really important distinction among M.P.s of this period was not that of party, but that of "type," and that the three leading types of members were essentially the same as those of the mid-eighteenth century—the courtiers and placemen, the "politicians" under their various leaders, and the independent country gentlemen. Furthermore, Walcott maintained that the chief form of organization among the politicians (the most numerous type of member) was, as in the 1760s, the connection—linked together by ties of kinship, neighborhood, dependency and interest. He then went on to isolate each of these connections and to identify their members in the Parliament of 1701–1702, basing his findings on electoral, biographical and genealogical data. Altogether he reckoned there were seven such connections, which, though they might at times merge into two opposed bodies, nonetheless preserved their separate identities and often acted independently in pursuit of their principal goal—the attainment and enjoyment of office. Hence, while some of these connections could be considered "Whig" and others "Tory" in outlook, they neither constituted two united parties nor did they consistently act in accord with their supposed political principles.

In any case, these connections did not act in isolation, for though together they comprised the largest single segment of the Commons (an average of 218 in the Houses of 1701–1702, 1702–1705 and 1705–1708), the "organized" government interest along with other courtiers and placemen numbered 142 members and the country gentlemen 146 members on average in these three Parliaments. Walcott maintained that the courtiers and placemen supported the ministry in power almost automatically, while the more active segment of the country gentlemen opposed the current administration with almost equal consistency, regardless of either their own or the ministers' party labels. In fact, these two types of M.P.s might be said to personify the persistence of the old Court–Country split.

Walcott's reconstitution of the structure of parliamentary politics between 1689 and 1714 might, then, be summed up in the following fashion. While on such great issues as the Church and the succession there was a Whig and a Tory position in the country at large, within the Houses were to be found a series of shifting alignments between the rival political connections on one hand and the court and country elements on the other, instead of two united parties in conflict with one another. Each administration was made up of a combination of courtiers and members of one or more of the connections; each opposition was similarly composed of a combination of country gentlemen and members of those connections not in office. Thus, in place of a two-party interpretation Walcott advanced a multi-party one, with the various connections and unorganized elements within Parliament being ranged schematically around the perimeter of a circle on which Court and Country figured as the north and south "coordinates" with Whig and Tory as the east and west "coordinates"; it is then possible "to read the roster of party groups as though we were boxing the compass: courtiers, Court Tories, Churchill Tories, Harley Tories, Rochester Tories, Nottingham Tories, October Club Tories, Country Tories, Country Members, Country Whigs, Junto Whigs, Walpole-Townshend Whigs, Court Whigs, and so back to the Courtiers."

When Walcott's arguments were first rehearsed in print in 1941 they attracted only brief notice. But by the time his book appeared in 1956 they had gained wide currency, so much so that one reviewer could remark that his main findings "have generally been accepted." On the whole this work—in which Walcott's earlier hypotheses were now advanced in more definitive form—was well received by students of the eighteenth century. Not all were as enthusiastic as J. W. Wilkes, who proclaimed that "the vast and erroneous generalizations about eighteenth-century political life in England, begun by the Whig historians of the nineteenth century, have suffered yet another blow." Yet many were prepared to cite his conclusions without demur, whether in their reviews or in their own writings.

From the outset, however, other scholars—and particularly specialists in the 1689–1714 period—were more dubious about their validity. While ready to acknowledge the extent of Walcott's labors, they were also quick to observe that "studies such as [this] cannot tell us all we need to know, if we are to understand English politics." What is more, their reservations about Walcott's findings and his methods were confirmed and extended as the results of other researchers' explorations in the newly-accessible wealth of manuscript materials for this period began to appear in articles and dissertations in the early and mid-1960s. And even more recently, the "Walcott interpretation" has suffered new setbacks from J. H. Plumb in his suggestive survey of English political developments from 1675 to 1725 and from Geoffrey Holmes in his detailed analysis of politics in Anne's reign.

The grounds of the reservations and criticisms voiced by these scholars might be summed up under two principal heads: (1) evidence and methodology; and (2) specific conclusions. First of all, some of Walcott's examples and certain of his procedures have been sharply challenged. On the one hand, it has been observed that in choosing to focus on the 1707–1708 session he selected a most unusual example, for the conjunction of "high Whig" and "high Tory" during the early months of that session astonished contemporaries, while the session as a whole was certainly the most chaotic of Anne's reign. On the other hand, his method of isolating the political connections and identifying their members has come under heavy fire for loose use of what electoral and parliamentary data he did invoke and especially for his heavy reliance on genealogical evidence. It has been calculated that of the 212 M.P.s whom he placed in one or other of the connections in the 1701–1702 Commons, no less than 96 were so allocated seemingly on the sole basis of kinship.

Now, to be sure, Walcott did recognize that almost any two aristocratic families of the period will be found to be related; nonetheless, his efforts to demonstrate the political significance of the family groups which he did identify as the bases of his seven political connections are strewn with pitfalls. Take, for instance, the case of the "Finch connection" headed by the second earl of Nottingham and chiefly composed, on Walcott's reckoning, of the nominees and clients of that earl's noble kinsmen. Walcott, it is true, did not include all Nottingham's relations and their associates in this group, but only those who seemed to take the same general political stand in Parliament as did the Tory earl himself. But even after removing some of the potential members of this connection because of evidence about their political behavior, to suppose that the residue constituted an effective parliamentary grouping can be very misleading. Indeed, a closer look at the available evidence reveals that some of Nottingham's *Tory* kinsmen were estranged from him by personal enmities, that others had no personal dealings with him, that some of the supposed nominees of his titled relations were not chiefly dependent on those kinsmen for their elections, and that others allocated to his connection were in practice more closely associated with such political leaders as Rochester. Nor is the Finch connection the only instance in which Walcott's procedures appear to have led him astray; similar strictures have been levelled against the construction of his "Newcastle–Pelham–Townshend–Walpole" and "Hyde–Granville–Gower–Seymour" connections. In short, as W. A. Speck has put it, "the slender branches of the family trees, so carefully cultivated by Walcott, will not bear the weight of the political fruit which he seeks to graft upon them."

Secondly, Walcott's critics have contended that his atypical "examples" and faulty use of Namierite techniques have skewed his conclusions in several vital respects. For one thing, it has been suggested that the connections must be conceived in broader terms than those in which he presented them. In particular, it would appear that they attracted into their orbits not merely the professional politicians per se, but also other M.P.s including many country gentlemen who, if not ambitious for office, were wont to follow the lead of men such as Rochester or Nottingham, Harley or the Junto. For another, it has been argued that political attitudes and issues had a considerable impact on parliamentary alignments. Many of the political leaders of the day were bent on gaining office not merely for its material rewards, but mainly for the influence which it offered, and great politicians such as Rochester and Wharton did refuse, or resign from, office when they felt their views would not carry due weight in the royal councils. Similarly their followers were linked to them not simply by ties of family, proximity, dependency and interest, but also (and in some cases chiefly) by the bonds generated by common convictions. The result was that many, perhaps even most, of a leading politician's adherents might refuse to stand by him should he appear to deviate from the policies or principles he had previously upheld: the Junto suffered many desertions when it backed a standing army in 1698–1699, while Nottingham's following almost melted away after he chose to oppose the peace in 1711–1712 in conjunction with the Whigs. Finally it has been maintained that Walcott's concentration on the rather unusual alignments of the 1707–1708 session, coupled with his distortion of the composition and character of the followings of the chief political leaders, has obscured the ample evidence for the subsumption of these groupings under the two parties, Whig and Tory, and for the magnetic attraction and repulsion of intra-party loyalties and inter-party differences.

For the most part Walcott has suffered these and other criticisms in silence, but in 1962, he did briefly and obliquely respond to his early challengers. There were, he agreed, a few controversial issues which stirred M.P.s during these years, but after making this concession he went on to reiterate his main conclusion: "within the walls of Parliament as it concerned itself with the day-to-day work of government in the intervals between controversy over some great issues (most of them religious), the apparent division into two national parties dissolves into the multi-party structure normally associated only with the reign of George III."

But despite Walcott's restatement, the discovery of new division lists for the period has thrown further doubt on his analysis by suggesting that the broad division between Whigs and Tories in the country as a whole "was carried over in Parliament" not only on religious questions, but also on those "which involved no principle" —questions such as the vote on Harley's South Sea scheme in May 1711 or the contest for the Speakership in November 1705. Neither of these votes involved a direct clash of ideas, but rather opposition to or support of the current administration. Yet what is striking about the voting behavior of the individual members, as recorded on these lists and correlated with other extant ones, is "the small number whose voting habits were irregular" and the "considerable number of members who voted consistently along party lines."

*   *   *

Here we cannot provide an account in full of the shift in the pattern of parliamentary alignments between 1689 and 1702, but a bare outline of the main developments may be briefly sketched. To begin with, we should note that despite the general revulsion against James's rule which the Revolution revealed, the Convention Parliament was soon riven by the pre-Revolution division between Whig and Tory over such questions as Protestant dissenters' political privileges, the treatment of James's servants and collaborators, and the regulation of municipal corporations. Furthermore, the General Election of 1690 saw bitter partisan conflict as Whigs and Tories sought to besmirch each other's reputations with the publication of "black lists" of M.P.s who had opposed the crowning of William and Mary or supported the purge of the corporations proposed under the "Sacheverell clause."

But though the rancor of the election campaign was carried over into the first session of the 1690–1695 Parliament, especially in the struggle over the terms of the Act of Recognition, by the autumn of 1691 Williams' preference for mixed administrations and the effects of the costly and largely unsuccessful war effort were combining to confound the partisan division and to accentuate Court-Country differences. As Robert Harley (destined with his kinsman Paul Foley to become the leader of the so-called "New Country party") wrote to his father early in the 1691–1692 session: "the House seems in a very strange temper and which way the parties will determine is very difficult to say, but at present very much intermixed and jumbled together." Thus, during the remaining sessions of this Parliament, party questions, such as abjuration bills and attacks first on Tory and then on Whig ministers, jostled uneasily with Court–Country questions, such as Place bills, treason trial bills and triennial measures. Moreover, though William reluctantly but gradually reconstructed his administration between 1693 and 1695 by removing Tories from positions of influence and replacing them with members or adherents of the emerging Whig Junto, at the same time the New Country party —a fusion of "old" or "true" Whigs such as Foley and Harley with pre-Revolution courtiers such as Sir Christopher Musgrave—gained strength in the Commons.

Nor did the General Election of the autumn of 1695 reverse the trend in favor of anti-Court measures and men, and in the opening months of the 1695–1696 session the New Country party, with Tory backing, appeared to be on the verge of toppling the Junto. Even the great ministerial undertaker, the earl of Sunderland, seemed to be ready to throw his support to Foley and Harley. But the sudden disclosure of the assassination plot against William late in February 1696 gave the initiative back to the Junto, and they quickly capitalized on this windfall by reviving the issue of loyalty to the Revolution regime as a partisan question both with the Association and with the bill of attainder against Sir John Fenwick. The upshot was that the second half of the 1695–1696 session and also the 1696–1697 session saw a reversion to a partisan axis in alignments within the Commons, while the Junto's hold on office was consolidated.

However, the conclusion of peace with France in the autumn of 1697 was the signal for the reopening of the Court–Country breach, and the General Election of the summer of 1698 was fought along those lines. As Lord Somers dolefully observed to the duke of Shrewsbury in the autumn of 1698, "the elections were made on an ill foot; uneasiness at taxes, and the most dangerous division of a Court and Country party; so that there is reason to doubt of the behavior of many of your best friends." And Somers's gloomy prognostications proved only too accurate, for the two sessions of the 1698–1700 Parliament saw the New Country party, in conjunction with the Tories, in command of the Commons and the members of the Junto forced or edged out of office.

In turn, the General Election of the winter of 1700–1701 was followed by new successes for the increasingly close alliance between Harley and the old Tory leaders during the spring session of 1701— especially the passage of the constitutional provisos of the Act of Settlement with their strictures against placemen, secret councils and foreigners. On the one hand, then, the 1701 Parliament saw the virtual completion of the transit from Whig to Tory ranks that Harley and other "old" Whigs had begun in the early 1690s. And on the other, the old Tory or "Church" party (with its bias in favor of royal prerogative) had by this time been no little transformed by the infusion of new blood and the adoption of a marked Country bias. As the author of an outspoken Whig pamphlet wrote after the close of the 1701 session:

> *The Tory Party, as they affect to be called, is that part of the House of Commons which has governed this session. . . . If we consider the men, and compare what they have done with the pretended principles of their party, 'twill hardly seem odder to see Sir Edward Seymour bring in a bill to prevent bribery, or Mr John How exclaim against exorbitant grants, or Sir Christopher Musgrave violent either against grants, or a standing army . . . than to see them assume the name of Tories. Is not Robert Harley a ringleader in this Tory party? . . . Does he not attend all Ordinances, and as constantly every weekday frequent the service of the Church (for his is a Church-party) in St Stephen's Chapel, as he does the Conventicle every Lord's day? Are not the Foleys, Winningtons, St John, Harvey of Weymouth, Barnardiston, Hammond, Randyl, and others of that leaven, members of this fraternity?*

Yet the reconstitution of the Tories, coupled with their vindictive attacks on the Junto lords, their slowness in taking strong measures against the revived French threat on the continent and at sea, and their lukewarm adherence to the Protestant successor, also set the stage for the revival of Junto fortunes and the orientation, once more, of the Commons on a Whig–Tory axis. The General Election of December 1701 was chiefly fought as a party struggle, and the last Parliament of William's reign—with the conflict over Whig proposals for a voluntary abjuration of James III coupled with Tory attempts to resurrect the impeachments of the preceding Parliament —was dominated by party rivalry. Thus, despite the shifting and often confused alignments of the 1690s, the chief parliamentary groupings in the final year of William's reign were—as they had been in its earliest years—Whig and Tory, though in the interval the Whigs had lost the Harleys and their associates to the Tories. By the spring of 1702, then, there had emerged a pattern of parliamentary politics which, despite occasional intra-party fissures and temporary relapses into a Court–Country division, was to continue to prevail throughout Anne's reign.

As we look back from the vantage point of the late 1960s upon the recent debate over the structure of parliamentary politics between 1689 and 1714, two final notes might be briefly recorded. Firstly, it is evident that Walcott's revisionist interpretation has not succeeded in holding the field. Rather, the findings of more recent studies would seem to suggest that the differences between the politics of the post-Revolution years and those of the mid-eighteenth century are greater than their similarities. But secondly, it would be mistaken to assume that the scholarly activity of the last decade, sparked in no small part by Walcott's provocative conclusions and "Namierite" methods, has resulted in a mere recasting of older accounts. For one thing, despite their disagreements with many of Walcott's conclusions, most political historians of the period have accepted the utility of Namier's techniques, when carefully applied and used in conjunction with traditional approaches. Current research, then, is based on the application of a variety of modes of analysis to a far wider range of sources than was used or available in the past. Furthermore, though by no means all the results are in as yet, already a good deal of illumination has been cast on hitherto dimly lit corners of post-Revolution politics. And, above all, it is now possible to conclude, with greater certainty yet with more subtle shadings than ever before, that the clash of the Whig and Tory parties was the prime, though not always the prevailing, element in the complicated and sometimes very fluid structure of parliamentary politics between 1689 and 1714. In sum, we may at last have reached the stage where knowledge of the structure of parliamentary politics has been sufficiently clarified for political historians to feel free to take up once again the work of narrating the course of politics in the days of King William and Queen Anne.

Robert Walcott, Jr.
THE REVOLUTION AND UNREFORMED FACTION

Professor Robert Walcott, Jr., born in Boston in 1910, studied at Harvard and in England. He settled at the College of Wooster in Ohio in 1946 where he is now a professor of history, a specialist in the late Stuart era. His excellent work in political history is matched by his research in economic and bibliographical studies.

The accepted traditions about political parties and their constitutional function are so common even in the latest histories that one hardly need multiply examples. In a well-known one-volume history of England, often used as a text, one reads that the work of the Revolution of 1688 "was inevitably to transfer the executive power from the control of the Crown to that of a party." Trevelyan in his one-volume treatment of the Stuart period tells us that after 1688 the "rule of England by the contests of the two parties now began in earnest"; while the author of another interpretation of the same period writes that "Anne's reign owes its importance largely to the fact that it was the age of apprenticeship for English parties." "Her reign is remembered for the first appearance of complete party government," and "the failure of the coalitions in 1705 and 1711 proved that party government was inevitable."

This is the orthodox view; now for recent heresy. First, from a fairly recent study of politics in the later years of George III: "Practically all the evidence points to the conclusion that neither the framers of the Revolution Settlement nor the first three rulers after 1689—William, Mary, and Anne—anticipated the constitutional developments of the next three quarters of a century." "Neither the two-party system nor the cabinet solidarity and joint responsibility of the nineteenth century was dreamed of in 1689." The parent of this heresy, Professor Namier, confines his generalizations to the second half of the eighteenth century. Between the politics of that period and those of the present day, he tells us, "there is more resemblance in outer forms and denominations than in underlying

Reprinted by permission of the publishers from pp. 2–6, 71–73, 75–82, 91–95 of Robert Walcott, Jr., *English Politics in the Early Eighteenth Century* (Cambridge, Mass.: Harvard University Press, 1956). Footnotes omitted.

realities, so that misconception is very easy. There were no proper party organizations about 1760, though party names and cant were current; the names and the cant have since supplied the materials for an imaginary superstructure." He concludes that "the political life of the period could be fully described without ever using a party denomination."

Namier's conclusions are based on meticulous study of the political correspondence of that period and are now generally accepted—at least for the 1760s and 1770s. Professor Barnes has shown that they hold for the later years of George III's reign; but no one has made a comparable analysis for the early years of the century. Can the political life of that period be fully described without ever using a party denomination? Are the underlying realities of its politics disguised beneath an imaginary party superstructure?

Any generalizations about the actual workings of the English constitution in the early eighteenth century must be based on accurate information about a number of interrelated questions. Into how many parties was the legislature actually divided? How were these parties organized, and who led them? If a careful analysis reveals not two parties but numerous party groups, if it shows that the ministries of this period were inevitably coalitions of several party groups and that there are no examples of a single party in office faced by a single opposition party, then surely the traditional interpretation of how the constitution worked in this period needs revising. If the legislature was divided into a number of party groups, and if the largest and best organized of these groups was made up of officials and dependants of the court, then the position of the sovereign and his chosen advisers must have been rather different from that generally assumed.

With a bloc of regular government supporters in the Commons the executive would be far less amenable to pressure from the party leaders. Moreover, if the nongovernment Members were divided at all evenly into Whig and Tory segments, the chief ministers might well hold the balance between them. According to several authorities Marlborough and Godolphin were in precisely such a position during the first six years of Anne's reign. However, should analysis show that the Whig and Tory segments were themselves divided into divergent groups each under individual leadership, the traditional picture would prove badly out of focus.

Any disunity within either the Whig or Tory camp, any personal or political differences between individual party leaders would further strengthen the executive. Instead of being forced to choose between a set of Whig masters or of Tory ones, the executive could select allies from a wide variety of party groups. With a substantial nucleus of government Members comparatively few additional votes would be required for a working majority in the Commons. When it came to bargaining for these votes, the executive would be in a stronger position than the party leaders. It alone had places to give; the party leaders, until given office, had only the votes of themselves and their immediate followers with which to barter. Should analysis show that no individual leader could be sure of more than a score of reliable followers, and that no combination of leaders could hold together their combined following for long in the face of disagreements among themselves and defections to the court, the generalizations so often made about the early eighteenth-century constitution would no longer be tenable.

If neither the Whigs nor the Tories were effectively organized as national parties, there could hardly have been a "two-party system" in the usual sense. Without two well-organized parties there could have been little progress towards a cabinet system as generally understood. Instead of the majority party in the lower chamber of the legislature controlling the executive, the executive could conceivably control instead the legislature—through its bloc of government Members reinforced by additional votes lent by individual party chiefs in return for a share of office and a subordinate voice in the determination of policy.

Which of the two—the traditional picture of early eighteenth-century government with two parties contesting for power; or the alternative view sketched above—comes closer to describing how politics actually worked in Queen Anne's reign ought to be decided on the basis of such evidence as is available and pertinent. This should include detailed data on the electoral system, on the composition of the House of Commons, on party organization, and on individual party members. The last point is important. The more we know about individuals, the better we can understand the actual workings of politics; and in this connection it should be pointed out that the material presented on individuals in this essay represents the distillation of every scrap of biographical data on some 1,200 Members of Parliament that could be collected over a period of some fifteen years.

*   *   *

The history of party in the thirty years before the accession of Anne is extremely complex—more so than most authorities on the period seem to realize, except for Feiling; and he tends to force the details of party history, which he knows thoroughly, into the two-party pattern, although with considerable difficulty. Feiling assumes that the reign of Charles II saw the creation of the two historic parties, and in this assumption he is joined by most historians. Given this point of departure, most of the literature on party history is concerned with origins, with attempts to determine at what date the two parties were born and what the relationship of these parties was to the political divisions which separated the English people in preceding and subsequent periods. Most historians now seem agreed that a Whig and a Tory party were both organized on a national basis in the late 1670s, that they were descended from the Roundhead and Cavalier parties of the Civil War respectively, and that they have persisted with little fundamental change of identity down almost to the present day.

Regardless of the accuracy of this view (and we do not intend to challenge it at this stage) its general acceptance has so colored party history that it has become almost impossible to discuss any political figure or group without assigning them a place in one or the other of the two historic parties. This, however, is exactly what we intend to do. By dealing with each of the political groups described in the last chapter as though it were an individual we shall try to discover its politics not in terms of Whig or Tory, but with respect to its position towards the king's government and the stand which it took in parliament and out on the more important issues of the day.

To small groups, such as we have analyzed above, it is perfectly feasible to assign "ages." They will be relative, of course, and somewhat arbitrary (being a composite of the ages and political experience of the leaders and principal lieutenants of each group); but data on the seniority of party leaders and most of their followers as of 1700 are available and indicate marked differences in the "ages" of the various groups—differences which are significant and which at the same time simplify our problem.

It appears at once that the various political connections range in age from the Hyde and Seymour groups, with leaders in their late sixties and henchmen who had entered politics in the days of Charles II's "Pensioners' Parliament," to the Townshend–Walpole connection, whose leaders were not even born until some fourteen years after Rochester, Seymour, and Musgrave first entered the Commons. In between come the Marlborough–Godolphin group, most of them in their fifties; the Finch connection, of whom Nottingham and his brother were in their fifties while most of their followers were younger; the Junto group, all of them except Wharton in their thirties or forties; and the Harley interest, of whom Harley, the eldest, was still in his thirties.

When arranged on the basis of age the party groups clearly fall into two classes: those which played an active role under Charles II and James II; and those which at the time of the Glorious Revolution were comparative newcomers to politics. The Hyde–Seymour, Marlborough–Godolphin, and Finch connections clearly belong in the first classification; while the others belong as clearly in the second. Only in the case of the three "older" connections need we go back much beyond the year 1688. . . .

The Revolution of 1688 was the most important issue in English politics in the years between the Exclusion controversy and the accession of Anne. One might expect to find the various "Tory" groups at least as united in opposing the deposition of a king as they had been in opposing Exclusion; but this was not the case. Of the "older" party groups all but one joined in the Revolution instead of opposing it. It will be worth our while to trace briefly the policy of each of the groups during the crisis of 1687–1688 in search of further illustration of the functioning of party groups in an actual situation.

Danby's following was the first to belie traditional "Tory" reverence for royalty and engage in sedition. Among the seven signers of the famous July 1688 "Invitation" to William of Orange, requesting his presence in England, were three Danbyites: Danby himself; his cousin Henry Compton, Bishop of London; and a connection, Lord Lumley. The idea of the invitation was hatched a year and a half earlier at an interesting meeting in January 1687 at the house of Lord Shrewsbury, kinsman, ward, and at that time political disciple, of Halifax. There were present: Halifax, Shrewsbury, and Nottingham —of the "Trimmers"; Danby—of the "Courtiers"; and Edward Russell, the future Lord Orford, and Mordaunt, Wharton's cousin—both with Junto connections. Soon after this meeting Shrewsbury and Russell went to Holland, reporting back that the Prince of Orange would come to England if invited by a group of sufficiently important English leaders.

Within the next year the conspirators lost the support of the Halifax–Finch connection, Shrewsbury excepted; so that the Danbyites were the only group actively engaged in the project prior to William's landing. Seymour, because of his close association with Danby, was early let into the secret, but he remained neutral until some time after the prince's landing at Torbay. His friend Danby, however, was not only one of the original signers of the Invitation; his early and successful raising of the North for William of Orange was one of the most important military actions taken by any party leader during the crisis.

Danby's action was in contrast to that of his rival Halifax. The great "Trimmer," together with Nottingham and their cousin Weymouth, was among the first to oppose the illegalities of James II; but the Halifax–Finch connection avoided any course that could be called treasonable, remaining loyal in deed, if not in heart, to the king—at least until after his second flight from the realm. The policy of the Hydes, the Granvilles, and the Seymours was less forthright, vacillating between Danby's bold treason and the strict neutrality of Halifax and the Finches. Clarendon and Rochester themselves refused to recognize the "usurper" William—Clarendon for the rest of his life; Rochester, until after the Revolution was an accomplished fact—but a number of their kinsmen and henchmen were among the first to come into the prince's camp at Exeter. Seymour likewise took the plunge at this stage. He and his followers were the first important West Country group to "come over to the prince."

The Marlborough–Godolphin connection, last of the "older" groups to be considered, played perhaps as decisive a role in the deposition of James as any other group. The superbly timed defection of Marlborough with his regiment and those of his officer friends on the eve of battle forced upon the king the realization that resistance would be hopeless and thus ensured the "bloodless" nature of the Revolution. The defection of Lady Marlborough was possibly just as decisive. She was responsible for persuading the Princess Anne to forsake her father and take refuge in Danby's north country, accompanied not only by the countess, but also by Danby's kinsman, the Bishop of London. Contemporaries considered the princess's desertion the final blow that led her father to abandon his kingdom.

Thus it was only the Halifax–Finch connection and the more responsible leaders of the Hyde connection who remained loyal to the *de jure* government of James during the prince's halt at Exeter. During this period the two groups had almost a fortnight in which to frame a common policy; but cooperation between the two proved impossible, and "ten precious days were lost by a sharp difference between the two wings." Halifax, Nottingham, and Weymouth refused to work with the Hydes, who had connived in some of the illegal policies of the king.

There was no common Tory policy, then, during the Revolution of 1688; and there is some question whether there is any point in speaking of "the Tory party" at this time. It remains to be seen whether a united Tory party developed after the Revolution; but first we must enlarge our field to take in the activities of one of the "younger" party groups, the Junto, most of whom first appeared on the political scene during the crisis of 1687–1688.

Just as Danby is usually considered the founder of a long-lived united Tory party, so Shaftesbury has been recognized as "the principal founder of that great party which, in opposition to the prerogative and uniformity, has inscribed upon its banner poltical freedom and religious toleration"—in other words a lasting and united Whig party. Undoubtedly Shaftesbury did contribute important elements to later "Whiggism": the idea of political alliance between a section of the aristocracy and the Nonconformist trading element, and the germ of a political philosophy later given classic and lasting definition by the earl's friend, John Locke; but of the actual parliamentary coalition organized and led by Shaftesbury in the 1670s little remained by 1700.

At its height in 1679 that coalition apparently numbered about thirty peers and sixty Members of the Commons, but many of these were aging veterans of Civil War politics. Of the peers all but three were dead by 1688; and while a number of the younger men in the Commons were still active at the time of the Glorious Revolution, very few of these had owed their seats of their primary allegiance to Shaftesbury himself. The Country party of Shaftesbury, like Danby's Court party, was not a unified party, but included a number of distinct elements. The inner core, Shaftesbury's personal followers in the Lords and Commons, was small—probably only a dozen or so. Far larger was the group, less closely identified with Shaftesbury, which can most conveniently be described as the Sidney–Capel–Howard connection—an extraordinarily extensive family alliance which included many of the titled houses which at one time or another sided with Parliament during the Civil War and which in the 1670s numbered at least a dozen in the House of Lords and probably twice that number in the Commons. Three leaders of this group did allow themselves to be drawn into the extremist plots of 1681 and died as "Whig martyrs," but the group as a whole stood to the right of Shaftesbury and did not follow him into the Duke of Monmouth's fatal undertaking.

The third element of Shaftesbury's coalition were the rake-hells: Thomas Wharton, heir to the Puritan lord and a future Junto leader; and five or six young nobles of similar dissolute habits. There was finally a lunatic fringe: Wildman and Ferguson "the Plotter," and young Hampden, among others. Some of this last group had personal ties with Wharton and his cronies, who in turn had ties with Lord Cavendish and Lord Wiltshire of the Capel–Sidney–Howard connection. This made it easy for Court spokesmen to stigmatize the entire Country coalition as "phanaticks" and "Commonwealth men"; but actually very few men from the Country groups followed Shaftesbury into treason, the great majority hoping instead for a new day under an Orange dispensation.

By 1687 Shaftesbury was dead; most of his following had deserted him, had died, or had dropped out of sight; and only a fraction of the old Country coalition participated in the Revolution of 1688. Some Country veterans did, but alongside them appeared a group of younger men: Edward Russell, John Somers, and Charles Montagu, among others. These new recruits joined forces with Wharton, Lord Wiltshire (later Duke of Bolton), and one or two older members of the Russell family, to form what was essentially a distinct new group—easily recognizable as the Junto connection of 1700.

This group was obviously active in the Revolution. Lord Wiltshire and Wharton's cousin Mordaunt were among the first Englishmen to join William in Holland. So was Edward Russell, and he and his kinsman Lord Cavendish were signers of the Invitation. Later the group acted as though they had brought in William and Mary with no help from the Tory groups; and the impression that the Revolution was "a Whig affair" and that William III was "the Whigs' king" gained strength from the fact that within a year of James II's forced "abdication" the various Tory groups were doing their best to disavow the revolution they had done so much to bring about. Virtually all the party groups had agreed that James must go and had helped him on his way. They were agreed, also, in accepting the Prince of Orange as *de facto* ruler for the time being; but how to settle the government on satisfactory new legal foundations was a problem on which they violently disagreed.

The issue did little to divide the Country groups, who argued that William and Mary should now be declared king and queen by parliamentary right, James having forfeited the crown by subverting the original contract between sovereign and people. The older Tory groups were united in opposition to any such "commonwealth" theory of contract, and they voted together against a Country-inspired declaration that the throne was "vacant," with its implication that parliament was free to fill the throne as it saw fit. To declare the throne vacant was to transgress the sacred principle of indefeasible hereditary right; but how to remain loyal to this principle and yet place the government where nearly everybody agreed it must be put —in the hands of the Prince and Princes of Orange—was a problem for which the older party groups had different answers.

The solution offered by Danby and his party rested upon the fiction that James II was legally "demised," with the additional assumption that the throne had thereby devolved not upon James's Catholic son, but upon the Princess Mary, presumed his rightful heir. This strained interpretation of plain fact was too much for the Finches to swallow. To them James was still legally king; and while the Princess and Prince of Orange must in practice rule for him, it must be as regents. This solution became the favorite of the Churchmen and was ultimately supported by all the older party groups except the Danbyites and Lord Halifax, who on this point parted company with the Finches and even his own children.

When the regency proposal came before the Lords for a vote, it was defeated by two voices, Halifax and Danby both voting against it. The regency advocates then joined forces with the Danbyites in an attempt to declare the Princess Mary sovereign in her own right; but they were unable to win over either Mary herself—who refused to reign without her husband as co-ruler—or a majority of the Commons. There followed a week-long deadlock, broken finally when nearly all the groups concurred in the famous "vacancy declaration." This combined a complete absence of logic with a fine practicality—gratifying each group in turn with a reference to its favorite constitutional premiss—and concluded by vesting the government in William and Mary jointly as king and queen of England.

The debates in the Convention mark an epoch in party history. If ever there had been a united Tory party, it disintegrated under the stresses of the years 1688–1689. "The change in the Tory party," writes Feiling, "was so great as to destroy its inner coherence." Certainly there was little evidence of Tory unity during most of William III's reign, to which we now turn.

*   *   *

What general conclusions can we draw from this analysis of the politics of the party groups in the period down to Anne's accession? First, we can probably accept the traditional interpretation of party politics to this extent: if the party groups are considered as forming a continuum, ranging from a republican Nonconformist Left to a royalist Anglican Right, the older party groups will in general fall to the right, the younger party groups to the left of some undetermined centerline. At any rate this would seem to be the case during such periods of political stress as the Exclusion controversy, the attempted Stuart counter-revolution, and the Revolution of 1688.

Can we go farther? Can we assume that, because there was a position later called "Whig," and one later called "Tory," in each of these crises, and because certain long-lived Members of both Houses took one of these positions in all three crises, therefore there must have been a united Whig and a united Tory party? We think not, mainly because such a thesis leaves too many factors out of account.

In the first place it dodges the important question of the "excluded middle." Certain leading Members can be classed as "either-or," as

FIGURE 4. "The Protestants' Joy" at the "Glorious Coronation of King William and Queen Mary": a woodcut from a popular English ballad-sheet, 1689. (*The Granger Collection*)

Whig or Tory on the basis of their voting record in a number of important divisions; but the more one studies the party history of the period, the more Procrustean such a procedure will seem. A number of party groups may have coalesced into a large entity under the pressure of some clear threat to the Church or the succession, but during the intervals between such periods of crisis the components of such coalitions were constantly dividing against each other. During these intervals the "either-or" analysis simply doesn't work: too many Members turn out to be neither consistently Whig nor consistently Tory. This was the situation under Charles II and again under James.

No doubt Feiling and others would say that such eccentric political behavior does not invalidate the two-party thesis, but is a natural consequence of the newness of the parties. Such dismissal of the inconsistencies shown by the various "wings" and "factions" becomes more difficult when one moves into the post-Revolution period. With the establishment of the New Country party by Harley and of its rival the reconstituted Whig party of the Junto, inconsistencies in party politics should practically disappear, when in actual fact they do not. Danbyite Tories refuse to cooperate with Seymour

Tories, and Country Whigs divide against Whigs of the Court. There are still "Courtiers" and "Country Members" in William's later parliaments; and "as late as 1702 it was commonly assumed that 'Court' and 'Country' were the normal divisions of politics."

The difficulty, it seems to us, lies in the inadequacy of the conceptual framework, the Left–Center–Right continuum used by Feiling and Trevelyan; for this concept, though apparently logical, is misleading. Members who do not vote regularly with the Left or Right are lumped in the Center, whereas in actuality they belong in two very different groups: those who have voted both "Whig" and "Tory" but usually *with* the court; and those who have voted both "Whig" and "Tory" but usually *against* the court. These irregulars need a more descriptive label than "Center," one to indicate their attitude towards the administration *qua* administration. In speaking of a Member—or of a group—we should indicate whether he is "Court" or "Country'" as well as whether he is "Tory" or "Whig."

In order to map the political position of the party groups, then, we need all four terms. "Whig" and "Tory" will be the "east" and "west" points; "Court" and "Country," the "north" and "south" points of our political compass. We can think of Parliament as a compass card than can be divided into a number of different segments, and in any one session we can expect to see it divided differently on different issues. Thus on a straight party issue like the contest between a Whig and a Tory for Speaker there will be an "east-west" division; but on a standard Country issue like a bill barring placemen from the House there will be a "north-south" division—Court against Country.

There will thus be four main segments: Whig, Tory, Country, and Court. In addition there will be subdivisions within each main segment: a nucleus of stalwarts (courtiers who always vote Court, and Whigs who always vote Whig), together with other groups—Court Tories, and Country Whigs, for example—which occupy an intermediate position. . . . If it will serve to explain some of the inconsistencies in the usual interpretation, if it will clear up some of the confusion in the party history of Anne's reign, we can accept [this conceptual framework] as a useful working hypothesis. Before examining the party history of Anne's reign, however, it might be useful to look first for significant changes in constitutional practice during the preceding reign.

In this connection the effects of the Revolution of 1688 seem commonly to have been exaggerated. The Bill of Rights did restrict the prerogative by specifically outlawing certain questionable devices used by William's Stuart predecessors and made it virtually impossible to upset the Anglican establishment so as to reintroduce Catholicism. Furthermore, the Revolution Settlement made it impracticable for the monarch to get along without frequent sessions of Parliament; but to say that the necessity for frequent meetings of Parliament "established the supremacy of the House of Commons over the king" is to jump to a conclusion not reached for a century.

The more one studies the history of the years just before and just after 1688, the more one is impressed by the absence of such a break in continuity as is usually assumed. William III had as high a view of the prerogative as the Stuarts and intended to rule like Charles II—selecting his own ministers, conducting his own foreign policy, and consulting Parliament only when it had to be called to grant funds. Ministers appointed by the king still believed it their duty to carry out the sovereign's wishes without respect to the party makeup of the House of Commons; and Parliament still seemed wedded to its traditional role of a permanent opposition. Sovereignty, as it had been ever since 1661, was still divided between executive and legislature.

The solution to the problem of divided authority—ministers responsible to the majority of the House of Commons, and the corollary, an organized majority party responsive to its leaders in office—lay far in the future. If some slight progress in this direction was registered during the decade after the Revolution, the financial exigencies of wartime were largely responsible. William experimented with ministries of every party hue: Old Country, Danbyite, Junto, New Country, and back to Junto; but gradually he and his advisers came to understand that a successful administration must include party leaders as well as "king's servants." The former were necessary to line up blocs of votes for government supply bills and against the inevitable Country insistence on redress of grievances at the expense of the government's program. The time had passed when the conduct of the king's business could be monopolized by courtiers with no parliamentary party behind them.

Court managers of this type could, of course, count on the bloc of "government Members" in the Commons; but that was never large enough to ensure a working majority; and alliance with some of the organized party groups was a necessity. Hence the government was always a coalition—built up, altered, demolished, and rebuilt, usually *between* elections. William finally saw the necessity of employing party leaders in order to gain the indispensable parliamentary reinforcements; but he did not feel bound constantly to change his ministries so as to bring them into conformity with the balance of parties in the Commons.

That every general election should be followed automatically by the appointment of an administration chosen from the party groups most successful in that election would have struck William III as absurd. . . .

J. H. Plumb
THE REVOLUTION AND THE EMERGENCE OF POLITICAL STABILITY

John Harold Plumb, professor of modern history at Cambridge University since 1966, was born in England in 1911. The rich variety of his works largely reflects his interest in eighteenth-century politics. His biography of Robert Walpole is perhaps his greatest achievement, though he has also published studies on exploration and the Italian renaissance.

In delivering these lectures I had two intentions: one was to attempt to clear up some of the confusion that has been growing in the political history of late seventeenth-century England, the second to reintroduce something that has proliferated in economic, but been at a severe discount in political history—namely a concept, in this case the growth of political stability.

The political historians who grew to maturity before the First World War—Stubbs, Lecky, Freeman, Maitland, Trevelyan, and many

From J. H. Plumb, *The Origins of Political Stability in England, 1675–1725,* also published in England under the title *The Growth of Political Stability in England, 1675–1725* (London, 1967), pp. xiii–xviii, 1–3, 19–23, 26–30, 60–69, 71–72, 126–131, 132–138, 157–158. Reprinted by permission of Macmillan, London and Basingstoke, and Houghton Mifflin Company.

others—had no fear of concepts. They discovered in English history the growth of liberty, the development of freedom, of representative government, of a two-party system, of the cabinet and prime-ministership. They traced them happily backwards and forwards in time, casting only a sideways glance at social structure or even at ideology in its precise chronological and social setting. Times have changed. Most of these concepts of political history have been dismissed under the convenient umbrella of Whig interpretation, and the greatest English political historian between the two world wars, Sir Lewis Namier, was preoccupied with the study of a very limited and precise political situation: the structure of the House of Commons in 1761. Political opinion, the political nation outside the House of Commons, the ideology of Whig oligarchy or that of provincial Toryism scarcely interested him. His demolition of the two-party system as a concept for interpreting the political events following the succession of George III was so shattering that not only was that particular concept blown sky-high, but others went with it. Concepts, as methods of interpreting political history, became totally unfashionable. Political historians turned to biographical methods, administrative history, or sheer narrative; social history claimed others, and the history of ideas more. Confusion was general, but the period from 1675 to 1725 fared worst. This was due to both the inherent difficulty of the period and to Dr. Keith Feiling.

Feiling, in a profoundly important book, *A History of the Tory Party, 1640–1714* (Oxford, 1924), had laid bare one of its major problems—the strange transition by which the party of Shaftesbury became the party of Harley and Bolingbroke. He clearly delineated the confusions and complexities of William III's reign and stressed the growing dichotomy of party after 1694, and its far clearer definition in the reign of Queen Anne. Unfortunately, in a subsequent volume, he trespassed, as we all tend to do, beyond the confines of his own highly specialized territory and wandered into the reign of George III. He had the folly to call 1760 a watershed in party development. The result was disaster, for Namier not only blasted that view but so lowered Feiling's reputation that young scholars, particularly R. R. Walcott, fascinated by Namier's methods, rushed in to demolish the exceptionally valuable analysis that Feiling had put forward for the earlier period. In 1956, Professor Walcott published his *English Politics in the Early Eighteenth Century,* in which he insisted that the structure of politics of this period was similar to that in the 1760s. His book has been widely used and widely quoted, with the result that confusion now prevails. Although there is much in Walcott's book of value, at least for the expert scholar, it is basically very unsound. Walcott all too frequently mistook genealogy for political history, and creates factions out of family relationships without even considering the political actions, ideas, or attitudes of the men in question; his case-histories are badly chosen, and at times untypical. His failure to consider his analysis in the total structure of politics is little less than disastrous. Also, his narrow chronological limits bred myopia. Two simple but profoundly important facts eluded him. One was that the late seventeenth century witnessed the growth of a large political nation with voting rights. Secondly, more general elections, and more contests at these elections, took place between 1689 and 1715 than for the rest of the eighteenth century. Indeed, more general elections took place between 1688 and 1714 than at any other comparable period in the history of Parliament, excluding medieval times. In the seventeenth century a political nation was in ferment, locked in a war for power, with ample opportunities for battle, and whatever their personal ambitions or intentions, politicians had to try to dominate a majority of that active, voting political nation. This could only be done by the attitudes, ideas, and organization of party. Hence the huge output of political party literature, the parade of Dr. Sacheverell through the provinces, the concern of men in Norfolk for the fate of the Kentish petitioners, and so on— all these and many more are facts of politics of a higher importance than the relationship of the Earl of Nottingham to Sir Roger Mostyn, which looms so large in Professor Walcott's vision. . . .

Political stability is a comparatively rare phenomenon in the history of human society. When achieved, it has seldom lasted. But perhaps one should define political stability: by this I mean the acceptance by society of its political institutions, and of those classes of men or officials who control them. Conspiracy, plot, revolution, and civil war, which has marked the history of most societies of Western Europe in modern times, are obviously the expression of acute political instability. Its momentum will depend on the degree of support that they achieve, and the frequency with which they are repeated. One of the many ironies of history is that political instability in Europe before the Industrial Revolution went hand in

hand with exceptional social stability. For the majority of the population knew only an unchanging world in which the patterns of belief,
of work, of family life and social habits changed with glacier-like
slowness. Wild political conflicts and instability had curiously little
effect on this immobility of social habit. But industry, and particularly
scientific industry, requires a politically stable world in which to
operate with anything like efficiency; so perhaps, as the political
world becomes more adamantine in its structure, society itself will
be subject to quicker and more violent change. Man's need for
action and variety may find its sustenance in quickly changing social
habits rather than in the shock and drama of political action.

Whether that be so or not, lasting political stability itself is not
a common political phenomenon until recent times; it is certainly far
rarer than revolution. It has, however, been much less studied. There
is a general folk-belief, derived largely from Burke and the nineteenth-
century historians, that political stability is of slow, coral-like growth;
the result of time, circumstances, prudence, experience, wisdom,
slowly building up over the centuries. Nothing is, I think, farther from
the truth. True, there are, of course, deep social causes of which
contemporaries are usually unaware making for the *possibility* of
political stability. But stability becomes actual through the actions
and decisions of men, as does revolution. Political stability, when
it comes, often happens to a society quite quickly, as suddenly as
water becomes ice. After all, Mexico had experienced generations
of constant political turbulence, but within a decade, the 1930s,
achieved stability. Russia, too, had been in turmoil for more than
half a century, when it seemed suddenly to acquire political equipoise
in the fifties. France experienced frequent political catastrophes
and experiments throughout the nineteenth and twentieth centuries,
but now appears to have found stability under the leadership of
de Gaulle. Such political stabilities have yet to be tested by time,
and they may not last. But whatever has brought about such sudden
political stability merits inquiry. Stability, like revolution, is a part
of social and political change to which Western Europe has been
extremely prone this last five hundred years. It seemed to me that
a classic example of the process existed in English history. The
contrast between political society in eighteenth- and seventeenth-
century England is vivid and dramatic. In the seventeenth century
men killed, tortured, and executed each other for political beliefs;

they sacked towns and brutalized the countryside. They were subjected to conspiracy, plot, and invasion. This uncertain political world lasted until 1715, and then began rapidly to vanish. By comparison, the political structure of eighteenth-century England possesses adamantine strength and profound inertia. . . . We are more than dimly aware of the causation of revolutions; some of the greatest historical minds of many generations have subjected them to fruitful analysis. There is as great a need, if not greater, to study how societies come to accept a pattern of political authority and the institutions that are required for its translation into government. In England, as I hope to show, there were three major factors: single-party government; the legislature firmly under executive control; and a sense of common identity in those who wielded economic, social, and political power.

The Background to Politics in 1688

By 1688 conspiracy and rebellion, treason and plot, were a part of the history and experience of at least three generations of Englishmen. Indeed, for centuries the country had scarcely been free from turbulence for more than a decade at a time. How to achieve political stability had haunted men of affairs since the death of Cecil. James I, Charles I, Cromwell, Charles II, and James II all failed, and as we shall see, William III did little better. Neither monarch nor minister was able to create a system of control by which the social, economic, and political life of the nation could be given coherence and order. The necessities of state only occasionally secured a precarious precedence over local needs and private will. Policies were frequently adumbrated both by those concerned with the need for strong government and by those intent on preserving their liberties. For both parties success was usually fragmentary and often transient. Few in 1688 believed that the liberties of the gentry had been firmly secured, and William III himself viewed his own prospects with disquiet. And many who were responsible for his coming were soon hankering after the Stuarts, drawn reluctantly towards those principles of strong government that they seemed to embody—principles that were heightened by the political chaos that followed the Revolution when ministers and ministries, from left, right and center, toppled and changed like a kaleidoscope tossed by a gale. By 1700

England seemed to have escaped the danger of arbitrary government only to succumb to political anarchy. Yet in 1722, England was to survive the most violent financial crisis of its history with throne and Whig party undamaged. In the years immediately following, Walpole enjoyed majorities in the House of Commons that scarcely varied from session to session, majorities that had been unknown in Parliament since the Restoration. Indeed, by the middle 1720s the English political system had begun to assume the air not only of stability but also of historical inevitability; it had become a child of Time and of Providence, an object of veneration, the Burkeian fantasy, and a halo of glory was forming about those muddled, incoherent events of 1688, events that had so very nearly spelt anarchy and ruin to the English nation.

How the political chaos of the late seventeenth century was transformed into the adamantine stability of eighteenth-century oligarchy is an exceptionally complex process that I propose to investigate at greater length in subsequent chapters. In the first chapter, I wish to draw attention to certain long-term factors that were driving English society to a closer-knit political and constitutional structure. Nevertheless, as we shall see, these forces were also encountering many obstacles, many intractable political, constitutional, and even personal situations that frustrated their development. There was no certainty by 1700 that the factors for stability would triumph; indeed, it seemed as if they might fail. Even as late as that date, it looked as if England's development might run counter to the experience of the rest of Western Europe. In contrast to England, the growth of political stability had been a marked feature of seventeenth-century Europe from the Baltic to the Mediterranean—a fact that many contemporary Englishmen understood and deplored.

*   *   *

The key to political instability was Parliament, a medieval institution launched by the Tudors into a world for which it was unfitted. The need to identify the authority of the ruling class with the acts of the Reformation arose out of the Tudors' own lack of a trained professional class of royal officials, capable of controlling and ordering provincial England. So long as the Crown, the gentry, and the merchants were involved in social revolution, religious crisis, and external danger, the relationship with Parliament, although often strained, worked. No permanent system of control of the Commons was devised; clientage and the creation of boroughs strengthened the Crown's influence but did not establish it, nor did it give any permanent security to the monarchy. Already in Elizabeth I's reign the Commons were managed with difficulty, and their capacity for intransigence, obstinacy, and violent criticism was frequently and amply demonstrated. After 1601, they were fundamentally out of hand—difficult to screw money from and a hotbed of criticism; no one could manage them for long, neither James I, Charles I, Cromwell, nor Charles II. Before the legislature, the executive was often impotent. Of course, attempts were made to control it: through managed elections—Charles I and Oliver Cromwell both tried that, but to no avail—or through exploitation of loyalty, well warmed with pension and place, and kept steady by a patriotic foreign policy; that too had been tried. Danby, who saw the possibilities of this approach more realistically than any other seventeenth-century politician, also failed. The Popish Plot and the Exclusion crisis blew his party to smithereens, and like so many others he finished in the Tower.

Because of its inability to control Parliament, the monarchy was starved of its necessary supplies in the pursuit of profit and power throughout the seventeenth century. The Scots in Ripon and the Dutch in the Medway were both results of the failure of the executive to exercise reasonable control over the legislature, or get money without it. An unbridled legislature, combined with an empty exchequer, is half-way to political anarchy.

The deep sense of independence, with its attendant suspicion of the court, that ran through the Commons, was based on the position of the gentry and provincial merchants in local government. The extent of social, political, and judicial power in their hands was formidable; and behind this power lay the sanction of arms, for in the last resort they controlled the militia. As Sir Henry Capel told his fellow squires in the Commons in 1673, "Our security is the militia: that will defend us and never conquer us." Local royal officials, apart from the Lord-Lieutenants, had become nonentities, and the gentry, as Justices, bore the whole weight of administration. But their power was more extensive than this; they were very largely their own judges and, . . . judicial investigations and decisions that were properly a matter for Chancery were often delegated to them.

Of course, they were subject to supervision: first Star Chamber, then Judges on Assize, could belabor them for incompetence, punish them for tyranny, and exhort them on behalf of the Crown. But only Cromwell and Charles II attempted to reduce their power; both failed. By 1688 the gentry were as deeply entrenched in their neighborhoods as the baronage of Henry III. And they possessed a like intractable nature: both felt that, if the need arose, they had the right to rebel. The power of the seventeenth-century gentry was sanctioned by violence—riding out against their enemies, hamstringing their neighbor's dogs, beating their farmers' sons, or shooting down their riotous laborers. They played ducks and drakes with the law when it suited them, breaking with impunity what they were supposed to maintain. At Wigtown in 1708 the magistrates were involved with a large gang of smugglers who attacked and wounded the customs officers and seized a large cargo of brandy. Robert Walpole, a J.P. of Norfolk, had smugglers call regularly at his back door at Houghton and even used an Admiralty barge to run his wine up the Thames. He held government office at the time. Justices frequently closed alehouses for no other reason than that it drove custom to the one they owned themselves. Their quarrels, usually about rights of property, were frequent and bloody. A sea of turbulence washed about the gentry's lives, and they deeply resented any threat to the freedoms that they felt belonged to them as gentlemen. Since the days of the Tudors no government, royal or republican, had got to terms with them. Like Charles I or Charles II, Cromwell had failed absolutely to take the gentry into his control, and so made Restoration inevitable. Charles II's failure nearly toppled his throne. James II's was more complete; they chased him out of his kingdom. To bring the independent country gentry into some ordered relationship with government, or to diminish their role in it, became an absolute necessity if political stability was ever to be achieved. The Bill of Rights, however, underscored their liberties and privileges no less heavily than Magna Carta had done for John's barons. Magna Carta, indeed, played the part of Moses' tablets of stone in the political beliefs of the gentry. On 11 December 1667, L. C. J. Keeling was bitterly attacked in the Commons for calling Magna Carta "Magna Farta," which was "thought to be tending to arbitrary government in the judicature." And in many ways the Bill of Rights makes more sense if seen in a medieval context of charters than as the cornerstone of the modern constitution. Parliament and the structure of local government were the key problems for centralizing monarchy, but there were others, less powerful but equally intractable, or so it seemed. . . .

Less obvious, and more difficult of solution, was the whole question of freeholds and liberties, a matter that James II had made worse by his attacks on the universities, the Army, and the Navy. A university fellowship, a commission in the Army or Navy, a benefice in the Church were considered to be freeholds, to be property. The whole experience of the seventeenth century had added limpet-like strength to men's attachment to such possessions. And England was littered with them, myriad marks of status, of possession, of profit: stewards of hundreds, precentors of cathedrals, beadles of corporations. Usually these offices were held for life and they all enjoyed standing and status within the community they adorned; most of them carried a vote. Such freeholds bred independence, truculence, a willingness to fight and litigate that bordered on neurosis, and yet when they conglomerated, as in the universities, the cathedral cities, and the parliamentary boroughs, they could build up into formidable heaps of political influence. Difficult to discipline, secure in their self-importance, their holders, with the gentry, became the leaders of political opinion outside London and the great towns, an opinion that proved easy to influence—through newspapers, pamphlets, and ballads—but hard to manage. Yet if Britain was ever to enjoy political peace, it was necessary to harmonize their interests with those of the national government; or, at least, to give them that sense of security of which the policy of the Stuarts, and indeed of Cromwell, had deprived them.

Such men, simply because they possessed vested interests, were potentially manageable. These men, with the landowners and merchants, great or small, were the men of property for whom John Locke wrote his "Two Treatises," the necessary nerves and sinews of the state.

The perturbations of politics in seventeenth-century England, however, had called into being a wider political nation than this, and one far less easy to control. Inflation in the sixteenth and early seventeenth centuries had reduced, almost to triviality, the property qualification—a 40s. freehold—of voters in the county electorates, which brought the parliamentary franchise not to hundreds but to thousands of small farmers, shopkeepers, craftsmen, and owners of modest freeholdings. At the same time the growth of the population, although slow, had increased the number of men qualified. The same is true of the boroughs with wide franchises—Bristol, Norwich, Hull, Coventry, Nottingham, Exeter, and the rest. Often two to three thousand men now possessed a vote. This would have been of little consequence had their betters lived in harmony, for elections could have been managed without consulting them, as, indeed, at times they were. But throughout the seventeenth century the gentry were deeply divided on a plethora of issues, as were the merchants and professional men of the large corporate towns. Naturally, they tried to use the electorate as a weapon in their battles. The consequence was a huge outburst of contested elections the like of which Parliament had never known. During 1690 nearly four thousand voters polled in Norfolk and the number steadily rose, reaching about six thousand by 1710. Norfolk was contested at almost every general election from 1679 to the death of William III. Essex differed little from Norfolk; the number of voters was somewhat fewer—about four thousand—but they went to the poll seven times in twelve years in William III's reign. Many other counties had similar electorates and similar experiences. In the large towns there was a similar increase; this increase in votes is very marked between 1689 and 1715, and is a measure both of party strife and of political awareness. After all this was a time when, according to the demographers, the population was static. If one remembers the comparative smallness of the population at this time, extracts from this the women and children and, of course, the laboring poor whom no one considered worthy of political rights, then the number taking part in politics at election times in these constituencies is very impressive. The total number of voters is very difficult to estimate, but a conservative figure for William III's reign would be about 200,000—perhaps one-thirtieth of the entire population. An electorate, therefore, for the first time in English history, had come into being. This new political nation proved very mettlesome, very contrary, very fickle in its moods; above all it helped to give substance to parties and give them added power. As Charles II and James II realized, until this electorate was reduced, subjected, or prevented from voting, there was no hope whatsoever that England would achieve political stability. The battle to control this new electorate is a vital issue in this period, to which I shall return again and again. It called into being new methods of propaganda and electioneering; it was subjected to vicious attacks by the Crown and to subtler forms of corruption and manipulation by the aristocracy and gentry. Its subjection was a prime necessity either for arbitrary government or rule by oligarchy.

In addition, some would add, as a final factor in the creation of political instability—tradition. The fact that Englishmen had for centuries rebelled against kings and ministers, conspired and plotted against them, risen often in riot and violence, had so conditioned them to a life of political instability that change might prove almost impossible. Traditions are quickly bred and quickly destroyed and they snap suddenly in a world of rapid social change. Historians too often think of rapid social change as creating conditions of turbulence; but societies can move as quickly into stability as into revolution, and between 1688 and 1725 Britain did just that. And traditions changed just as rapidly: by 1730 Englishmen were congratulating themselves on their tolerance, on their capacity for political compromise, on the preservation of their liberties. In 1688, however, it seemed as if the forces of political instability had won, for the Revolution had been undertaken by those forces in society that were thoroughly opposed to strong executive government. For the Revolution of 1688 was a monument raised by the gentry to its own intractable sense of independence.

*   *   *

James II and his advisers turned their attention to local political power in a wider sense than the parliamentary boroughs, which they could influence by charter. They wanted to secure control over the county representation if they could do so; more than that, they wished to see local society dominated by men on whom they could rely absolutely. So the Lord-Lieutenantships were purged; peers such as the Earl of Rutland in Leicestershire, who had been sympathetic to the remodelling policy of the early 1680s, were thrust aside and replaced by their hereditary enemies—in this case the Earl of Huntingdon, who was completely sympathetic to James II. Elsewhere Court hacks—Preston, Dover, Jeffreys, Petre—acquired Lord-Lieutenancies. The pattern of a century was broken as savagely as it had been at the time of the Civil War. As with the Lord-Lieutenants, so with their deputies; out they went in purge after purge, the Justices of the Peace following the Deputy-Lieutenants. Not since the Norman Conquest had the Crown developed so sustained an attack on the established political power of the aristocracy and major gentry. But the attack, which after all had begun in the 1670s, had to be renewed again and again, for each onslaught alienated a new group of gentry until men as loyally royalist as Sir John Reresby, the ardent High Anglican, dedicated Tory, Governor of York, wrung their hands in despair. Reresby just could not understand a policy that turned out such men of substance as Sir Henry Goodricke, Christopher Tancred, Sir John Kaye, and Sir Michael Wentworth, men whose acres were so broad that they could command dozens of the minor gentry and hundreds of freeholders, and replaced them by men who possessed scarcely any land in England, let alone in Yorkshire, and by one man, at least, who by reputation could neither read nor write. Such a reversal of power caused tempers to flare, and at times was accompanied by riot and violence.

By September 1688 this policy had so obviously failed that James II switched rapidly into reverse. The traditional men of power were restored, recent charters cancelled, new Commissions of the Peace promulgated. But it was too late; not only were events destroying James II and his narrow circle of advisers, but also the total alienation of the majority of the aristocracy, gentry, and commonalty lost him the slightest hope of mass support, so that when the Revolution came, he was rejected by the nation, by Tories as well as Whigs— indeed, by everyone. Even the Clarendons, Rochesters, and Ailesburys realized the forlorn nature of their cause. True, neither the aristocracy nor the gentry rose *en masse* against James II, and it has been calculated that only 10 percent of the peerage gave William III active support during his march on London. This is not surprising; in the autumn of 1688 James II possessed an excellent professional army, based on London; the militia had been deliberately neglected for more than two years; the Lord-Lieutenants who controlled it were James II's most ardent supporters. It must have struck even the meanest intelligence among the aristocracy that James II could only be beaten by a professional army; hence the need for William III rather than a civil war. Nevertheless, when the crisis came, it was the Dutch professional army that men joined and James II's from which they deserted in flocks; and the reluctance of such pillars of James II's Court as the Duke of Beaufort or the Earl of Bath to stir themselves, the ease with which Nottingham and Halifax changed sides at the last opportune moment, underlines, if underlining be needed, the total rift that had taken place between James II and the natural political establishment of the country. The universality that permeates the Revolution of 1688 arose not only because of James II's specific attacks on the Anglican monopoly of the Church, the Army, Navy, and universities, or from his determination to secure toleration, but also because of his outright onslaught on the very basis of political power, which if successful would have made the Stuarts as absolute as their French or Spanish cousins. It is this attack on the natural leaders of society in their country neighborhoods that must be regarded as the most fundamental cause of the Revolution of 1688.

The drive towards absolutism on the part of Charles II and James II involved more, of course, than an attack on parliamentary franchise. As we shall see, a deliberate, conscious drive had taken place to secure administrative reform and to plan the armed forces on the French model. In consequence, one of the critical features of the Revolution was the fear that new methods of administration and the innovating administrators would not survive the political crisis. The danger for the future political stability of England in 1688 lay not only in the independence of Parliament, but also in the likelihood that an effective executive would be overwhelmed and the machinery of the state circumscribed at every turn. Whether this would happen or not depended on how far the country party, whose resurgence was a political fact as soon as James II restored the charters, could establish its authority at the center of political life. The parliamentary situation seemed to favor them. William III was pledged to regular and freely elected Parliaments. The situation in almost all parliamentary boroughs was full of opportunities for the radicals. The possibility of prosecuting the lackeys of the Board of Regulators and that far larger body of Tory-inclined corporation men, who had surrendered their charters with such alacrity in the early 1680s, seemed to men like William Sacheverell almost a certainty; prosecution meant proscription and a world safe for Whigs. Such hopes, however, were to be quickly dashed. Parliament needed to be preserved; that was agreed, but little else.

The Revolution of 1688 marks one more failure of the Crown to secure control over the legislature. It was an emphatic act by the gentry to insist on the maintenance of their local power and their peculiar institution—Parliament; for that is what they meant by those clauses in the Bill of Rights that stressed the need for frequent Parliaments and free elections (by free elections they did not mean elections free of their influence, but of the king's). The supreme authority of Parliament was also stressed in the new Coronation Oath, and to make doubly sure that Parliaments met regularly William III's supplies were initially granted for a few months only. And like Magna Carta of old, the Bill of Rights had its sanctions clauses— there was to be no standing army and Protestant gentlemen were to be allowed arms; the right of rebellion is implicit. The gentry had asserted their rights. To whom those rights would belong was, however, a matter not of unity but of discord. Years of conflict had created two bitter factions among the gentry—Whigs and Tories, and these parties were not merely in conflict about ideological matters—the extent of religious toleration, the role of prerogative, and the like. They were fighting for power in the constituencies. The gerrymandering that had gone on in corporations and counties for more than a decade had, in the vast majority of boroughs, created two parties bidding for control, which meant power over charities, jobs, property, real estate, and freeholds of all kinds, as well as parliamentary influence. All this was to give teeth to the party conflict, and to increase the instability of English political life, which is such a marked feature of politics from 1688 to 1715. There was a solid economic and social basis to the conflict between Whig and Tory, which represented not so much a conflict of ideology in a national sense, although that had importance, but personal and factional vendettas at the local level. Every maneuver to bring Parliament to heel had failed; in 1689 the Commons enjoyed a freedom and an independence that they had not possessed since 1641. As well as freedom, they had acquired a certain, continuing place in government; no year was to pass without their meeting, and this they knew would be so. And after the execution of Charles I and the flight of James II, few could dispute where sovereignty ultimately lay. The problem of the control of Parliament seemed to have been solved to the satisfaction of its back-benchers —that control was impossible. Parliament, it seemed, was free to harry monarchs, topple ministries, cut supplies, refuse taxation, concern itself with peace and war, formulate those constitutional changes that it felt necessary for its protection, and generally ride rough-shod over the administration. For the next twenty-five years the pattern of politics resembled this description: governments teetered on the edge of chaos, and party strife was as violent as anything England had known since the Civil War. The Revolution, however, strengthened the two processes, the development of oligarchy and the growth of the executive, which were in time not only to reduce the power of the independent Member, but also to secure single-party government, and this was to achieve that subjugation of the legislature that the Stuarts had frequently attempted but never achieved.

The Growth of Oligarchy

It proved easier to win a revolution than secure it. Within twelve months the country party registered a number of defeats, and by February 1690 the king had decided to see whether a fresh general election would bring him a more amenable Parliament, or, rather, one with a less instransigent core, for the Convention Parliament, in full session, was moderately rather than violently Whiggish. The Bill of Rights, which in the first flush of the Revolution promised to be a comprehensive constitutional document, had been quickly watered down to a string of condemnations of James II's actions, followed by a number of hopeful generalizations about the way in which executive power should be used in the future. The ultra-Whigs protested at such flabbiness; as William Sacheverell urged the Commons, "Since God hath put this opportunity into our hands, all the world will laugh at us if we make half a settlement. . . . Secure the right of elections and the legislative power." What was worse, from a Whig point of view, was that little punishment was meted out to those who had been responsible for the destruction of their party after 1681. To their chagrin they failed to obtain their cherished Corporation Act by which those responsible for surrendering charters, or acting under the new ones issued by Charles II and James II, would have been incapacitated for seven years from playing any part in corporation affairs—an essential step if the world was to be made safe for the Whigs. The issues were perfectly clear to Sacheverell's supporters and their opponents. Serjeant Maynard, that aged relic from the Long Parliament, told the House in a voice so frail with age that Anchitel Grey could scarcely hear him, "If there be no penalties, you had better like what King Charles and King James did. If these sur-

renders stand, they may make what Parliament they will at court."
Or as Foley put it more violently, "We have ill ministers, and they
are concerned that the same thing may be done again. Men have
done all they can to annihilate their corporations, and we must not
annihilate but restore these men." His sarcasm was wasted. The
Tories were well enough aware that proscription would mean their
ruin, and they also knew that their policy of moderation was William's
policy. They surveyed their own necessities with a warm and generous
feeling. "If all these," Sir Henry Goodricke, Danby's henchman, told
the House "whom avarice, force and easiness have induced to surrender their charters, if all these must be left out, whom will you
have to act; whom will you have to choose Parliament men? None.
Harmony must save us." But the chance had been lost, a bitter
struggle in the chartered corporations was inevitable.

The failure of the extreme Whig party was due to a variety of
causes. The success of William III's invasion had followed so rapidly
on James II's reversal of his charter policy in October that little or
no time had been available in many constituencies to undo the years
of preparation by his secretaries: over 45 candidates, for example, out
of 102 recommended by Sunderland in the summer of 1688 were
returned to the Convention Parliament in 1689. Probably less than
a third of the Commons were old exclusionists, and the balance of
power was certainly held by men who had never previously sat in
Parliament, and significantly their names are not to be found in the
two division lists—one Whig, one Tory—which throw light on the
more intransigent groups in the Commons. The Whig situation in
the House of Lords was weaker still. Only with considerable reluctance had the peers been brought to accept the idea of a vacancy
of the throne, and they were totally uninterested in making the world
safe for the country gentry. They had burst back into the lush pastures
of court favor, and their attention was consumed by far more serious
business than constitutional principles. Most of them had been happy
enough with the late Charles and early James. The majority of the
peers found it difficult to accept William III with whole-hearted grace;
and the wrangles about regency, vacancy, and abdication had displayed clearly enough their yearnings for a fixed and immutable
world. What had broken their spirit was their steady exclusion by
James II from authority in their neighborhoods and from the rich
pickings of executive office. Now all was changed; and although their

loyalty might be dubious, their appetite was not. The Spencer House Journals, the notebooks of the Marquis of Halifax, in which his conversations with William III are recorded, are concerned principally with questions of place—who should get what—and the aristocratic professionals and their henchmen created the major problems; be they suitable or unsuitable, niches and rewards had to be found. Although William III thought the Duke of Northumberland a great blockhead, he had to have a troop of horse and be sent to Holland; young Hampden might be weak in the head, but the offer of an embassy was important; Delamere was repugnant to the king, but he became Lord-Lieutenant of Cheshire; Sir Henry Capel, Lord Essex's brother, was thought to be incompetent, but he moved steadily up the ladder of promotion. As to Danby, said William III, "hee knew not what to make of him. All his kindred and dependence voted against him. He could not live with a man at that rate." But live with Danby, William did. He could not escape him. In the next five years Danby moved first to a marquisate, then a dukedom, and he stayed in office until 1699, enjoying both salary and perquisites, although at times without the power it conferred. The aristocracy and gentlemen of influence were back where they belonged, at court and in office. They were never to be dislodged again by any narrow clique of purely king's friends; instead, so deeply entrenched did they become, as decade succeeded decade, that neither social change nor extension of the franchise made much difference. They were still there in the reign of Queen Victoria. Although it has long been realized that the Revolution of 1688 could be expressed in the equation "property equals power," this is too coarse a statement to describe the reality. What the Revolution did was to confirm the authority of certain men of property, particularly those of high social standing, either aristocrats or linked with the aristocracy, whose tap-root was in land but whose side-roots reached out to commerce, industry, and finance. And their authority was established not so much because Parliament became a continuous part of government but because they settled like a cloud of locusts on the royal household and all the institutions of executive government. For these prizes, they fought each other —at least for thirty years or so after the Revolution—after which Walpole sliced up the cake for them and reduced their quarrels to bickerings about the crumbs. . . .

Both at Westminster and in the constituencies the fight for power was on, and the peerage was more active in general elections, if contemporaries are to be believed, than ever before. Be that as it may, one fact is certain: there were more general elctions to be active in. Between 1689 and 1715 twelve general elections were fought, only one less than for the rest of the eighteenth century; indeed, more general elections took place in that short time than in any other period of parliamentary history, before or since—a fact unmentioned by historians, yet of immense significance. Not only were general elections exceptionally frequent, but they were strongly contested. Scarcely a borough avoided a poll, and the majority were fought time and time again. This was true of the counties, and of boroughs with large electorates, medium electorates, and, significantly, of tiny, electorates. Only in the two decades immediately preceding the Reform Bill of 1832 were parliamentary seats of all kinds so fiercely contested, but even then not so frequently.

*   *   *

The years immediately following the Revolution witnessed a considerable extension of government activity and efficiency, although this must not be exaggerated; the increase was in terms of what had gone before. This, with victories in the field, gradually bred confidence in the political nation—in the ability of the government to govern and to win its wars.

The growth of the executive had also created more places, and in the ensuing scramble for patronage, political considerations more often than not dominated the decisions as to who should get which place. But between 1689 and 1715, there was no single-party government; there were two parties, *pace* Mr. Walcott, and many factions, and the scramble for place did not immediately lead to political stability—indeed, quite the reverse, for during this period there grew up the beginnings of a spoils system. It was never fully comprehensive, but it helped to keep party and factional animosity alive. After 1689, all Catholics were naturally purged from office, and with them went nonjurors; after 1696, those who would not sign the Association were scheduled to follow, but if the customs service is anything to go by, the process was slow and inefficient. Whigs had a rough time in 1702, and again in 1711 and in 1714. Bolingbroke swore he would have every Whig out of office within six months. Of course, these purges were a hit-and-miss affair, and a discreet Tory or Whig, whether in a high office or a smaller one, could survive for years. Godolphin was rarely out of office between 1689 and 1710, and William Blathwayt was only out of office for a few months after the Revolution until the Whigs finally purged him in 1707. Others survived frequent ministerial changes because they held their offices for life. Nevertheless, swings in party fortunes could play ducks and drakes with place-holders. Members of Parliament became conscious of the risk of office. For example, a dozen or so Tory place-holders who voted for Bromley as Speaker in 1705 were summarily ejected from office.

Even with the extension of place, the majority of M.P.s, however, had little or no share of patronage. This growth of the executive was viewed with disquiet by the back-benchers, who were contracting debts and mortgaging their lands to meet the ever-increasing costs of elections. As scene after scene of corruption was revealed to them —exposure of frauds; swindles in the Treasury, Customs, and colonial accounts; deficiencies in naval supply—moldy biscuits, bad beer; fraudulent Army contractors and false musters for dead men's pay— all of these things turned disquiet to anger and fed the flame of party animosity. There is thus a twofold result of this rapid growth of the executive: on the one hand, an intensification of factional strife at the center, a more ferocious battle for power among the professional politicians, if not among the professional civil servants; and on the other hand, an increased bitterness between court and country. For the independent squires or the back-benchers, the liberty of Parliament seemed to be threatened by this growing cancer in its midst, a mood that was quickly sensed and half believed by Robert Harley. It was exploited by him in order to influence party politics to the advantage of himself and his friends. For the whole of William III's reign and for most of Queen Anne's, the growth of the executive increased the instability of English politics, and the independent interests fought every inch of the way to prevent the domination of Parliament by the executive. The growth of place, like the growth of oligarchy, initially fed the rage of party.

The Rage of Party

"This I say; it is time for every man who is desirous to preserve the British Constitution, and to preserve it secure, to contribute all he can to prevent the ill-effects of that new Influence and Power which have gained strength in every reign since the Revolution; of those means of corruption that may be employed one time or another on the part of the Crown and that proneness to corruption on the part of the People, that hath been long growing and still grows." So wrote Bolingbroke in 1734 in his *A Dissertation upon Parties,* whose thesis was that increased taxation, brought about by the wars of William III and Queen Anne, had created fresh sources of patronage, and so defeated the major aim of the Revolution, which had been to secure the independence of Parliament. His hope was a renewed, reinvigorated country party—by 1734 a hope as utterly futile, as ridiculously unrealistic, as the rest of Bolingbroke's political philosophy. Yet it had not always been so. Bolingbroke's analysis was correct enough and his own early experience had demonstrated the power and effectiveness of the country party in action. The back-benchers, led usually by Tory or crypto-Tory groups, were quite as clear-sighted as Bolingbroke about the developments that were taking place between 1689 and 1714, and made resolute attempts to stop them. The rising cost of elections, the growth of government patronage, combined with inefficiency and corruption, so inflamed the passions of the average Member of Parliament that party strife became, between 1689 and 1720, as violent as at any time in our history. In this rancorous upsurge of political feeling old lines of party division were blurred, if never eradicated, but a cleavage between Whig and Tory remained one of the basic facts of political history. The confusion, the complexity of politics in this period does not derive, as Walcott would have us believe, from the absence of a two-party system, but from the failure of either party to secure effective domination over the other, a situation that was further complicated by the needs of two great wars. Coalitions were forced on both parties by circumstances; principles at times were moderated by events; and, of course, there were desertions and conversions, loss of nerve and beady-eyed compromise—all of which factors help to create a sense of confusion at the center. At least for historians; contemporaries were less distracted and they rarely had difficulty, at least after the middle 1690s, in distinguishing Whig from Tory. When lists of Members of the 1713 and 1715 Parliaments were drawn up, probably for the enlightenment of George I's Hanoverian ministers, the compiler had no hesitation in dividing the majority of the House of Commons quite simply into Whigs and Tories. And to politicians of these two reigns, Whigs and Tories were as discernible as day or night.

There were broad party principles to which most politicians acknowledged allegiance, one way or the other. Of course, political commentators tried to give a more exact description, as, indeed, political commentators do today: Church Tories, Country Tories, Court Tories—these help to explain the bias of a particular Tory. Again, the use, for the purpose of analysis, of court and country interests is exceptionally valuable, for here is a real dichotomy, as we shall see, but it does not break the reality of either Whiggism or Toryism. And the same is true of factions: whatever coalitions are made, factions remain Whig or Tory. As Feiling showed over forty years ago in his *History of the Tory Party*—which still remains the best political analysis of the period, the most profound, the most scholarly, and the most realistic—the separation and definition of party becomes clearer each year after the Revolution, and the only period of gross confusion was between 1690 and 1698, when the New Tory party, which was to base itself as solidly on the country interest as Shaftesbury himself, was being forged. . . .

Traditionally, the conflict of power in seventeenth-century England had revolved about the role of the gentry, who had come to regard the House of Commons as their own peculiar institution which, if kept independent, could secure them a world to their liking. With this attitude to Parliament, they had maintained a loathing of standing armies—Cromwell's as well as Charles II's or James II's—a loathing based on the fear, not groundless, that they might have to fight again for Parliament. It was natural, therefore, that men who had opposed James II's tampering with the boroughs, or been supporters of Shaftesbury at the time of Exclusion, should view with equal concern the rising cost of elections, the growth of powerful oligarchical patronage in the boroughs, and the spreading influence of the aristocracy in county politics. The danger to the freedom of Parliament was, in their eyes, further increased by the proliferation of placemen and the growing opportunities for corruption in a tax system that seemed designed for their ruin. As Sir Charles Sedley thundered in the Commons in November 1691, "The country is poor, the nation is racked, the courtiers hug themselves in furs, and the humble country gentleman is half-starved." His sentiments in that debate were echoed by both Whig and Tory, for in 1691 party politics were in flux. The old exclusionists—Garraway, Sacheverell, Lee— had been deeply disappointed by the Bill of Rights and by their failure to secure draconian measures against the Tories who had supported James II. They and their supporters felt that the Revolution was half complete. And they had their friends and allies at court, for the leading Whigs, Shrewsbury included, did not take very warmly either to William III and Mary's obvious regard for Nottingham or their dependence on Carmarthen. Between 1690 and 1694 the Whigs were at a disadvantage at court, and the prospect was far from remote that the king might establish his government on a purely Tory basis. Hence the Whigs were alert to the dangers of long Parliaments in which the effects of patronage might damage their future. They were also concerned by the growing number of placemen. Hence we find Whigs such as Shrewsbury in the forefront of the battle to secure a Triennial Bill, and the strongest opposition to it coming from the Tory Nottingham and the king himself. The Whigs, too, may have felt that frequent elections would strengthen rather than weaken their position in the Commons. About the Place Bills, pushed forward in this Parliament, the Whigs, or the bulk of them, were more circum- spect; but what Whiggish support they achieved came from the old intransigents, the exclusionists, the immovable anti-court, Country Whigs and the new radicals associated with Harley. These years 1692–1694 witness the beginning of a realignment of party forces in the Commons: the fusion between the Whig and Tory "country" interests, which came about at a time when the members of the old country party—Sacheverell, Garraway, and Lee—died, so giving an opportunity for Robert Harley to emerge as the new leader of the opposition to the court. But the changes in the *persona* of party go deeper than that. These are the years of the Whig party's volte-face. There emerged not only a New Tory party but a newly orientated Whig party, based on the House of Lords. Sixteen ninety–ninety-four had proved two things: first, that no Tory leader could secure effec- tive leadership either in the Commons or at court, and secondly that coalition government had been disastrous in the prosecution of the war. There was a fundamental contradiction in the Tory position, which Sunderland, back at court, had been quick to realize. As he wrote to Portland in 1694:

I have so often repeated my opinion concerning Whigs and Tories that it is vain to do it any more, but I must however say, that the great mistake that has been made for five years together has been to think that they were equal in relation to this government, since the whole of one may be made for it, and not a quarter of the other ever can. Whenever the government has leaned to the Whigs, it has been strong; when the other has prevailed it has been despised.

Behind this acute analysis of Sunderland's lies a change in every way as dramatic as the rise of a new Tory party, and one ultimately of far greater consequence. The efforts of Shrewsbury on behalf of the Triennial Bill is the last stand made by any Whig leader to secure major constitutional change on behalf of the independence of the legislature. It is the end of Whig aristocratic support of those radical constitutional principles that stretch back to 1641. Of course, many Whig aristocrats had been unhappy with their radical allies before 1688, and there had been an inner contradiction in Whiggism since the early 1670s. The right wing, represented by such peers as Viscount Townshend or the Duke of Rutland, had wanted power, not constitutional change, but events had forced them into a radical alliance with the anti-court gentry. After 1694, all truck with the moderate radicalism goes. The Whigs solve their inner contradiction, as the Tories acquire theirs. After 1694, the Whig aristocracy is concerned not to limit but strengthen monarchy and authority. They oppose the reduction of a standing army; they vote against the Act of Settlement; they actively negotiate the Act of Union with Scotland—a method of strengthening the Crown and increasing royal authority in the Lords and Commons, it should be remembered, that had been seriously considered by Charles II; they force through the Septennial Act; and they reduce the democratic franchise of the City of London. A strange Whiggery this! Sixteen ninety-four is one of the great watersheds in the development of party, far more significant than 1760 or 1794. From this time the Whigs, in constitutional principles, become deeply conservative but not, and this must be stressed, in political practice and management. There, they remained innovators. Whether consciously or unconsciously, the most powerful groups in the Whig party became preoccupied with the processes rather than the principles of government. They wanted to capture the government machine and run it. Of course, they had a policy, both long-term and short-term; but they felt that, given the king's full patronage, they could make the government work both in the national interest and in their own. Personal strains and animosities continued within the Junto; intrigue among Whig leaders did not stop in 1694, nor close contact with the country Whigs abruptly cease. When it suited him Wharton could rouse his squires to action with the skill of a Harley. But this situation did not last long. With each passing year country and Tory became increasingly closely identified, and Whig and country further separated.

In the too ready acceptance of Professor Walcott's analysis of party, the emergence of a coherent, effective, and reasonably united Whig leadership has been overlooked. The Whig Junto saw its way to effective power through a more thorough exploitation both of the electoral system and of royal patronage. They realized quickly enough that they were a minority, and this imposed on them a unity that they might not otherwise have achieved, a unity that was deliberately strengthened by active social intercourse—race meetings and house parties in the summer and frequent junketings during the parliamentary session at the Kit-Kat, founded in 1698. Their main strength lay in their territorial magnificence, enabling them to influence elections out of proportion to their numbers. Although, throughout the reigns of William III and Anne, committed Junto Whigs always remained a minority in the House of Commons, they were from 1694 onwards the largest coherent unit in the House of Lords, where, by 1713, their strength was such that Queen Anne could only obtain ratification of the Treaty of Utrecht by the unusual exercise of her prerogative in the creation of twelve new peers on 1 January 1712. Yet, and this must be stressed, they were always a minority. And in this lay their party strength. They might quarrel, but they did not break into factions. In William III's reign they parted with much of their old country Whig support, with Jack How and his friends, but their leadership was never riven with the animosities that marked the Tory leadership—the bitter feuds between Nottingham and Leeds, the hatred of Bolingbroke and Oxford. It requires considerable ingenuity on Professor Walcott's part and a considerable opacity to the facts to factionalize the Whigs. His separations will scarcely bear analysis. There were men of great power in the Whig party—the Dukes of Newcastle and Somerset are cases in point—who by the very extent of their possessions and eminence of social position acted in a more circumspect and courtly fashion, but, as I have shown elsewhere, reluctant as they were to follow Junto decisions, they could not bring themselves to support for more than a few months a Tory ministry. Again, on those occasions, as in 1694 and 1708, when supporters of the Junto managed to obtain a foothold in a coalition ministry, they began to work, deploying all their skill, to obtain places for the rest of the Junto. At no time are the leaders of the Tory groups found working for each other with the same dedication.

This greater sense of unity was forced upon the Whigs by their minority position; so, in a sense, was their attitude to elections and patronage. From 1694 onwards the Junto began to take a much more practical attitude to place-holders. Henry Guy, the Secretary of the Treasury, was broken by Wharton; expelled from the Commons for peculation, his management of the Commons was taken over by the Junto and place-holders taught to learn the duties of their place, a system that was intensified in the next Parliament. A similarly dexterous use of the Assassination Plot was made by Somers in an attempt to secure a firmer political base for Junto Whiggery among the gentry. The loyal Oath of Association was imposed and a promise obtained from a reluctant William III for a thorough purge of the Commissions of the Peace. Again, in the election of 1695, Wharton conducted a more complex and vigorous campaign in his territories of Wiltshire, Buckinghamshire, Cumberland, Westmorland, and Yorkshire than they had witnessed since the days of Exclusion, if not entirely with success. The most notorious election bribery of William III's reign was perpetrated by the Whigs of the New East India Company, who attempted to suborn a number of boroughs in Wiltshire in 1700 and were expelled from the House for their pains. The Whigs, too, were often quicker than their rivals to print and circulate defamatory lists, and had so positive a success with their Black List of 1700 that most of the M.P.s on it lost their seats, a fact that Professor Walcott observes, but whose significance for the party conflict between Whig and Tory he fails to realize.

*   *   *

Surveying these years, it is impossible to deny the ferocity of party strife, Whig versus Tory, in Parliament and in the constituencies. The impeachments—Somers, Portland, Wharton, Sacheverell, Marlborough, Walpole—were all party impeachments; the growing ruthlessness in the use of place; the keen struggles in county and borough elections; the acrid attacks in speeches and pamphlets: all these bespeak a world of politics totally different from that observed by Namier for the middle years of the eighteenth century. The needs of the state forced temporary coalitions, but they never lasted; they merely took party strife into the departments of state and the cabinet. Concepts of property, the pull of patriotism, an inbred sense of service owed to the Crown could, and did, confuse party issues and weaken party feeling at the center. But party division was real and it created instability; indeed, it was the true reflection of it.

The problem of government, however, went deeper than party. Could either party, Whig or Tory, ever secure continuing majorities in the Commons? The Tory party had demonstrated time and time again the power of the back-benchers and their intense dislike both of methods of government and of the way in which they felt the ancient constitution was being violated, to say nothing of the fears that they felt for the Church. Every ministry from 1689 onwards had run into difficulties in the Commons and failed to manage it for more than a session or two. And behind this intransigence of the Commons towards the executive, there was a century of tradition. Although in 1714 the materials for oligarchy everywhere abounded, it seemed as if no party could use them and that political instability, which had been such a marked feature of English life since the Revolution, would continue. Within a decade all was changed: aided both by events, and by the tidal sweep of history, a politician of genius, Robert Walpole, was able to create what had eluded kings and ministers since the days of Elizabeth I—a government and a policy acceptable to the court, to the Commons, and to the majority of the political establishment in the nation at large. Indeed, he made the world so safe for Whigs that they stayed in power for a hundred years.

Suggestions for Additional Reading

The burgeoning literature on the Revolution era is thoughtfully introduced by two contributors to this volume. Robert Walcott has his *American Historical Review* article, "The Later Stuarts (1660–1714): Significant Work of the Last Twenty Years (1939–1959)," reprinted in *Changing Views on British History,* edited by Elizabeth Furber (Cambridge, Mass., 1966), pp. 160–180; while Stephen Baxter wrote on "Recent Writings on William III," *Journal of Modern History* (September, 1966): 256–266. The latter is particularly strong on European writings for the period.

Approaching the Revolution from the broader context of the entire seventeenth century, readers might start with Christopher Hill's *The Century of Revolution, 1603–1714* (New York, 1966), which emphasizes economic and social history; or Maurice Ashley's *England in the Seventeenth Century* (Harmondsworth, 1954), which is a superb political narrative. Sir George Clark's work is in greater detail, *The Later Stuarts, 1660–1714* (Oxford, 1955). For a master summary of the immediate Revolutionary period, aside from David Ogg's *England in the Reigns of James II and William III* (Oxford, 1955), which is excerpted in this anthology, it is very difficult to match the nineteenth-century liberal classic by Thomas Babington Macaulay, *History of England from the Accession of James II,* in the Everyman's Library edition.

A number of superb closeup views of the Glorious Revolution have been provided by Maurice Ashley's *The Glorious Revolution of 1688* (New York, 1966), and John Carswell's *The Descent on England: A Study of the English Revolution of 1688 and its European Background* (New York, 1969), both studies focusing on the Revolution's international ramifications. An older but solid constitutional analysis is by I. Deane Jones, *The English Revolution, 1688–1689* (London, 1931). One classic contemporary history written by a participant, Bishop Gilbert Burnet, should not be ignored, *History of His Own Time* (London, 1850). Finally, the excellent set of essays describing the causes of the Revolution, from which Professor Horwitz's essay was reprinted, should be cited, *Britain after the Glorious Revolution, 1689–1714,* edited by Geoffrey Holmes (London, 1969).

There are a number of fine political biographies, equal to Professor Baxter's *William III.* Danby, one of the signers of the invitation to

William, is treated in Andrew Browning's *Thomas Osborne, Earl of Danby* (Glasgow, 1944–1951); J. P. Kenyon, in his *Robert Spencer, Earl of Sunderland* (London, 1958) studies James II's last minister; and Henry Horwitz's *Revolution Politicks: The Career of Daniel Finch, Second Earl of Nottingham* (Cambridge, 1968) analyzes the role of an arch-conservative. The aristocracy's collective role is assessed in J. P. Kenyon's *The Nobility in the Revolution of 1688* (Hull, 1963).

As this collection has pointed out, much of the new literature about 1688 has been about the growth, or lack of growth, of a two-party system, and whether the Revolution was a turning point in party history. Robert Walcott began the issue with his "English Party Politics (1688–1714)," published in *Essays in Modern English History in Honor of Wilbur Cortez Abbott* (Cambridge, 1941). He furthered it with the book, parts of which are excerpted here, and concluded it with an article, "The Idea of Party in the Writing of Later Stuart History," *Journal of British Studies* 1 (May, 1962). J. H. Plumb's response to Walcott, extracted for this anthology, attempted in part to revive the traditional views of Trevelyan, but particularly of Keith Feiling's *History of the Tory Party, 1640–1714* (Oxford, 1924). The debate has increasingly shifted to Queen Anne's reign with the editorial commentary of Geoffrey Holmes and W. A. Speck in their *The Divided Society: Parties and Politics in England, 1694–1716* (New York, 1968). Mr. Holmes has a splendid discussion of the party issue as it relates to the Revolution in the introduction to his *British Politics in the Age of Anne* (New York, 1967); but for disagreement with Holmes, see D. Rubini, *Court and Country, 1688–1702* (New York, 1968). Finally, to complete the political spectrum, the lost cause of Jacobitism is discussed in George Hilton Jones's *The Main Stream of Jacobitism* (Cambridge, 1954).

The Anglican church's role in the Revolution has not been slighted, and for the most comprehensive survey, see John Stoughton's *The Church of the Revolution* (vol. V. of the *History of Religion in England,* London, 1901). Dudley Bahlman's *The Moral Revolution of 1688* (New Haven, 1957) suggests that the Revolution inspired a great moral resurgence. George Every's *The High Church Party, 1688–1718* (London, 1956) is a fine outline of the church's politics, while L. M. Hawkins's *Allegiance in Church and State* (London, 1928) may still be the best study of the nonjurors. Gerald M. Straka's *Anglican Reaction to the Revolution of 1688* displays the tortuous path followed by Anglican political thinkers after 1688.

Political and social theory and its relation to the Revolution necessarily centers on John Locke. Three complementary studies should be consulted: Peter Laslett's *Locke's Two Treatises of Government* (Cambridge, 1964); John Gough's *John Locke's Political Philosophy* (Oxford, 1950); and C. B. Macpherson's *The Political Theory of Possessive Individualism, Hobbes to Locke* (Oxford, 1962). The broader context surrounding Lockean ideas is surveyed in two works: G. P. Gooch's *Political Thought in England, Bacon to Halifax* (London, 1960); and Harold Laski's *Political Thought in England, Locke to Bentham* (London, 1955).